Fortunes and Fables

Fortunes and Fables
education for hope in troubled times

Robin Richardson

Trentham Books

First published in 1996 by Trentham Books Limited

Trentham Books Limited
Westview House
734 London Road
Oakhill
Stoke-on-Trent
Staffordshire
England ST4 5NP

British Cataloguing in Publication Data
A catalogue record for this book is available from the British Library
ISBN: 1 85856 047 0

Cover: Ceramic sculpture by Graham Piggott, 'El Baile de las Aztecas', Bladon, Oxon, 1993.

Designed and typeset by Trentham Print Design Ltd., Chester and printed in Great Britain by BPC Wheatons Ltd, Exeter .

Her father loved me; oft invited me;
Still questioned me the story of my life,
From year to year — the battles, sieges, fortunes
That I have passed.

Othello, Act I, scene iii

Mutato nomine de te
Fabula narratur.

With a change of name it's about yourself
This tale is told.

Horace, Satires

In memory of
Peggy
born 8 February 1912

and for the future of
Rizwaan
born 8 February 1995

Contents

Acknowledgements ix

INTRODUCTION

1. Fabulous 3
— *the hope of the storyteller*

SOMEHOW WE SURVIVE

2. Let Us Now Praise Teachers 27
— *for their work at this time*

3. Never Mind the Crisis, Feel the Quality 45
— *scarcity, equity and public services*

4. Who's the Partridge in the Peartree? 61
— *literature, literacy and fabulous children*

5. Review of the Decade 79
— *a period piece, perhaps*

6. A Great White Paper 85
— *musings for a vision statement*

7. Returning Home 89
— *tribute to a tireless comrade*

TURNING INWARDS

8. **All the World's a Keystage** — *schools and the politics of spirituality* — 109

9. **Paradise Postponed** — *in the meanwhile, hell of an in-tray* — 127

10. **The Monarch and the Inner Life** — *seasons and the spirituality of politics* — 131

11. **Roots and Routes** — *journeys of a lifetime* — 143

PROJECTS

12. **They Struggled Here** — *bearing witness and telling tales* — 149

13. **The Answer Lies in the School** — *contexts and conditions of change* — 169

14 **Yes, Of Course, Of Course** — *dreaming a future* — 173

15. **What We May Be** — *curriculum for national identity* — 177

16. **Permits and Power** — *checklist for the journey* — 197

BEGINNINGS

17. **A Week in a Life** — *influencing friends and making people* — 203

18. **The Two Towns** — *self, other and looking forward* — 207

19. **A Day to Remember** — *headlines for a young friend* — 211

20. **Unfinished** — *toward a theory of justice* — 215

21. **The Keys of the Country** — *we hold them in our hands* — 219

ENDINGS

22. **Reprise** — *taking stock, again* — 227

Notes and references — 233

List of works cited — 245

Acknowledgements

The papers collected here all began as lectures or parts of lectures. I am grateful to the organisations which requested or commissioned them and to the individuals who contributed to them through encouragement, criticisms and advice.

Individuals to whom I have reason to acknowledge special debts of gratitude include the following: Kaushika Amin, Madhu Anjali, Ranjit Arora, Roland Azor, Sally Barnes, Maud Blair, Waltraud Boxall, Elaine Brittan, Catherine Burt, Tom Buzzard, Teresa Clark, Paul Coleman, Geoffrey Court, Kerry Crichlow, Shirley Daniel, Shirley Darlington, John Eggleston, Debbie Epstein, Chris Gaine, Ros Garside, Robin Grinter, Jagdish Gundara, Susie Hall, Andy Hannan, Clifford Headley, Lola Henry, Chris Henshaw, Anita Higham, Maurice Hobbs, Karin Hutchinson, Jo Jolliffe, Frances Jowell, Celestine Keise, Akram Khan-Cheema, Anna King, Gillian Klein, Jane Lane, Don Lee, Norah McWilliam, Berenice Miles, Rehana Minhas, Tariq Modood, Terry Mortimer, Bhikhu Parekh, Giti Paulin, Chris Power, Sam Sharma, John Simpson, Kawal Singh, Iram and John Siraj-Blatchford, Pam Smith, Jayant Tanna, Monica Taylor, Enid Tickle, Joan Todd, Michael Vance, Angela Wood and Moeen Yaseen. Views expressed or implied in these pages are my own responsibility alone. They do not represent the views of any of the individuals listed here, nor of my employers.

I am grateful to Angela Wood for her example, wisdom and inspiration as a storyteller and co-worker, and for permission to reprint versions of some stories first written in collaboration with her for our book *Inside Stories: wisdom and hope for changing worlds*, published by Trentham Books in 1992. They appear here as chapters 9, 13 and 20. I thank Ester Gluck for permission to reprint A Day to Remember (chapter 19). It is her property. I thank Ben Richardson, Pauline Richardson and Barbara Doubtfire for their company and patient support and Gillian Klein of Trentham Books for her heartening encouragement over many years and for her expert practical assistance as an editor. The ceramic sculpture featured on the cover of the book is entitled 'El Baile de las Aztecas' and is used with grateful acknowledgement to Graham Piggott of Bladon, Oxfordshire.

Organisations and institutions which are especially close to texts in this book include the London boroughs of Brent, Newham and Westminster (parts of chapter 1), Lambeth Primary Headteachers (chapter 2), Scottish Library Association (3), National Association of English Advisers (4), University of Warwick and National Union of Teachers (5 and 17), Birmingham City Council (7), Brahma Kumaris World University (8), Enfield Standing Advisory Council for Religious Education (10), University of London Institute of Education (12), the School Curriculum and Assessment Authority (14), West London Institute of Higher Education (18) and the London Borough of Haringey (21). A version of chapter 7 first appeared in *Multi-Ethnic Education Review* and in a booklet published by the Development Education Centre, Birmingham; versions of chapters 5 and 6 have been published in *Multicultural Teaching*.

As indicated on an earlier page, the book is dedicated to the memory of Peggy, who was born on 8 February 1912, and to the future of Rizwaan, born on 8 February 1995.

Introduction

1

Fabulous

the hope of the storyteller

On the night before the battle of Agincourt, according to
Shakespeare, the King of England rallied his troops not by
winding them up to hate the external enemy but by
emphasising that the real battle was within, on their own
shores. The real battle was to forge a new national identity
in a divided and diverse society. The king pictured for his
people their own story over the years to come, its import
and dignity.

*Reflections on the nature of storytelling and the role of
stories in sustaining and feeding hope. Therefore, an
introduction to this book as a whole.*

1. Fabulous
the hope of the storyteller

We are all of us fabulous. We are heroic characters in stories of import, stories which contain warnings and wisdom, meanings and lessons. This book is for and about fabulous teachers and headteachers, and the fabulous people who assist and hearten them, as advisers, lecturers, governors and inspectors. In the background there are fabulous pupils and students, and their fabulous parents and carers. In a range of ways and voices these pages recollect the story and stories through which we are all living, and in which we're acting and featuring, in British education in the 1990s. The times are troubled. Valuable enterprises are cramped and confined, or are shrivelling and crumbling away. Damaging projects are being let loose in their place. But there are teachers and headteachers everywhere who are continuing to hope and to embody their hope, relentlessly, fabulously, in hard work. The aspiration in these pages is to give expression to such fabulous hope and, in this way, to help it thrive.

To hope is to tell and to absorb stories. The opposite is true also: narrative not only embodies hope but also inspires it and nurtures it. Hope, it has been said, by a twentieth century figure who is both a politician and a storyteller, is 'a state of mind not of the world .. It is an orientation of the spirit, an orientation of the heart ... It is not the conviction that something will turn out well, but the certainty that something makes sense, regardless of how it turns out.'[1]

The stories in these pages have various kinds of relatedness to facts, feelings and truth. There is both anecdote and grandish narrative, both fabling and factuality, both accuracy and embroidery. There is a range, therefore, of moves, invitations and gestures towards the audience, the reader. Here is one kind of tale, to begin setting the scene.

A headteacher was asked one day if she would give a brief talk to the governors of her school, to bring them up to date with changes which had been happening since 1988 in the world of education. The governors were aware that all sorts of things had changed since they themselves were at school and they felt baffled, even overwhelmed sometimes, by the hurricane of papers which they had been receiving through the post from the local authority and from the school itself. All those forbidding new pieces of jargon and those arcane acronyms. Could the head please explain it all to them in terms they would understand? The head said she would try.

The day of the governors' meeting arrived but the head still hadn't managed to prepare a talk with which she was satisfied. She decided to tell the governors a cock-and-bull story. Not confident that she was adequately up-to-date, she told them, she had rung the Department for Education and Employment in London and asked to be put through to a senior official in the policy section.

> 'Do you have,' she had asked, 'a simple guide to all the recent changes and developments in education?'

> 'Funny you should ask that,' replied the Grade Three civil servant at the other end of the phone, 'because yes, we're just working on a new publication, the *Idiot's Guide to What's What in Education.*'

> 'Is that the official title?'

> 'No, that's the in-house working title. The official title is *The Aims and Management of Education in the 1990s — A Guide for School Governors.*'

> 'Oh how wonderful! Is it quite short? I mean, could you fax it to me right now? I need it for a meeting I'm going to later today.'

> 'Well yes, it's quite short. We're writing it in the form of a Victorian nursery rhyme. You see, we reckon there are 26 main changes in

education in the 1990s, and we're describing these with the 26 letters of the alphabet—'

'That's just what I need! Do please fax it to me.'

'I'd like to help, but we haven't finished it yet. We've only done the first 22 letters so far. In fact, strictly between you and me, we're having some difficulty with the last four letters. I'd rather not send it to you in its unfinished form.'

'Oh please, *please*, I'm desperate.'

The voice at the other end of the phone relented.

'All right. I'll fax it to you. And—'

'Yes?'

'I'll highlight the words and phrases which we think are particularly important.'

'Oh thank you so much, I can't tell you how grateful I am.'

The fax had come through to the school, the head told her governors, a few minutes later. But alas, the civil servant's highlighting pen had rendered several parts of it illegible. She had consulted members of her staff, however, and between them they had managed to guess, they reckoned, what the illegible words and phrases must be. Also, they had composed the last four lines. They were aware that on the printed page the doggerel didn't scan. But when read aloud, with judicious pauses, cadences and emphases, they found that the infelicities disappeared. Or, any way, they faded. This is what the head read out aloud to her governing body:

A is accountancy and appraisal, auditing all we do,
B's bottom lines and business units, but back to British basics too.

C's competition and customers, good, and coursework, bad,
D is drill and discipline, their decline very sad.

E's the educational establishment, to be kept in its place,
F is factual knowledge, and the financial facts we must face.

G's GM schools and grammar schools — you know, good schools,
H is the horrors of hellfire, if you don't keep the rules.

For the line beginning H, the head provided a gloss. In summer 1992 a politician who shortly afterwards became Secretary of State for Education wrote an article for *The Spectator* in which he lamented that not enough young people nowadays are being brought up to believe in hell.

I is indicators of performance, to measure heart, mind and will,
J's joined-up writing, the epitome of skill.

K is keystage testing to show who is best,
L is league tables, to encourage the rest.

M is markets and marketing, making all things rational,
N is this Nation, the one whose curriculum is national.

O is the Ofsted framework and Ofsted visitations,
P is therefore panic — and polished public relations.

Q is quality and the assurance of quality, sweet QA,
R is right and wrong, and therefore religion every day.

S is standards — service levels, sats, streams and sets,
T is trendy teaching, and treacherous Tory wets.

U is the unions, and the unrest they all breed,
V is vocational education, viz what the masses most need.

W is wisdom, and the wide world out there so many are afraid of,
X is xenophobia — what hearts and minds can be made of.

Y is the young, and their youth, which is hell, but
Z is the zeal and the zest, with which they'll one day rebel.

She interpreted the doggerel briefly, with six not 26 main points. First, she spoke with regard to the overall device of hanging everything on an ABC. Changes in education in the 1990s frequently come at us as one damn thing after another, apparently unconnected, like the arbitrary and meaningless ordering of letters in an alphabet. It may well be that the changes are unlinked to each other even in the minds of the civil servants and politicians who conceive and perpetrate them, or any way that some of the spellings which they create are neither clearly predicted nor consciously intended.[2] Be that as it may, what certainly seems to be the case is that the apparently disparate events, policy-decisions and tendencies of the 1990s combine and mingle, and — as it were — spell out messages. The messages seem to be consistently wearisome and depressing. We are surrounded in education by decay and loss, said the headteacher, and too many of us, for too much of our time, are gripped by an internal paralysis. We do not feel hopeful.

If, so someone has claimed to observe, you put a frog in a saucepan of boiling water it will immediately jump out and in this way save its life. But if you put it into cold water, and then slowly bring the water to the boil, the frog won't notice the increasing heat and will then quite quickly die. It is gradual and imperceptible change which is life-threatening, not sudden change. If the disparate trends named in the doggerel verse had come together and spelled out danger and death much earlier, we might have done something about it, might have nipped them all in the bud. As it is, things seem to have crept up on us slowly and separately, and their consequence has become clear too late.

Second, the head pointed out that the doggerel allegedly received from the DFEE refers to the mechanising of education, the increasing use of metaphors and assumptions which might be true of engines and machines, but which are not adequate to understand and describe processes of teaching and learning, nor the pleasures and pressures of being a member, as adult or as child, of a school. Of course, just as machines have their real uses and successes, so are metaphors derived from mechanics often illuminating when applied to education. They come not only directly from mechanics but also, often, via a sojourn in the world of accountancy, where they acquire further nuances and implications. Whether from mechanics or from accountancy, discourse of performance indicators, targets, quality control, quality assurance, auditing, bottom lines and so forth can provide a valuable focus on the importance in education, as elsewhere, of accuracy, rigour, precision. But accuracy and precision are not absolute values, unrelated to any others, least of all in education. In the art and craft of being a headteacher or classroom teacher there is a place for intuition as well as for facts, speculation and wondering as well as for right answers, unpredictability and uncertainty as well as for clear objectives. There are severe problems in education, the headteacher emphasised, when metaphors and ideas from mechanics and accountancy are not balanced and corrected by metaphors from organic growth and development, in other words from processes which are in essential respects unpredictable, unquantifiable and immeasurable, and never complete.

Third, the headteacher referred to what she and her staff called the marketising of education. Mechanising and marketising are closely linked to each other, she reminded the governors, and feed on and off each other — they are mutually reinforcing. Now again, she readily conceded, illuminating insights can be derived from comparing any institution, including schools and educational systems, to a market, a place where producers compete for custom, keeping the costs low, the demand vigorous and the quality high. Much teaching and learning, and much school management, involves haggling, negotiation, bargaining and dealing, analogous to the negotiations and manoeuvrings in a marketplace. Throughout education it is important to be concerned with image and reputation as well as with reality, analogous to the ways in which commercial enterprises promote and sell their wares and their trademarks.

But as with mechanics, the headteacher continued, so with markets: metaphors from marketing need to be corrected and balanced by metaphors from other spheres. This is particularly important since real markets, like real machines, can do damage if left unregulated. The hidden hand of a free market helps the strong not the weak, and typically leads to a growing gap between rich and poor. If schools and education systems are run like markets, said the headteacher, there will be damage, for two separate though linked sets of reasons. On the one hand, metaphors and assumptions from markets are inadequate to describe, understand and guide what goes on. On the other, large numbers of children, together with their parents, communities and neighbourhoods, and with their teachers and headteachers too, will be losers for the same reasons that there are losers in real markets.

Fourth, the headteacher talked further about inequalities. She pointed out that the education system in the 1990s works not only as a mirror of inequalities in wider society but also as a mould, creating and re-creating the very inequalities which it also reflects. The doggerel she had read to the governors had referred to ways in which central government, consisting of senior civil servants as well as ministers and their political advisers, seems totally complacent about the causal, two-way links between inequalities in wider society and inequalities in the education system. The doggerel referred also, she added, to the ways in which policy trends and decisions in the 1990s seem to be consciously, even callously, designed to cement and increase the inequalities of, as the term sometimes is, a three-speed society.

The children of parents in the wealthiest and securest third of society attend well-resourced schools with stable staffs. They receive in due course a university education and get well-paid jobs with sound career prospects.

They do not imbibe, even from their schooling let alone from their parents, a sense of responsibility and concern for the rest of society and have little or no awareness that their own good fortune is achieved at the expense of others. On the contrary, they are groomed to opt out from public space, public culture, public services. People in the second third of the population are weighed down by the insecurities of negative equity, down-sizing and redundancy, the malaise and stagnation of a pervading feel-bad factor. They teach their children to admire and envy the first third and to dread falling into, or being contaminated by, the poorest third. Children born to the poorest third of the population attend schools which are likely to be in dilapidated buildings and to have overcrowded classes and high staff turnover; they are unlikely to go to university or to have a secure future. They do not learn from their schooling that their fortune is human-made and could be different. Certainly they are not taught the skills and assertiveness which they need to set about changing their fortunes. It was always broadly thus, yes of course. But in the 1980s and 1990s, particularly as a direct result of the new legislation introduced since 1988, the gaps between fortunes have become both wider and sturdier, and are growing day by day.[3]

Fifth, said the headteacher, there are issues of identity, particularly cultural identity. It is no accident, she added, that inequalities of income and well-being are accompanied by increases in xenophobia and claims to cultural purity. There was a time recently in education — its high point was around 1985 with the publication of the Swann Report, *Education for All* — when it looked as if cultural pluralism would be acknowledged, indeed generously celebrated, as a new proud strength in British society. Pupils with a range of cultural, religious, ethnic and linguistic identities would feel that they belonged to British society and had a stake in it, a welcome and welcoming future. But in the event it has been 'back to British basics': a vicious narrowing of public concepts and feelings of Britishness, a narrowing which serves the material interests of a smallish but powerful minority of white people, but no-one else. That is bad enough, said the headteacher to her governors. What brings the staff and myself close to despair, she went on, is the way so few white people seem to care about what's happening. In the English school system as a whole, black and ethnic minority pupils make up just over a tenth of the total school population. In most urban schools the proportion is at least a half. But for DFEE policy-makers, and for their counterparts in town halls and county halls up and down the country, these children and their fortunes are frequently invisible. Debates about national identity, and the role of education in fostering national identity, seem to be increasingly banal and superficial.[4]

I could go on, said the headteacher wearily. Not least I could complain about the way government ministers and their supporters on the back-benches and in the press have declared an open season on teachers these last few years and are continually criticising us, and continually implying that the country's troubles are all our fault, and in no way to do with themselves. Stress levels amongst teachers have never been higher, and a major cause of this is the low esteem in which teachers are held by the government and by sections of the media. But I'll leave that point for the present. My sixth and last point is the one which the staff and I coded into the last line of the doggerel which we prepared for you.

We referred to 'the zeal and the zest' with which children and young people will one day rebel. This is our faith, our hope. We believe that the human spirit is alive and well and is strongest in the young. One day it will throw off the lunacies and the crimes which have disfigured education in this country these last few years, and there will again be a system of teaching and learning which the staff and I will be thrilled to take part in. In the meanwhile, we're on the children's side. We invite you to join us.

She paused and looked each governor in the eye. There was a silence. Let us leave them there, in their stillness. This story, like all stories, has a myriad of possible continuations. There is no final closure. The story has sketched in general terms the subject-matter and concerns of this book. Let us begin looking at the book's overall shape, and the assumptions it makes about the nature of stories, and the nature of links between fortunes and fables.

As indicated in the table of contents, material in the book has been clustered under four main headings — (a) 'somehow we survive' (b) 'turning inwards' (c) 'projects' and (d) 'beginnings'. The distinctions between these four are admittedly not entirely sharp. The pattern is intended to be as follows. The items gathered together with the term 'somehow we survive' focus on the contexts in which teachers now work, and on the courage, determination and hopefulness which they bring to school each day. There are chapters on stress, coping and leading (chapter 2), working in a public service (chapter 3), using story and storytelling with children and students (chapter 4), coping with the changes heralded by new legislation (chapters 5 and 6), and reviewing and engaging in antiracist education (chapter 7). These practical tasks are undertaken against the background of increasing inequality in British society and of increasing parochialism, racism and intolerance. But although these chapters on coping and survival all have a practical emphasis and starting point, they also continually touch on inner attitudes, feelings and outlooks: all contain reminders that how we see and classify the outer world around us, and react to it within our own minds and intentions, is as important as what we do. Dennis Brutus once suggested, writing in South Africa when the country was still a racist police state, that the word 'tenderness' might be a valuable key term with which to name and to sum up the human values which he and his comrades were determined to defend: 'Somehow we survive, and tenderness, frustrated, does not wither.'[5]

Tenderness implies fragility, vulnerability and sensitivity and also (as in 'of tender age') the nature and situation of children, their hopefulness and their potential. Brutus recalled the boots and clubs which break down your door in the middle of the night, but: '... somehow we survive severance, deprivation, loss.' All the land, he said, is scarred with terror and is rendered unlovely, and the people are sundered and separated from each other, but 'somehow tenderness survives'.

The items gathered with the term 'turning inwards' are concerned with inner attitudes, feelings and outlooks, particularly those which involve the nurture and care of, in Dennis Brutus's term, tenderness. They therefore explore discourse in education about, as the term sometimes is, spirituality. (Hope, Vaclav Havel has said, is 'an orientation of the spirit, an orientation of the heart'.) It would be disingenuous to claim that such discourse is not also latently political, not also about — if indirectly — conflicts, agendas and negotiations in the outer world as well as about inner feelings and beliefs. But the focus in the first instance, in discourse about spirituality, is on inner feeling and orientation. The subtitles of the two longer chapters on this theme emphasise, however, that inner and outer worlds intertwine and are not readily or for long separated out: respectively they contain the phrases 'the politics of spirituality' and 'the spirituality of politics'. The one subtitle (for chapter 8) refers to the clashes and arguments, and to the alliances and settlements, which surround and shape whatever may be meant by this admittedly obscure and disputed term spirituality. The second (for chapter 10) refers to the inner feelings and sense of self which affect how we conduct ourselves in outer arenas. This section of the book also contains the text of a hand-out (chapter 11) originally compiled to accompany the lecture printed as chapter 10 and an Arab folktale about the inner life (chapter 9).

The term 'projects' in the table of contents refers to attempts in the outer world to promote greater equality in British schools. One of the chapters here (chapter 12) is about a project in the London borough where I worked in the 1980s. The project was heavily criticised by the national media and by right-wing politicians, both locally and nationally. It came to an end without ever fulfilling its potential. Another (chapter 15) is about a publication created to provide guidance to schools on issues of personal, cultural and national identity in the curriculum of all schools. Other chapters in this third main section of the book are to do with aspects of the management of change. They all take the form of brief stories and are respectively about school ethos (chapter 13), images of the ideal (14) and basic ingredients and factors (16).

The term 'beginnings', finally, refers to various short pieces of material which explore and illustrate the nature of hope within specific tiny situations: a fantasy week in the life of one person (chapter 17), the end-of-term musings of two teachers as they make changes in their careers (18), the life-situation of a young friend on the day she celebrated becoming Bat Mitzvah (19), a refugee family talking and wondering about their future (20), and a bunch of keys held in a hand (21). Throughout, the book tries to embed its grander themes and narratives in tiny fragile moments such as these.

Every chapter in the book is introduced by an extract from itself. The final chapter (22) is a reprise of these extracts, to revisit and re-state the book's recurring themes. Notes and references right at the end acknowledge debts to others and the sources of ideas, and make cross-references between different parts of the book.

Nearly all the items in the book were first written to be presented out loud to an audience. The texts which appear here are similar to, but not precisely the same as, those which were used at the presentations themselves. They are all slightly longer than when first presented. This is partly through the addition of extra sentences and phrases, occasionally indeed extra paragraphs, which incorporate points, afterthoughts and clarifications which arose in discussion. Partly also it is because the original texts contained material which in the event, because of pressure of time, was not used. I have removed local, personal and topical references which would be out of place on the printed page but have retained various indications that the texts were intended to be heard in the first instance rather than to be read. There are frequent references to the lecture situation itself, for example, and to the itch which I have to understand more about the nature of a lecturer's art and craft, and about the texture of a relationship between a lecturer on the one hand and an audience on the other.

It is relevant to reflect further here, in this introductory essay, on the nature of lecturing. What are the features of a good lecture? What are the features of a right relationship between a lecturer and an audience? What are responsible and respectful ways, as distinct from selfish and manipulative ways, of using the lecturer's tricks and techniques of trade and of exploiting the situation's asymmetry and dependency? Are there relevant similarities between the lecturer/audience relationship on the one hand and the teacher/pupil relationship on the other? In what ways is the lecturer *qua* lecturer a manager or leader, similar to headteachers and educational administrators, such that an analysis of lecturing techniques could illumine styles of management and leadership in other settings? If it is said that a lecturer is 'inspirational' what exactly is the meaning? Is the word being used in the same way when we speak of inspirational teachers and headteachers? These questions are touched on quite frequently — though by and large subliminally and tangentially, not in so many words — in the pages of this book.

One approach to such questions, one which is adopted in many of the texts gathered here, involves observing or claiming that the skills of a lecturer are similar to those of a storyteller. This is partly, of course, because lecturers use stories as illustrations and to provide variety, in much the same way that they use visual aids, or quotations from fiction and poetry. But the similarities are much deeper than that. A lecturer was once having great difficulty in gaining and holding her audience's attention. She had prepared her facts and arguments entirely adequately, spoke audibly and clearly without rambling or interrupting herself, smiled pleasingly but had no distracting mannerisms, used the overhead projector with crisp efficiency ... but the audience wasn't really listening, she knew, wasn't taking much in ... her words were falling on stony ground. She suddenly put down her notes, moved away from the lectern and spoke as follows: 'Once upon a time the prime minister of India went for a walk with a swallow and an eel.'[6] Everyone now was hanging on her words. She had the audience in the palm of her hand. This was not just because she was using a new kind of material, analogous to a statistical diagram projected on a screen, or a piece of video, or an arresting quotation. It was because, resulting from the words 'once upon a time' and the images which they introduced, the texture of the relationship had changed. The new relationship was the one which she in fact sought for the lecture itself, and which (incidentally) is entirely achievable without the use of conventional stories. It was switched on by a storyteller's tricks and techniques, but could alternatively have been switched on by other means. The switch came from the use of a stock starting formula ('once upon a time') and then through a stock type of juxtaposition — the prime minister, the swallow and the eel: what are these three doing together? — and through a stock movement into the unknown. They went for a walk. Anything could happen.

In any consideration of storytelling it is important to recognise that the 'once upon a time' type of story is coextensive with, and embedded in, a process in which all human beings engage all the time. We are all of us fablers and fabulous, as we narrativise our days and our lives. What's new? What did you do in school today? Where have you been? What did you do there? In these and in a myriad of other ways we ask to be told stories, and we tell stories ourselves. Most of the stories which we exchange are about the trivial round and common task of daily life, furnishing much (though seldom if ever all) of what we need to ask, in our human need and desire for a sense of meaning, pattern and purpose in our experience. Some stories, however, are about traumas, events which defy all templates and patterns which we have hitherto found sufficient in order to make sense of what is going on. And some are life-stories, autobiographies, pictures and sequences of our selves and our loves over time, the big things we have done, the big things which have happened to us. To cope with traumas, and to get our life-stories together, we draw on the resources and achievements of — as it were — professional storytellers, not only those of ourselves. We need nourishment, challenge and solace from 'once upon a time' stories.

My mother once told me something which she in her turn had been told by her mother. It was for both of them, I am sure, a fragment of private not shared experience. It was imparted to me as something which only they knew, a kind of family secret, something puzzling and possibly shameful, a story not be talked about outside the home. When my grandfather returned from the trenches in 1918 he sat at home for week after week totally silent, barely moving. My mother was six years old at the time, but had no memory in later life of this aspect of her father's homecoming. Slowly the young man found his voice again but he never, in the three decades during which he continued to live, spoke other than fleetingly and sparsely about what he had seen and experienced in the war. And he never regained the sparkle, articulacy and gaiety which my grandmother remembered from the days of their courtship and early marriage. Years later I came across some words in an essay by Walter Benjamin, originally written in German in the 1930s.[7] They helped me to understand the kindly yet irritable grandfather whom I barely ever got to know, and to place aspects of our private family story within a European-wide pattern of domestic silences and waste:

> ... The art of storytelling is coming to an end ... It is as if something that seemed inalienable to us, the securest among our possessions, were taken from us: the ability to exchange experiences ... With the World War a process began to become apparent which has not halted since then. Was it not noticeable at the end of the war that men returned from the battlefield grown silent — not richer, but poorer in communicable experience? ... A generation that had gone to school on a horse-drawn streetcar now stood under the open sky in a countryside in which nothing remained unchanged but the clouds; and beneath these clouds, in a field of force of destructive torrents and explosions, was the tiny, fragile human body.

At best, professional or 'once upon a time' storytellers help their audiences to make sense of current shared experience, particularly of traumatic experience, and give them a sense of hope and power. Hope, Vaclav Havel has said, quoted here earlier, 'is not the conviction that something will turn out well, but the certainty that something makes sense, regardless of how it turns out.' This overall function of making sense has many sub-tasks. In terms of time and sequence, one of the first sub-tasks is to summon and re-construct recognisable realities in the outer world. For example, going for a walk. Second, storytellers give voice and recognition to worries and fears, the feelings which they and their audience have that the outer world is chaotic and threatening, and out of control. They frequently do this with images and symbols rather than directly. For example, real enigmas and absurdities may be evoked through imaginary fantasies: a prime minister goes for a walk with a swallow and an eel. Or they may do it more directly and literally, though still artfully and with a playful sense of absurdity and fantasy, as when the headteacher told her cock-and-bull story about a faxed ABC. Third, storytellers remain in control of these feelings of anxiety, they are not overwhelmed by them. They therefore inspire and they justify trust that, in spite of everything, a sense of pattern is humanly achievable. They do this, fourth, through their skill in communicating experiences, their tricks of trade — devices to create and maintain suspense, conjuring of images, choices of cadence and sound, throwaway remarks and one-liners, teasings and jokes, anticipations and reprises. Fifth, they show respect and liking for their audience and pleasure in the audience's company. They do this through various kinds of more or less transparent flattery, of course, but also, much more riskily, through leaving their story and pattern tantalisingly incomplete and unclosed, open to a range of different inter-pretations and understandings, and to a range of possible continuations. Sixth, they give members of the audience a sense of their own worth, their own strengths and likeableness: they give them, in short, and to repeat, hope. These six sub-tasks are not only those of a storyteller but of a lecturer (or essayist) too. Some of them were performed for myself by Walter Benjamin in the passage quoted above. He referred to a deep trauma in recognisable shared experience and placed it for me in a pattern. He indicated too through the use of imagery ('nothing unchanged but the clouds ... the tiny, fragile human body') that he was in control of his and my fears, could be trusted.

At an admittedly high level of abstraction these same six sub-tasks are not only those of a storyteller and lecturer but also those of a teacher or headteacher — (1) rooting everything in recognisable particularity and shared experience; (2) acknowledging and naming fears; (3) inspiring and justifying trust; (4) using tricks and techniques with skill; (5) showing respect and liking by, amongst other things, leaving certain matters incomplete and unclosed; and (6) nurturing a sense of pattern and hope. The relationships of lecturer/audience and storyteller/storylistener are homologous, this is to say, with those of headteacher/staff and teacher/learner. The broad pattern is shown in the summary on page 18.

When relationships are homologous — that is, when they have the same general shape and dynamics, with similar structure and potential — they influence each other in two separate ways. On the one hand, they act as models for each other. For example, a headteacher provides a model to her staff, in the way she treats them, for how they in their turn will treat children. Also, there are ripple-effects. A class teacher who receives a sense of her own worth from her headteacher, for example, will be better able to develop self-esteem in her pupils.

The dual converse, alas, is true as well. Poor models and examples can be set forth as well as enlightening ones. Ripple-effects can pass on bitterness and depression as well as generosity and hope. Storytellers, for example, are not always or intrinsically benign. They may use the tricks of their trade to manipulate and close down, not to free, may flirt and flatter for their own self-satisfied arousal and sense of disposing power ('he had them in the palm of his hand' ... 'they hung on her every word') rather than to attend to the real audience here at this moment, now in this place, these people's distinctive likeable features and strengths. They may tease and promise but arrive nowhere. May leave things incomplete and unclosed and never return. Yet you can't get it right if you don't risk getting it wrong. You can't avoid using tricks and techniques nor the elementary duty to use them well, deftly. You can't avoid working for acclaim and applause. Any way, one person's praise may be another person's seduction, and vice versa. The need for vigilance is eternal. For the better the telling of the tale the higher the stakes. 'She bade me,' says Othello, claiming not to discern the power of his own narrative, and implying that Desdemona does not grasp fully what is happening either:

> ... if I had a friend that lov'd her
> I should but teach him how to tell my story,
> And that would woo her. Upon this hint I spake:
> She lov'd me for the dangers I had passed,
> And I lov'd her that she did pity them.

'We desire to desire,' observes a contemporary writer about narrative, 'but far from being insatiably randy animals, we need to be coaxed into desire. Very often we are sluggish and difficult. Tricks and techniques are needed to get us going.' Therefore 'the technical craft of the storyteller, like that of the film editor and the seducer, is the craft of building up, sustaining and pacing an emotional development.' He says also that 'the stories we can tell about our own lives have various sub-plots and loose ends. They are constantly threatening to break down or become incoherent. We have to keep on improvising, stitching and patching, amending our histories. We are indeed like Scheherazade, who told tales to keep her life going.'[8]

In the thousand and one nights of her testing Scheherazade used the teasing tricks of her trade not only to keep physical death at bay but also to stave off the dying of her spirit. For she constructed her stories not only to intrigue and tantalise the one-person audience outside of herself but in order to face emptiness and lack of meaning within: 'Narrative fills time with meaning and structures it ... Story structures time and the world, and keeps darkness and death at bay — at least for a while ... Scheherazade ... putting off death by telling tales through the night. Narrative, only narrative, conquers darkness and the Void.' Eventually, though, Scheherazade and the tyrant to whom she tells her bewitching, tantalising tales are both transformed. They fall in love. Her stories are benign and graceful, finally, not flirting and manipulative. At the end, there is hope and generosity in both teller and listener, as also in the case of Desdemona and Othello. Well, so the story goes. It's the story of storytelling but — I am suggesting — of lecturing too, and of teaching and headteaching also.

Storytelling, lecturing, teaching, headteaching ... they require a mix, a holding in tension, of the local and general, personal and political, bodily and mental, here and there, now and history, the individual and the collective, text and context. So does, of course, compiling a book such as this. As Walter Benjamin, quoted here earlier, might have put it, the mix takes in both the tiny, fragile human body and the unchanging clouds. In Toni Morrison's novel *Beloved*, set in the United States in slavery times, the character Baby Suggs preaches at one stage an inspirational sermon to her fellow slaves about the tiny, fragile human body.[9] She celebrates the specific, that which is closest to her audience, closer than any words of hers or indeed of theirs, in order to rally their spirits and energy for political action in the wider world, beneath the unchanging sky:

> She did not tell them to clean up their lives or to go and sin no more. She did not tell them they were the blessed of the earth, its inheriting meek or its glorybound pure ... 'Here,' she said, 'in this here place, we flesh; flesh that weeps, laughs; flesh that dances on bare feet in grass. Love it. Love it hard. Yonder they do not love your flesh. They despise it. They don't love your eyes; they'd just as soon pick em out. No more do they love the skin on your back. Yonder they flay it. And O my people they do not love your hands. Those they only use, tie, bind, chop off and leave empty. Love your hands! Love them. Raise them up and kiss them. Touch others with them ...'

If Baby Suggs were here, reading this quotation from her yanked from its context, she might well be angry and exasperated rather than amused, let alone pleased. For it would not be at all self-evident to her, I think, that the interests of herself and her people were being served. She has been

The relationship between a storyteller and
those who are listening

*is similar in its structure, dynamics and
potential to*

The relationship between a lecturer and the
audience

*is similar in its structure, dynamics and
potential to*

The relationship between the head and staff
of a school

*is similar in its structure, dynamics and
potential to*

The relationship between a teacher and class

co-opted, she would probably feel, into someone else's storytelling, a long distance from herself and her people. Whenever a privileged and privileging person, for example the author and compiler of a book such this, cites words from the oppressed it is appropriate that there should be distrust. Particularly if the emphasis in the quotation is on the bodily, the erotic, the immediate. But it would be worse, surely, not to call Baby Suggs and her situation to mind here at all. The purpose of storytelling is to quicken and nurture hope, love and rejoicing. But these are not ends in themselves. The purpose of hope, love and rejoicing is to create justice, a world with no slavery, no manacles. Not that justice is an end in itself, either. Its purpose is to make the world safe, or safer at least, for hope, love and rejoicing. Justice and joy: each is the ground and the fruit of the other.

But any way, there is no point apologising. It's not possible to avoid quoting and co-opting, nor to avoid being quoted and co-opted in one's turn. The struggle, through our risky intertextual borrowings and takings, our perilous givings and lettings, is to combat manipulation and despair and to nurture, if we can, generosity and hope. And the struggle is to engage in the struggle, not drop out from it, not take early retirement. These are struggles in inner worlds. At the same time there are other struggles, as the headteacher reminded her governors with the doggerel ABC, struggles in outer worlds.

Each item in this book, then, whether long or short, and whatever its style and format, is a kind of story — it's about, in Othello's words, some of 'the battles, sieges, fortunes that I have passed' in the outer world, and about inner struggles too. Most of the struggles evoked in these pages involve adults in the first instance, not children or young people. But just as the stories gathered here would be insufficient if they did not call to mind the need for justice in the wider world so they would not be sufficient if they did not, since this book is about education, call to mind the young. The headteacher in our opening story ended her ABC with a recollection and affirmation of the young, their zeal and their zest. And now this opening essay draws towards its end by evoking the situations which any book about education must be, finally, all about. This closing evocation is from the diary of a teacher, a fabulous teacher, the sort of teacher for whom this book has been compiled, and by whom it is inspired.[10] And it is about a fabulous young person, just one of the millions who are unfolding and claiming their identity and their story in the diverse and divided Britain of the 1990s:

> ... I need to make some notes about Ridwana before I forget. She was in school today, still looking rather low, and after 8Z's history lesson, at lunchtime, she walked not so much with me as beside me. She said, 'You'll think I'm silly, Miss. You'll say I should be able to cope.' And she talked and talked, more words than I have ever heard from her, about her difficulties in understanding the work, about her feelings of not being appreciated, about feeling guilty for not being able to understand, about staff anxiety when she uses her first and second languages, and about her own fear that she is losing those languages.

> I listened in sorrow, but also with a degree of awe, for I felt she spoke for so many of our students. And I asked her to come and see me after school and to allow me to tape what she was saying. And she came and she talked with the same sad and articulate power and I listened again and recorded her and she has said that I may transcribe (and anonymise) her tape and then use it with staff. For I am sure that staff

have no sense of the power and powerlessness, frustration and ambition, that moves her. And she can tell them better than I, but I can provide the space for them to listen.

'Growing up is something you don't want to do. It's something that's wrong with your life. I feel like I'm not being used. They're always putting me to one side,' she ended.

Depressing words for the week's end. But I shall take Ridwana's tape with me and I shall use it, for all our Ridwanas.

On the night before the battle of Agincourt, according to Shakespeare, the King of England rallied his troops not by winding them up to hate the external enemy but by emphasising that the real battle was within, on their own shores. The real battle was to forge a new national identity in a divided and diverse society. The king pictured for his people their own story over the years to come, its import and dignity. The battle would be on St Crispin's Day. Not everyone would live to tell their tale, but:

> They that shall live this day and see old age
> Will yearly on the vigil feast their neighbours
> And say 'Tomorrow is Saint Crispin.'
> Then will they strip their sleeves and show their scars,
> And say, 'These wounds I had on Crispin's day.'

This is how it is in British education in the 1990s. It's one long Crispin's day. There is an outer struggle about national identity in a divided and diverse society and there is an inner struggle to combat manipulation and despair, in our attitudes towards each other and ourselves, for the sake of generosity and hope. For and out of both kinds of struggle, outer and inner, we tell and we absorb stories, day by day. Stories are for ever incomplete, but with loose ends not dead ends. In that story of the headteacher and the ABC, what did the governors say and what did they do? And then what happened? In the story within the head's story, what did the civil servants at the Department for Education and Employment do? That lecturer who used a 'once upon a time' story, did she keep her audience's attention? How come, in the story within a story, the prime minister was with a swallow and an eel? Where did their walk take them and what did they do there? What happened to my grandfather? Ridwana? Her teachers when they listened to her tape? All our Ridwanas? We shall never know. Nor shall we all of us survive to tell our own tales in as many words. But many of us will, yes, survive. And there will be days, yes there will, when we shall strip our sleeves and show our scars. And this is what we shall say, or something like it: 'These wounds I had in British education in the 1990s ...' We shall share warnings and wisdom, meanings and lessons.

> ... And there are folk in England now abed Who shall think themselves accursed they were not here; And hold their honour cheap, whiles any speaks That fought with us upon Saint Crispin's day.

We are all of us fabulous.

Somehow We Survive

2

Let Us Now Praise Teachers

for their work at this time

Let us praise teachers who fill their schools with unfinished stories; know a good story when they see one; tread deep into the underworld for the sake of love; bargain and negotiate; are both spiritual creatures and political animals; are unknowing; have bodies; give seed and birth to carnivals; take part in politics and attendant wordsmithery; develop their governors; are multicultural persons; are midwives of new ethnicities; make images of exuberant and generous beauty; experience dismemberment, yet rejoice; and sing.

Lecture at a conference of a local authority's headteachers, spring 1995, in the form of a letter written to the conference convenor. The title of the conference was 'Valuing Our Schools, Valuing Ourselves'.

2. Let Us Now Praise Teachers
for their work at this time

Dear Elaine.

Various voices and veins within me prepare to be with you next week at the headteachers conference. There's in consequence adrenalin in me for both coming forward and backing off, for both engagement and retreat. In some of my parts there's an intrigued, even an interested, anticipation — for I'm strangely keen to find out if I can do what you've asked me to do. But in other parts of me, the parts your flattering remarks on the phone could not reach, there is dread — I'd rather not know what I fear on Wednesday I'll find out, though thank you for inviting me Elaine, that I'm a failure, a wasn't-ever, someone quite incapable of doing for you and your colleagues what you say you want.

Words are reluctant to wriggle up out of me even to define the task in the first place — this task that you have offered me and which crazily I have somehow accepted. Actually trying to accomplish the task doesn't, just at the moment, even bear thinking about. But this, as a first rough outline, is what I understand the task to be. In the keynote speech at the start of your conference on Wednesday I am to praise you and all your headteacher colleagues. And I am to bestow this praise in such a way that the heads feel released to praise their staffs and through them the children in their care, in order that they too, in their turn, may praise, celebrate, exult and rejoice. This will be wholesome for the children, and wholesome for society, the spreading of joy. That's what you want me to do, Elaine, as I understand the matter, and I'm not at all sure that I can.

I watched a video film which someone had lent me, in order to help me assemble and focus my thoughts for this, this, er, lecture. (Yes, Elaine, what is this? A lecture is *une lecture,* a reading, and well I'm going to be reading this, out loud, word for word, more or less. So. But does that really make it a lecture? Would a *mot* more *juste* be speech, or address, or talk? Or is this a sermon, a homily, a presentation, a performance, a discourse? Discourse, interesting word. It means running around, going backwards and forwards, creating ever widening circles. From the Latin *discurrere,* formed from *currere,* to run, plus *dis,* implying apart, asunder, separately. You didn't really want to know that, Elaine, did you, I do realise, I'm awfully sorry. Yes, this could be a discourse, tearing about all over the place, scattering bits and pieces here and there, with no immediately apparent rhyme or reason. Continually returning and repeating. Another thing this could be, and oh dear perhaps it ought indeed to be, is a hymn, an anthem, a eulogy. Or is it merely a story? Though what's wrong with stories? Why do I say 'merely'? Perhaps that's precisely what I am to be with you and your colleagues on Wednesday, a storyteller. The sort of storyteller who tells stories to teachers, there ought to be a word for it. It might help if I were to sort this all out before I come, Elaine. But any way.)

The video I watched was about a carnival which took place last summer, involving six of the schools to be represented at the conference next Wednesday. (Lecture, speech, discourse, praise, story ... the word 'epistle' is interesting, too. A combination of the Greek prefix *epi,* meaning close to but more of and in addition to, and *stellein,* to send. Something which is sent but, as it were, more than sent. First use in English is for the descriptions of chapters or sections of the *Ancrene Wisse,* also known as the *Ancrene Riwle,* 'a book of devotional advice', an encyclopaedia says, written in about 1220 AD by a monk at Wigmore Abbey in north-west Herefordshire for the nuns of Limesbrook. I don't know which county Limesbrook is or was in, sorry, but I don't suppose it's important. Advice on 'wisse', wisdom, and 'riwle', rule of life. There are chapters on, amongst other subjects, Elaine, penance and love. Also the sin of accidie — apathy, listlessness, torpor, sloth, dryness of spirit. Apparently the nuns of Limesbrook got accidie pretty bad. When you've got accidie, this monk said, you don't praise, you grumble. But Elaine, about this carnival I was mentioning.)

The carnival involved vigour, fun, colour; all the arts, performing, visual, plastic, literary; all the children and all the teachers; streets as well as classrooms; bodies, limbs and hearts as well as minds. Unselfconsciously inclusive and multicultural, fed and resourced by a generous range of humankind's tradition, heritage and custom. There used to be an awful phrase in and around British schools, 'multicultural children'. It was a sort of genteel euphemism in the minds of people who used it. But in some ways they spoke more truly than they knew or intended. Let's hear it for multicultural children, and multicultural teachers also, people fed and resourced by a generous range of humankind's traditions. Everyone who took part in the carnival, said a teacher on the video's sound-track, will remember it for the rest of their lives, that time of celebration, of praise. It was as if the children and the teachers, and everyone else involved, were rejoicing along with Michael Tippett's third symphony (do you know it, Elaine?): 'O, I'll go walking with my nostrils Quiv'ring and my eyeballs Flashing and my mouth Round open laughing and my tongue, My tongue on fire ... O, I'll go prancing with my toe-tips Flying.'

Tippett celebrated his ninetieth birthday just a few weeks ago. He's still composing, still singing and praising. In an essay written many years ago he described how he saw his own function in life, and how he saw the role of all artists. It is an inspiring though daunting job description also for teachers, and for anyone who meets with teachers, or with headteachers, Elaine, with the intention of saluting them, praising them:

> My true function ... is to continue an age-old tradition, fundamental to our civilisation, which goes back into pre-history and will go forward into the unknown future. This tradition is to create images from the depths of the imagination and give them form whether visual, intellectual or moral. For it is only through images that the inner world communicates at all. Images of the past, shapes of the future. Images of vigour for a decadent period, images of calm for one too violent. Images of reconciliation for worlds torn by division. And in an age of mediocrity and shattered dreams, images of abounding, generous, exuberant beauty.[1]

Praise, celebration, *Freude,* joy. Images of vigour, calm and reconciliation, and of abounding, generous, exuberant beauty: this is wholesome for children, for teachers and headteachers, for society. But you don't want empty, insubstantial praise, Elaine, do you, or flimsy and contrived images. Empty words and predictable images would fail to give you what you have asked for. Also, they would make things worse, accidie would be exacerbated. They would make you and your colleagues even more depressed, dry, demoralised, drained, despondent and downright suicidal than you and they already are. They would not be wholesome, but would on the contrary keep each person scattered, sundered, unassembled. You know, like the kid in the barrack room song:

> A handsome young private lay dying,
> At the edge of the jungle he lay.
> The regiment gathered around him,
> To hear the last words he would say.
> 'Take the trigger-guard out of my kidneys,
> Take the magazine out of my brain,
> Take the barrel from out of my backbone,
> And assemble my rifle again.'

To be wholesome, praise has to be grounded not only in recognition of real achievements but also in terms such as 'any way', 'in spite of' and 'however'. The opposite of praising is not cursing, said the wise monk, but grumbling. Wholesome praise takes place in spite of things to grumble about, not in their absence. I think (as Michael Tippett has frequently thought, incidentally, for example in *The Mask of Time*) of the story of Orpheus, who has God's plenty to grumble about. There is death and decay all around: any way, Orpheus sings. He sings till the trees bend, the beasts are entranced, the stones melt, and the moon and the stars stand still in their courses. Living is full of risk: however, Orpheus loves Eurydice and joins his life with hers. She dies: however, Orpheus will not let her go and he plumbs the depths of the earth to plead through his songs with the ruler of the underworld. He wins Eurydice back but being human he cannot be sufficiently unknowing and non-possessive in his love to keep her, and he therefore again loses her: but any way, he sings still. He is torn apart, head from body and limb from limb, and is thrown in his portions and pieces into the raging torrent of the river Hebron: any way, any way, any way, he sings and he praises still. A small child started nursery school. 'Was your teacher nice?' her mother asked her when she returned home at the end of her first day. 'Yes, mummy, very nice.' — 'Did you like the other children?'

31

— 'Yes, mummy, I liked them a lot.' — 'And the head, was the head nice?' — 'The head, mummy? I didn't see the head.' — 'Well do look out for the head tomorrow.' The next day the child reported back. 'Yes, I looked out for the head today, mummy, and I saw the head. But mummy, it was joined to a body.' Let us praise teachers who have heads joined to bodies.

We live and work in troubled times, times which seem to be doing their worst often to dismember us, tear us and drive us asunder. However, teachers and headteachers do keep themselves in one piece, by and large, they keep body and soul together. How do they do it? If I could answer that question, Elaine, my images and praise on Wednesday would not be empty or insubstantial. How and why are our times troubled? If I could fashion images for that too, Elaine, my praise would be grounded in a solid however.

Imagine. You are average height and you have average income. This is not a coincidence, for — imagine — the height of everyone in Britain has been miraculously changed to reflect their income. And another miracle: you are able to watch a grand procession in which every adult member of the population passes before you in the space of one hour. If you lived in a society of perfect equality you would spend the whole hour looking directly into the eyes of your fellow citizens, all your fellow citizens, as they parade past you.[2]

And imagine this too. You yearn to live in a society in which indeed all people are equal. The respect and praise which you receive are from your equals. The respect and praise which you give are to your equals. But you do not live in such a society. You live in Britain in 1995. Here is how the parade unfolds.

The parade starts with the smallest people and ends with the highest. For the first half minute the people passing before you are barely one inch tall. But quite quickly they get bigger. Quarter of an hour, however, passes before there is anyone level with your waist. You find that you do not enjoy this — a quarter of an hour spent looking down at people who are less than half your own height. You wait for another 23 minutes before you are able to look people directly in the eyes — the parade is almost two thirds of the way through, in other words, before you see people of average income.

Slowly people get taller. During the last five minutes people are about nine feet tall. During the last ten seconds or so they are 90 feet tall. In the last split second before the parade finishes some people flash past who are several miles tall. With that picture in our minds' eyes, let us add some further key statistics:

- Whilst in 1995 it is a quarter of an hour before people reach waist high, in 1979 it was only six minutes: in other words, inequality of income has been growing: those living in relative poverty, as internationally defined, have increased in the last 15 years from a tenth (six minutes in the hour-long procession) to a quarter (15 minutes).

- There is only one industrialised country in the world, New Zealand, in which inequality has grown since 1979 faster and greater than in Britain.

- The average height of the people who passed by in the first six minutes is less now, in real terms, than it was in 1979: for the poorest tenth of the population there is more absolute poverty, not just more relative poverty.

- A third of all black and ethnic minority people in Britain passed by you during the first 12 minutes, compared with only 18 per cent of all white people. In the last 12 minutes, however, only 11 per cent of the country's black and ethnic minority people were represented, compared with 22 per cent of the white population.

- A third of all children in the country live in households whose adult members passed by during the first quarter of an hour.

Those are all statistical and uncontestable facts.[3] If you teach in a school where many, most or all of the children belong to households represented in the first quarter of an hour, as a third of all children do, then these are some of the facts of your daily experience:

- Your school receives less money per child than do other schools, and in consequence you have larger classes and your staff work with fewer and poorer resources.[4]

- Morale amongst staff is frequently low, which means that there is more illness and absence, therefore more work and stress, therefore lower morale, therefore more illness and absence, and so the vicious circle goes on.

- You will be frequently told, if and when you have the time and energy to read a newspaper or switch on the television, that you and your colleagues are bad teachers and that your school is failing.

It is all, the message will continue, your own fault. This same message is implicit in the stream of vicious circulars (as the term might be) which your school receives through the post, day after day, from your local authority and from central government: *it is all your fault..*

- So you'd better work harder. Get to school each morning earlier. Leave each evening later. Read each vicious circular over and over again, with a palette of highlighting markers. Write more letters. Put up more notices. Organise more meetings. Get to school early, earlier than others, gripped by 'presentism', the mad craving to be at work when one should be resting. (The Government collects figures on 'unauthorised absence' amongst pupils. It ought also to be looking at unauthorised presence, as the term might be, amongst workaholic headteachers.) You have lost something, you know, but you have no time to name it, let alone to look for it, let alone to grieve for it.

Loss, grief, mourning. Orpheus went deep into the underworld to find and retrieve, if he could, his beloved. Watching that procession just now was a kind of descent to the underworld. We saw a lot but not enough. Let us look further, in the shadows of the underworld. Here is a story. It's entitled 'To Be Continued':

It's Monday. 'Wake up, mum, wake up.' She wakes. The normal morning routine for a weekday in term time. Gets the two oldest off to school. Takes the youngest by bus to nursery. Not a long journey, but there's a long wait for the crowded bus. Hears from the headteacher that the nursery is to close at the end of term. Shock, she can't absorb it. Bus to job centre. A couple of part-time jobs, poorly paid, for many reasons not worth it. Calls at surgery on way home, given an appointment for Wednesday morning. Watches TV, sees the wider world. This story is to be continued.

It's Tuesday. 'Wake up, mum, wake up.' She wakes. Normal morning routine. A message comes from the school attended by one of the older children, asking her to go there as soon as possible. Wearily goes, difficult bus journey. Informed that her child has been fighting viciously, violently, in the playground. Is to be suspended for the rest of the week. 'We cannot cope with such violence at this school.' Shock, she can't absorb it. Watches TV, sees the wider world. This story is to be continued.

It's Wednesday. 'Wake up, mum, wake up.' She wakes. Not so normal morning routine, for there's a child at home who usually goes to school. Goes to surgery. 'You're suffering from stress, there's a lot of it about.' Antidepressants. 'Be sensible, now. Read the instructions carefully.' Shock, she can't absorb it. On way home hears that local youth centre is being closed down, and youth workers are to be made redundant. Watches TV, sees the wider world, takes a pill. This story is to be continued.

It's Thursday. 'Wake up, mum, wake up.' She wakes. Hears today that the home help who visits her mother has been made redundant. Happens to meet on the street an acquaintance who works in the local branch of a building society. The branch is closing, her acquaintance is being made redundant, is in tears. This too a shock, she can't absorb it. Watches TV, sees the wider world, takes pills. This story is to be continued.

It's Friday. 'Wake up, mum, wake up.' She wakes, with difficulty. Watches TV, sees the wider world, all day. Glamour in the advertisements. Success and power in the stories and films for some, jagged failures, hassles and violence for many. Pills during the day. Alcohol. More pills at night. This story is to be continued.

It's Saturday. 'Wake up, mum, wake up.' This story is to be continued.

It's trite, this story. I am embarrassed by the triteness but not by the intention which has led to it — the intention of shaping and offering, in the deep shadows of the underworld, an image of what is happening, an image of loss. We need stories, plays and images, to catch the conscience. Encoded in this particular story are seven main themes. First, the stress of poverty itself, the stresses and hassles, the daily and weekly treadmill, which is your lot if you are one of the people in that first quarter of an hour of the procession. Second, the collapse of various support networks and structures — nursery, youth service, home helps and so forth — which both singly and in combination help to maintain the infrastructure of community. Third, the collapse also of various other enterprises (the branch of a building society was mentioned) and the griefs which are caused: all such collapses, whether in public services or in the private sector, contribute to a sense of anxiety, insecurity and loss of control even amongst those who do not belong to the procession's first quarter of an hour. People in this broad area of society are correspondingly less able to help and care for people less fortunate than themselves.[5] They lack the 'feel-good factor', as the phrase currently is: they do not at all feel inclined to celebrate, to praise, even though they have reasonable wages and salaries. They do not, to recall the term in this conference's title, value themselves.

Fourth, there is an increase in violence, for example in school playgrounds as well as on the streets. Occupy space and territory, throw your weight around, hit first, ask questions if at all afterwards. There is an analogous kind of violence in classrooms — an American term for it is reported to be Attention Deficit Disorder, ADD for short. Keats, in a barely happier phrase, called it the absence of negative capability — the irritable reaching for instant certainty, the impatient rejection of unknowing, doubting, questioning. Fifth, the role of television and video, in two separate respects. On the one hand, in showing material goods and success which are beyond the reach of people in the parade's first quarter of an hour — it is through TV that those people know about the rest of the procession and have a sense of their own lowly place in it. On the other hand, in showing — without catharsis or solace — images of decay, violence and despair; and in not showing, as Tippett beautifully put it, 'in an age of mediocrity and shattered dreams, images of abounding, generous, exuberant beauty.' These five features of our times interact with each other to create the sixth, a sense of predictable yet unavoidable loss and tragedy. But, seventh, the story is to be continued. There is therefore hope. As long as the story is unfinished, there is hope.

So the first thing, Elaine, when we meet together on Wednesday is to assert this: the story is to be continued. We haven't lost yet, and we're never going to lose, because for ever the story is going to be continued. True, we're never, for the same reason, going to win, either. But that's a small price to pay — isn't it? — for never losing. Let me praise headteachers whose schools are full of unfinished stories, and of stories which are so good and strong that the children and teachers go back to them time and again, repeating, rehearsing, finding new facets in the familiar, exploring new depths in the already known. A story is unfinished not by virtue of ending in mid-air, not by teasing to an anti-climax, but by leaving layer on layer to be still unwrapped, and by inviting therefore repetition and return.

It's quite important, actually, that we should try to be reasonably clear about the features of good stories, the sort of stories we want to fill our schools with. Not any old (or new) damn story will do. TV and video fill our lives with stories but not, apparently, for the better. 'I'm not easily shocked,' says Arthur Miller, 'but when you turn on the TV and every programme is about shooting people, yet there's no pain, no suffering, the people around continue their lives as if nothing had happened, that can have a dulling effect.'[6] So do the tabloid papers, and they too do not exactly add to the gaiety of the nation. (Yeats: 'All things fall and are built again, And those that build them again are gay.') The story of Orpheus and Eurydice has the following eight features. It's not a bad checklist:

1. It's unfinished.

2. It's old — let us, yes, trust the wisdom of the ages, trust that stories searched, tested and tempered by time are worth staying with, and worth having to stay.

3. Nature is all around — rocks, trees, beasts, torrent, moon and stars.

4. It's a love story.

5. There is loss and grief.

6. There is magic and mystery, but no Big Bloke or Good Godmother getting everything miraculously sorted.

7. There is prohibition (don't look round, Orpheus, do trust, don't go for absolute certainty, don't go for possession, don't script everything, do go forwards with unknowing) and there is humanity's accursed yet blessed inability to accept prohibitions — our nature is that we cannot do the things we must.

8. There is, however, singing.

(Dear Tony Blair. About aims and values and attendant wordsmithery. I have read the replacement for Clause Four with interest. I regret to observe that it contains nothing about singing.[7])

Let us praise teachers who sing. Yes, but just at the moment let us return one more time to the underworld, the place of death and decay, we haven't finished there quite yet. When we were there recently we watched the procession — all the adult population of Britain walking past in one hour.

And we watched a week in the life and living death of one person. We need also, in that place of decay, to listen to the stories and images which people in the last quarter of the procession deploy to explain and justify the way things are:

> Ours is the first age in history in which the plebs, or the proletariat, or whatever polite word you conjure up for them, have no function in life ... If this class did not exist (roughly speaking it is the same class that reads and absorbs the *Sun*, video nasties, etc), nearly all the social problems facing this country would come to an end ... The prisons are overflowing with them. They have no intellectual energy — if they had it, they would cease to be proles and climb up the social ladder ... In a decent world, the obvious 'eugenic' solution — to sew up the wombs of all *Sun* readers' wives — cannot be contemplated. We, the bourgeoisie, are too gentle and kind to admit that there is a whole category of being ruining our country and whom we would be much better off without. (A N Wilson, *Evening Standard*, 8 January 1993).

> Those living in the bottom 10 per cent of income in Britain today have, in terms of consumption — TVs, videos, central heating, telephones — a higher standard of living than many surtax-payers enjoyed in Attlee's day. For example, more than half the poorest British families now own a car. In America ... obesity, not hunger, is the chief nutrition problem of the poor. (Ann Leslie, *Daily Mail*, 10 March 1995).

> The average IQ of the mothers of illegitimate children is 88; of chronic welfare recipients, 85; of recidivist criminals, 80; and of the long-term unemployed, 77. Collectively, these social problem groups are known as the underclass, and the bottom line is that the underclass has an intelligence deficit ... The average IQ of blacks is 15 points below that of whites, and 16 per cent of blacks have an IQ of below 70 and are mentally retarded, as compared with only two per cent of whites. There are therefore many more blacks in the low IQ range being sucked into the underclass ... The problem of the black underclass is likely to get worse in the future ... The underclass will turn more and more to crime because it has little to lose ... There is one thing the underclass is good at and that is producing children. These children tend to inherit their parents' poor intelligence and adopt their sociopathic lifestyle, reproducing the cycle of deprivation from generation to generation.

The underclass has more children than the rest of society ... Virtually all readers of this article will belong to this intellectual elite [i.e. the top two per cent of the population] or be close to it. Don't imagine the rest of the population are like you. They aren't. (Richard Lynn, a professor of psychology, in *The Times*, 24 October 1994.)

There has been a good deal of opportunity and reward in these years, not just for 'them that hath', but for most of us. The growing inequality is a symptom of a society with more incentives, not of exploitation. (Leading article in *Sunday Telegraph*, 12 February 1995).

The poor spend all day watching television when they could be out of doors growing their own vegetables. (Toby Jessel MP, House of Commons, 14 February 1995.)

This is the context, then, in which we praise, if we do, 'however'. With specific regard to the position of this borough within an unequal society, it is relevant to recall and note:

- In summer 1994 the Department of the Environment published figures which enable league tables to be calculated with regard to multiple deprivation. This borough was eighth in the league for degree of deprivation, sixth in the league for extent of deprivation, and third in the league for intensity of deprivation.[8]

- In January 1995 the School for Advanced Urban Studies at the University of Bristol published a report on social and economic distinctions in England. In a league table for poverty, based in particular on patterns of employment, this borough was eighth out of 366.[9]

What is the job of teachers in this borough, in view of such realities? To this question I now turn more systematically. Though, Elaine, I have already been wondering about it and suggesting things implicitly. The last time I met and worked with teachers from this authority they and I compiled a list of ten management maxims to crystallise what we reckoned we knew about the business of being a headteacher or deputy head. The list went as follows:

1. Your nerve and your knowledge
With regard to her work as a sculptor Barbara Hepworth once wrote: 'Perhaps what one wants to say is formed in childhood and the rest of

one's life is spent trying to say it.' Shaping a school is like shaping a sculpture, in two respects at least: you have to keep your nerve; and you already have all the knowledge which you need.

2. Second syllable stress

The headteacher is the head*teacher* — the leader of the teaching. This includes, but it is not the same as, managing. A head is more — much, much more — than a mere manager.

3. Not what but how

We don't change what children learn by changing what teachers teach. It's the how that matters, not the what. Process, relationships, the unique encounter.

4. Unlimited potential

We do not know and can never know the potential of any child, or any teacher, or any school. All potential is unlimited, and unmeasurable.

5. You can't do nothing

Not to decide is to decide. Being objective and honest, as distinct from deceptive or deceiving, or thinking wishfully, does not mean you can avoid taking sides, or that you can sit on the fence. There isn't a fence.

6. Counting

There are things which can be counted, and they should be. Quantification, test results, objective analysis of contrasts and comparisons, yes.

7. Inside and outside

This is true both of children and of headteachers: everyone needs, in order to survive and grow, both provocation and assistance from outside.

8. Good-enough

Many children, most parents and (it sometimes feels) all staff expect headteachers to be omnipotent and omniscient. The ideal, though, requires you to be no better than good enough.

9. Relent seldom, relax often

Do look after yourself, and after your staff. If you must feel guilty, feel guilty about not relaxing, not about your unattended in-tray.

10. Be a morning person

Carry on believing and hoping, greeting each new day, as for example Maya Angelou hailing what she hoped was a new era in American history: 'Here on the pulse of this new day You may have the grace to look up and out And into your sister's eyes, And into your brother's face, Your country, And say simply Very simply With hope — Good morning.'[10]

Elaine, I should like to unpack those points today in a slightly different form. This time, I wish to suggest seven main principles. First, a headteacher has to lead her or his staff at a time of growing inequality and has to help them understand this first main aspect of the context. So, in addition to the roles of chief storyteller, lead singer and main creator of images which I have already mentioned, and to the roles of spiritual director and crafty exponent of epistolary discourse, and to the role of headteacher as Orpheus figure, treading down for the sake of love into the depths and bargaining and negotiating on and on, there is the role of principal economist and senior political scientist. Key concepts include those of absolute and relative poverty, with that of relative poverty, in other words inequality, being particularly important.

Do you know the story, Elaine, of the class of children who were asked to write stories about poverty? One child began as follows: 'Once upon a time there was a very poor family. The daddy was poor. The mummy was poor. The children were poor. So was the butler, the chauffeur, the maid, the gardener and all three of the nannies ... '. I am not talking about some sort of idealistic utopianism — it is the decreasing of inequality, not the removal of it, that is the realistic task before us. We do not need to have a strategy for creating a society in which everybody has precisely the same monetary rewards, so that in that procession you spend the whole hour looking people directly in the eyes. Human beings do not know how to make a perfectly equal society, as distinct from the one we've got and always have had, and they do not know how they would maintain one even if they could make it. But such knowledge isn't, fortunately, necessary. Education has a role in decreasing inequality, though most certainly cannot do everything on its own. The headteacher's task is modest enough: to help her staff identify what education can do, what their own school can do, and do it.

It follows from this, second, that headteachers have to lead thinking on the implications for education and for their own school of the new Clause

Four. Yet without necessarily becoming involved in party politics. The prohibition on turning round, in the case of Orpheus, was amongst other things a prohibition on getting too much involved in the programmes and therefore internal politics of one, of any, political party. Well I *think* this may be the case, Elaine: we need tolerance of uncertainty, unknowing and ambiguity not only as spiritual creatures, as that monk in Herefordshire instructed the receivers of his epistles in the thirteenth century, but as political animals too.

Third, yet another statement of the obvious: a school is more than just the staff and the children, and the leadership role is correspondingly wide. I came across an infants school last week whose mission statement proclaimed an explicit aim 'to develop the governors, parents and local community'. Such bold and brave aspiration, Elaine, such praise-worthiness.

Fourth, the headteacher as organiser of carnivals and festivals, leading the seminal and gestatory work as well as the birthing. Fifth, the head-teacher as chief antiracist. This is not at all to do with political correctness, but with the development of new and more generous understandings of identity — personal, generational, sexual and geographical as well as ethnic, cultural and national. In Hanif Kureishi's new novel the main character is a teenage Pakistani-British boy who wishes at one stage that he could join the British Nationalist Party. 'Why can't I be racist like everyone else?'[11] The choosing of a racist identity, for white working class boys, is bound up with other choices also. It's crucial that anti-racism should attend to this elementary yet much neglected point. Sixth, the headteacher as transformer of vicious circulars: if I have a single practical suggestion, Elaine, it's that the headteachers of this borough should get themselves and their schools in a big way into *papier mâché,* and that their principal raw material for this should be letters, documents and papers received from the DFEE and the local authority. Seventh, I am not sure that it would be the best use of our time to take this list much further just at the moment. I will mention just one more role and task for headteachers: the headteacher as delegator.

So Elaine, let us now praise, as this epistolary discourse draws now to an end, teachers. It is, yes, meet and right so to do. Let us open our lips and praise teachers who:

- fill their schools with unfinished stories

- know a good story when they see one

- tread deep into the underworld, for the sake of love

- bargain and negotiate

- are both spiritual creatures and political animals

- are unknowing

- have bodies

- give seed and birth to carnivals

- take part in politics and attendant wordsmithery

- develop their governors

- are multicultural persons

- are midwives of new ethnicities

- make images of exuberant and generous beauty

- experience dismemberment

- rejoice, however, and sing.

Dear Elaine, one last return and repetition. Thank you, again, for inviting me.

3

Never Mind the Crisis, Feel the Quality

scarcity, equity and public services

Processes of otherising, demonising and racialising are kept alive and well, in any one community or society, by a range of stories and narratives — including grand narratives about the history and destiny of the nation as well all sorts of fables, legends and imagery, and anecdotes, gossip and travellers' tales. They therefore have to be resisted by, amongst other things, alternative narratives, alternative imagery.

Lecture at the annual conference of the Scottish Library Association, summer 1994. Between September 1993 and May 1994, following a by-election, there had been a British Nationalist Party councillor in a London borough.

3. Never Mind the Crisis, Feel the Quality
scarcity, equity and public services

For several weeks the two of them had lived together in their cell in reasonable harmony. They chatted and reflected, and exchanged stories, memories and dreams. Every day the gaoler would bring each of them a bowl of soup. Then one day their life-world changed: the gaoler brought just a single bowl of soup. 'New regulations,' he sneered as he dumped the bowl down, carelessly and contemptuously, on the stone floor between them. 'From now on you get just one bowl between the two of you.' The prisoners eyed the single bowl with craving, and they glared at each other with a new distrust.

So begins a famous story.[1] In the formulation of it which I shall be using here, the story will introduce three key notions with which this lecture is to be concerned — 'Quality, 'Generosity', 'Political Incorrectness'. Also, even more importantly, the story will evoke the context in which I am proposing to explore these three terms, and to apply them to the work of libraries and librarians. The imagery in the story of two prisoners and a single bowl of soup gives body and liveliness, that is to say, to the fundamental political and philosophical questions which will hover around us as I speak with you this morning. The lecture has a prologue — the story which I have already begun. There will then be some brief reflections on the prologue, and these will constitute the lecture's introduction. Then the main lecture has three parts. Part one will be about 'Quality', part two about 'Generosity' and part three about 'Political Incorrectness'. In a nutshell, I am against quality, in favour of generosity and against political incorrectness. I will explain and attempt to defend these prejudices in due course. Suffice to say just at present that I shall be problematising and criticising much discourse about quality; shall be pondering with you what it might mean to say that public services in general and libraries in particular should be generously resourcing generosity; and considering how, in pursuing this task, we may face and dare down a certain demonising tendency in contemporary culture — the tendency to project, from out of a fearful and ungenerous imagination, this thing named and known as political correctness. As I draw towards a close, there will be a recapitulation. This will be, as the term might be, an unadulterated piece of internal plagiarism — I shall repeat verbatim a handful of sentences from earlier parts of the lecture. Finally there will be an epilogue, which will be a continuation of the story with which I am beginning, the story of two prisoners with a single bowl of soup between them.

Suddenly each prisoner lunged forward to seize the bowl between them. In their struggle they knocked the bowl over and its precious contents were spilled across the stone floor of the cell. The next day the same thing happened. Each lunged for the bowl and the contents were wasted. And again the next day. The prisoners were becoming faint with hunger and increasingly frantic in their hatred for each other.

On the fourth day they were visited by a group of five prison visitors. The visitors listened to their complaints and then made a number of suggestions and recommendations. 'The basic problem,' said the first visitor, 'is that there isn't a system of quality assurance and total quality management in this prison. I'll get a Prisoner's Charter for you which will lay down standards as to how the gaoler should carry your soup, and require him to be polite and to wear a badge at all times with his name and photograph on it. What's more, I'll see to the introduction of GBLT's — Gaoler Behaviour League Tables — and I'll get a private sector partnership scheme going, and a soup hotline organised, so that you can complain whenever you want to.'

'As I see the matter,' said the second visitor, 'the basic problem is that the two of you are intolerant. Your attitudes are all wrong, you're prejudiced against each other. You must love each other, be generous to each other, and share the soup harmoniously. There is no excuse for intolerance, and I have absolutely no sympathy for it.'

'As for me,' said the third visitor, 'I can see grave dangers in the ways you are complaining. You cannot change your situation and therefore shouldn't even try to talk about it. Once you do start talking about it, with a view to trying to change it, you'll fall into the trap of arguing about the right terms and phrases. There's already more than enough political correctness in the world. I strongly advise both of you to keep your mouths shut.'

The fourth and fifth prison visitors worked as a pair. Each took one of the prisoners aside and spoke out of earshot of the other. Both said exactly the same thing: 'Look, the basic cause of all your problems is the other prisoner. You have noticed, haven't you, that the other prisoner is very different from you — you're aware of all sorts of signs and marks of difference, I'm sure, particularly these last few days. Basically the other prisoner isn't really a complete human being, but a sort of monster or demon, full of vicious malevolence towards yourself. I daresay you remember stories you've heard in the past which tell how people like the other prisoner have always been worse than people like you, and don't deserve to get as much out of life. I can sort all this out for you, if you would like me to — I could get the other prisoner removed, totally removed if you understand my meaning. What do you think?'

Each prisoner thought hard.

We leave them there. I shall return to this imagery later, with a continuation but — I give due warning — not a conclusion. First, some reflections on it. The imagery problematises this lecture's three key ideas. Is discourse about quality a cop-out for not talking about quantity and not talking about equity? In situations where there is a shortage of resources is discourse about generosity merely empty and hypocritical? Is the function of discourse about political correctness, by those who use it to criticise and demonise others, to divert attention from vital political issues about inclusion and exclusion?

Further, the story explores some points about the origins and dynamics of the phenomena sometimes known as 'otherising', 'demonising' and 'racialisation'. In certain circumstances, specifically in circumstances where there are conflicts over scarce resources, human beings believe that people with whom they are in conflict are 'Other' — beings quite different from themselves, with different needs and rights. They often then go on, as it were, to see others as demons or monsters, deeply malicious and malevolent, and they construct the idea that the human species can be divided into different races, and that membership of a race is marked by various visible features. It is incidentally very common, in racialisation processes as in competitive team games, for 'colour' to be used as a way of marking differences between oneself and others. Processes of otherising, demonising and racialising are kept alive and well, in any one community or society, by a range of stories and narratives — including grand narratives about the history and destiny of the nation as well as all sorts of fables, legends and imagery, and anecdotes, gossip and travellers' tales. They therefore have to be resisted by, amongst other things, alternative narratives, alternative imagery. These processes and their narratives are the backdrop for any occasion, for example this conference and this lecture, which seeks to attend to issues of human equality and inequality.

No imagery can say it all. This image of the two prisoners with a single bowl of soup, for example: it severely distorts reality in so far as it forgets that in real life and in real history, as distinct from in stories and in competitive team games, there are seldom if ever such things as level playing fields. Always we start unequal — powerful and powerless, oppressors and oppressed, topdog and underdog, senior and subaltern. Otherising and racialising take place not just in contexts of competition, but in contexts of unequal competition. In such contexts those with the greater access to and control of material resources are able to assert a cultural hegemony: they impose their representations of difference and otherness as entirely 'normal' and unproblematic. Typically, indeed universally, they represent themselves as superior and others as subaltern: it is the topdog who demonises the underdog, usually, not the other way round.

The term quality belongs to a body of discourse in which other recurring terms include 'customer', 'customer care', 'customer satisfaction', 'contract', 'service level agreement', 'excellence', 'charter' and so on. It combines with other words to yield the acronyms QA and TQM — 'quality assurance' and 'total quality management'. This whole body of discourse has its attractions and indeed its uses. But also it has some fundamental limitations and has implicit in it some considerable dangers. I wish to recall a number of the objections which need to be made to it. But first, let us acknowledge that it has a certain usefulness and confess that not all was well before its advent. There are weaknesses in public services which TQM and QA do to an extent address.

Such weaknesses are sometimes starkly revealed in loosely worded notices, and in careless attention to possible double meanings. It was reported in the press recently that there was a notice in a school corridor which said: 'Examinations in Progress. Do Not Pass.' And hospital staff showed a similar unawareness of double meanings with a notice on their institution's perimeter fence saying: 'Caution. Guard Dogs Operating Here.' Such a notice is symbolic of public service at its worst — a careless approach to language and communication, and an essentially fearful, distrusting view of the public. This is by way of saying that people who work in public services are as prone as anyone else to engage in processes of otherising and demonising. We have to confront these processes within ourselves — our structures and our organisational cultures — at the same time that we seek to address them in the wider world. An article a couple of years ago in the *Health Service Journal* described a training event at which public service managers had been asked to brainstorm around the term 'service users'. The words which they came up with, reported the article, were: 'difficult, critical, vulnerable, sick, inadequate, ignorant, ill-informed, manipulative, dependent — and just occasionally satisfied'.[2]

All of us who work in public services know the lures of solipsism — we dream of labouring in that delightful utopia where there is no public to serve. Teachers long sometimes to do their work of instructing, informing and educating in a school where there are no pupils, and nurses and doctors yearn to practise, heal and care in a hospital where there are no patients. Local government officials and elected members desire a world in which there are no local residents or voters, and national civil servants and politicians, as is all too well known, relish in their imaginations (and not only, alas, in their imaginations) a world in which there is no local government. Librarians, I venture to assume, sometimes have a gleam in their eye when they ponder the blissful possibility of working in a library which never has any users.[3] All of us, librarians and non-librarians alike, can sympathise and empathise with that tailor in Athens who put up a notice recently for his English customers in which, because of the slight imperfections of his English vocabulary, he perhaps disclosed his own utopian vision of an ideal world rather more clearly than he intended: 'Order your summer clothes now. Because of big rush all customers will be executed in strict rotation.'

A map without utopia on it, it has been said, is not worth consulting. Yes, but it matters what sort of a place the utopia is, and what sort of linkages it has with reality, and the kinds of path and route back to reality which it emboldens and clears. A utopian vision should help us to grapple with the realities we know, and to try to change them and improve them. I shall repeat these reflections about utopias a little later, when introducing a continuation of the story with which I began, about the two prisoners with the single bowl of soup. The main thing I wish to acknowledge at present is that discourse about QA and TQM does have the potential to dispel a serious weakness in the culture of public services.

However, quality in public services is surely a duty not a virtue. There is something deeply wrong with a system which elevates quality to some sort of absolute value, and forgets thus that it is merely a means to something, not an end in itself. It is particularly alarming and significant that all this new discourse about quality ('Quallispeak', as it might be called) has emerged at precisely the same time that there have been major declines in the *quantity* of resources being distributed through public services: and at the same time too, more seriously still, that there have been major increases in inequality between the richest and poorest in our country, and major declines in structures of democracy and accountability.[4] Quality discourse seems to have nothing to say about equity, and no way of critiquing and resisting the rise of quangocrats and quangocracies.

Quallispeak needs perhaps to be removed from our occupational and organisational cultures, and to be replaced with a different body of discourse — one which is bolder, braver, more keen-eyed and more passionate in relation to issues of equity and accountability. Alternatively, it needs to be immensely refined, enriched and added to. Either way, there are three main things which need saying.

First, we need to look very critically at this phrase 'providing services'. It is so familiar and so friendly, and so innocuous and so commonsensical, that we forget that there are other and more accurate ways of describing what we do. We do not provide services, merely: we distribute resources. And the key question is who benefits. Who gets more than their fair share of the resources which we pass on, and what do they do with them? What is the impact on patterns of inequality and injustice in the world around us? If we do not even ask these questions we invite comparisons with those legendary people who demonstrated excellent customer care when they put deckchairs out on the Titanic. Or, recalling the metaphor with which this lecture began, we invite comparison with prison gaolers who try not to be rude to their 'customers' when going about their business in a savagely oppressive regime.

Second, we need to talk much more about 'citizens' than about 'customers'. Our task isn't primarily to do with satisfying customers, it's to do with empowering citizens — giving them the resources they need to play a full part in social and community life. Third, we need therefore to envision that our accountability is to a whole community, a community in which there are very probably conflicts of interest and inequalities of power: our accountability is not merely to various individual 'service users'.

There are important insights for our work, to repeat, from the world of producer-customer and provider-user relationships. But there are other worlds, other relationships, from which to derive learnings, analogies, metaphors, models. For example, there is the relationship between therapist and client; the relationship between lovers; the relationship between artist or performer and audience. Even — dare I say this, just here and just now? — there is the relationship between a lecturer and an audience. This latter relationship is mercifully more terminable than the others but it has, alas, every bit as much potential as they for anti-climax.

What does a library look like when it takes on board these points about quality? When, that is to say, it sees quality as a means not an end; when it conceptualises its role as channelling resources rather than providing services; when it views its users as citizens to be empowered rather than as customers to be satisfied; and when it seeks to be accountable to a community rather than to various individuals? It is not for me, I believe, to answer this question with nitty-gritty detail.[5] I can offer, though, some broad-brush sketching of utopia. Such a library has a bias to the poor, the underdog, the colonised, the dispossessed, the subaltern: the voiceless and the textless. This bias is seen in, of course, its stock and in its activities, events and programmes. It is seen also in its understanding of what a text is or may be; in the attention it gives to the importance of information-sharing and networking; in its structures and procedures of accountability; and in what it chooses to store from the past and present for the empowering of citizens and of communities one future day. It is both old and new, and here are both past and future:

> New eyes each year
> Find old books here
> And new books too
> Old eyes renew;
> So youth and age
> Like ink and page
> In this house join,
> Minting new coin.[6]

Such a library, in a word, is generous. The word 'generosity', I wish to suggest, evokes an alternative to what earlier I have referred to as otherising and demonising. Also, it is a value which needs to be added to 'quality' in public services, and without which quality is not enough. Further, it is the opposite of so-called political correctness. I shall propose three main principles of generosity and shall summarise these with three quotations from, respectively, a novel, a play and a poem: 'There is no measure'; 'In you that journey is'; and 'There is a place for all at the rendez-vous of victory.' Subtitles might be, respectively: relativity; hybridity; and inclusiveness. To introduce the first principle of generosity, I should like to quote from Pat Barker's novel *Regeneration*. The book is a remarkable study of the work and secular faith of a doctor in a Scottish hospital in 1917. It takes its title from medical work to repair damaged nerve tissue, but is concerned with regeneration of the human spirit more than with physical or bodily regeneration alone. The main character is a Dr Rivers. He is both a neurologist and a social anthropologist. At one point he speaks as follows, in a conversation with a close colleague:

> 'I don't know whether you've ever had the ... the experience of having your life changed by a quite trivial incident. You know, nothing dramatic like the death of a parent, or the birth of a child. Something so trivial you almost can't see why it had the effect it had.'[7]

He then goes on to describe something which once happened to him in the Solomon Isles, where he was researching as an anthropologist. He was on a boat with a group of islanders and after he had finished asking them some questions, in his professional role of anthropologist, about their mores and values they turned the tables and put some similar questions to himself:

'They were *incredulous*. How could anybody live *like that?* And so it went on, question after question. And it was one of those situations, you know, where one person starts laughing and everybody joins in and in the end the laughter just feeds off itself. They were rolling around the deck by the time I'd finished. And suddenly I realised that *anything* I told them would have got the same response. They wouldn't've felt a twinge of disgust or disapproval or … sympathy or anything, because it would all have been too *bizarre*. And I suddenly saw that their reactions to my society were neither more nor less valid than mine to theirs. And do you know that was a moment of the most amazing freedom. I lay back and I closed my eyes and I felt as if a ton weight had been lifted.'

And he then explains the experience as follows:

'It was … the *Great White God* de-throned, I suppose. Because we did, we quite unselfconsciously assumed we were the measure of all things. That was how we approached them. And suddenly I saw not only that we weren't the measure of all things, but that *there was no measure.'*

The term 'post-colonial' is not ideal. But it does begin to capture the experience which Pat Barker is describing here through her character Dr Rivers. (Incidentally he was a real person, not just a character in a novel.) If there is to be an end of otherising, demonising and racialising then there has to be an end also of the colonial mentality — the belief not only that one's own ways and traditions are the measure of all things but also that there is a measure somewhere. The fact is, there is no measure.

The phrase 'In you that journey is' is from a speech at a funeral in Tony Kushner's play *Angels in America*. The person who has died was an immigrant to the United States many decades ago and was the mother and grandmother of many of the people gathered at her graveside. The rabbi taking the service speaks as follows:

'In her was — not a person but a whole kind of person — the ones who crossed the ocean, who brought with us to America the villages of Russia and Lithuania — and how we struggled, and how we fought, for the family, for the Jewish home, so that you would not grow up here, in this strange place, in the melting pot where nothing melted. Descendants of this immigrant woman, you do not grow up in America, you and your children and their children with their goyische names, you do not live in America, no such place exists, your clay is the clay of some Litvak shtetl, your air the air of the steppes — because she carried the old world on her back across the ocean, in a boat, and she put it down on Grand Concourse Avenue, or in Flatbush, and she worked that earth into your bones, and you pass it to your children, this ancient, ancient culture and home. (*Little pause*). *You* can never make that crossing that she made, for such Great Voyages in this world do not any more exist. But every day of your lives the miles that voyage between that place and this one you cross. Every day. You understand me? In you that journey is.'

Salman Rushdie has said that the migrant is the archetypal human being. We don't need literally to cross borders and frontiers to be in touch with the migrant sensibility, the hybridity, inside the consciousness of each one of us. In each of us the journey is. The Latin wisdom of long ago is not in all respects true, and perhaps it never was —*caelum non animum mutant qui trans mare currunt*, you change the sky but not your soul when you cross the sea. For souls do change when they mingle with other souls, people change through exchange, they become hybrids.[8] Particularly the offspring of migrants are new, even newer than other offspring, and of course people are changed by their own children and grandchildren even as they try to shape and point them into the future.

Philip Larkin once wrote beautifully about the importance of elsewhere. 'Lonely in Ireland, since it was not home,' he said, ' Strangeness made sense … Differences went to prove me separate, not unworkable.' But at home in England there is no such strangeness, and no relief for loneliness:

> Living in England has no such excuse:
> These are my customs and establishments
> It would be much more serious to refuse.
> Here no elsewhere underwrites my existence.

Well, hybrids and migrants do have an elsewhere to justify their existence. Of hybridity we may say, quoting (it so happens) a phrase from another poem by Larkin, 'may it always be there.' Knowing and celebrating hybridity is an essential strand of generosity, for we can no longer make a sharp distinction between the purity of the self and the impurity of the Other.

The statement that that there is 'a place for all at the rendez-vous of victory' is attributed to Aimé Césaire. Césaire was a Martiniquian poet and writer, associated with the celebration of *négritude,* black consciousness and culture. In his book *Cahier d'un Retour au Pays Natal* he wrote the sentence which, in a translation of it made by CLR James, has become famous and inspiring in many lands and locations throughout the world:

> No race possesses the monopoly of beauty, of intelligence, of force, and there is a place for all at the rendez-vous of victory.[9]

There is a place for the erstwhile oppressor as well as for the erstwhile oppressed, he is saying, in the new society of the future, the utopia of which he dreams. It follows that also in the search for utopia, the struggle to beat a path to it, there is a place for all. It is difficult, however, for a sensitive topdog to believe this! The principal protagonist of André Brink's *A Dry White Season,* set in South Africa in the 1970s, sees no future for himself at the rendez-vous of victory and no role in the journey. His ending as he sees it is defeat and despair. He writes:

> Whether I like it or not, whether I feel like cursing my own condition or not ... l am white. That is the small final, terrifying truth of my broken world. I am white. And because I'm white I am born into a state of privilege.... Even if I fight the system that has reduced us to this I remain white, and favoured by the circumstances I abhor. Even if I'm hated, and ostracised, and persecuted, and in the end destroyed, nothing can make me black. And so those who are cannot but remain suspicious of me.

> If I act, I cannot but lose. But if I do not act, it is a different kind of defeat, equally decisive and maybe worse... The end seems ineluctable: failure, defeat, loss.

Brink's narrator is in a kind of prison: ineluctable failure, defeat, loss. This lecture began by evoking a prison and it will end with an image of freedom from prison. As we consider the nature of generosity as formulated by Aimé Césaire, the apostle of *négritude,* and doubts and despair about it, as sketched by a white person in South Africa, it is fitting to recall a significant world event through which we have all lived in summer 1994. Despite decades on Robben Island there came the generosity of Nelson Mandela's speech of a few weeks ago, and the generosity of the circumstances in which the speech was embedded:

'This is a joyous night for the human spirit ... The calm and tolerant atmosphere that prevailed during the elections depicts the type of South Africa we can build. It set the tone for the future. We might have our differences, but we are one people with a common destiny in our rich variety of culture, race and tradition ... Let our celebrations be in keeping with the mood set in the elections, peaceful, respectful and disciplined ... Let us build the future together, and toast a better life for all.'

There is a world of difference, of course, between generosity and political correctness: so much so, indeed, that in explicitly commending generosity I have implicitly been condemning political correctness. However, so-called political correctness is seldom if ever an objective phenomenon. Mainly it is a demon or monster projected from the conservative imagination of those who criticise it. Generosity towards the demonising, monsterising tendency in conservative culture involves — amongst other things — a calm and cheerful mockery of its fears, and an assertion that people speak more truly than they know when they try to claim that everything's all right really. This frothy little piece of doggerel, for example:

Here Be Monsters

Give ear to me my friends, there's no need to have a fright.
Though monsters roam around, I'll get them sorted out:
I am telling you, everything's all right.

Eg political correctness — shrill bark and snarling bite:
Contemptuously ignore it, it's the outlook of a lout.
Give ear to me my friends, there's no need to have a fright.

These priggish p.c. people think they've seen the light,
But it's only trendy theory that tediously they spout:
I am telling you, everything's all right.

Envy drives their whining, and cynicism, spite,
But I'll pursue and hound them — it'll be a rout.
Give ear to me my friends, there's no need to have a fright.

One's useless, says their chatter, if one's dead and male and white,
But let's keep old-style wisdom, untroubled by a doubt:
I am telling you, everything's all right.

> If we just get back to basics, the future's very bright.
> True — monsters, devils, demons, there's a lot of them about:
> But give ear to me my friends, there's no need to have a fright,
> For I am telling you, everything's all right.

Undoubtedly there are fundamental philosophical questions to be clarified in the political correctness debate, and this frothy doggerel is no more than a very preliminary bit of psychological (not philosophical) ground-clearing. People who use the term 'p.c.' to demonise and denounce others must certainly be resisted. Such resistance must not be, in its turn, merely trite and trivialising. A real and rigorous debate is needed about terminology to name and to point towards new realities; and throughout the formal and informal education system, including in particular higher and adult education, there needs to be a serious debate about 'the canon' and about the unending interchange between heritage, present and newness: 'So youth and age/Like ink and page/In this house join/Minting new coin.' But I am not engaging any further in either of the two key debates, about terminology and the canon, here today.

I draw now towards the end by repeating a handful of sentences and quotations from earlier in the lecture. This brief anthology of material *déjà entendu* is in the first instance a recapitulation or summary. But it has a further purpose also: it is a way of setting the scene and the stage for a continuation of the story and imagery with which I began, about the two prisoners and the single bowl of soup.

Processes of otherising, demonising and racialising are kept alive and well, in any one community or society, by a range of stories and narratives — including grand narratives about the history and destiny of the nation as well all sorts of fables, legends and imagery, and anecdotes, gossip and travellers' tales. They therefore have to be resisted by, amongst other things, alternative narratives, alternative imagery.

Our task isn't primarily to do with satisfying customers, it's to do with empowering citizens — giving them the resources they need in order to play a full part in social and community life.

A map without utopia on it, it has been said, is not worth consulting. Yes, but it matters what sort of a place the utopia is, and what sort of linkages it has with reality, and the kinds of path and route back to reality which it emboldens and clears.

So youth and age
Like ink and page
In this house join,
Minting new coin.

The imagery in the story of two prisoners and a single bowl of soup gives body and liveliness ... to the fundamental political and philosophical questions which will hover around us as I speak with you this morning.

The relationship between therapist and client. The relationship between lovers. The relationship between artist or performer and audience. Even — dare I say this, just here and just now? — the relationship between a lecturer and an audience. This latter relationship is mercifully more terminable than the others but it has, alas, every bit as much potential as they for anti-climax.

The notion was, yes, for a moment attractive — the other as source of all their problems.

But when they returned to their cell and looked into each other's eyes, and when each guessed precisely, and at precisely the same moment, what the other was thinking, they simultaneously smiled. Each smile reflected, brightened, filled out, the other.

From that time onwards they fought shoulder to shoulder — fought the gaoler, fought the governor, fought the prison visitors. Often smiling, never hating.

Eventually they were set free. But their fight continued, it continues still.

A fight which is also a search. A search for the secret, their secret, the source of their hope, the source of their joint refusal to hate or to despair.

Yes, the fight and the search continued, and they continue still.

4

Who's the Partridge in a Peartree?

literature, literacy and fabulous children

To be very grand, indeed over the top, but seasonal: the stand-up comic deals in epiphanies. 'The most delicate and evanescent of moments,' said Joyce, 'when the soul or whatness of a thing leaps to us from the vestment of its appearance. The soul of the commonest object ... seems to us radiant. The object achieves its epiphany.'

After dinner speech at a conference of the National Association of Advisers in English, early January 1995, shortly before the traditional occasions known as Twelfth Night and the Feast of the Epiphany. The conference theme was children and young people as writers. The venue was the Green Dragon Hotel, Hereford.

4. Who's the Partridge in a Peartree?
literature, literacy and fabulous children

Sunday 25 December 1994 — One
A bare page

A bare page. Stay with it, the bareness of the present. A gift which we both receive and give, the present, its bareness. We move and tread into it, making first footprints on a long journey. The bareness is beautiful because it seeks, invites, holds. And is terrifying for the same reasons. Burden and danger as well as gift. Receive it, move into it. Beauty, terror. Gift, burden. Bareness, prints. The choice is between both or neither. We take, we are given, both or neither, this is the present.

I am proposing to walk across, through, bare pages these next eleven days of Christmas. From home here in Oxfordshire to there, the Green Dragon in Hereford. From family to work. From snug retreat to astringent new year. A bare page each day. Both or neither? Stay with it, move into it. Beauty, terror. Gift, burden. Bareness, prints. Both or neither, this is the present. And what is going to be unwrapped? That is the present question.

In the background, children and young people as writers, as fabulists, storytellers. Tomorrow and the next day I shall recall briefly what we want and need them to write about, and why, and ways it is difficult, and on these matters shall quote five people, for the sake of a preliminary *tour d'horizon*. One of them is R S Thomas, on the loneliness and terror of bare pages.

Thomas implies that a writer faced by a bare page glimpses what it's like to be excluded, cast off from the centre, denied love and liberty. Be that as it may, this eleven-day starry-eyed trek towards epiphany is, I hope and intend, going to be about connections between writing and society, textuality and equality, the joining-up not only of letters but also of people: it's going to be political. Also it's going to wonder and worry at this question: what's a partridge doing in a peartree? In other words, it's going ask about the inner nature of presents sent by a true love, as distinct from that of those sent by a false love. This too is a kind of politics. A writer, a storyteller, a speaker wraps and unwraps. And does so as true love or false love, or as some sort of mixture. You dis-cover yourself when the last layer of the wrappings is removed, and the partridge is made manifest.

This afternoon I read Antonia Byatt's story in Christmas Eve's *Independent.*[1] It's entitled *Dragon's Breath,* so perhaps is prima facie relevant for next week's venue, though Byatt's dragons are drab grey, not green. It could be that they are symbolic of an authoritarian government, accoutred with an authoritarian, reductionist and Philistine national curriculum. Byatt stresses that it is when the humans are bored and have lost the power to resist that the dragons emerge, slithering down with fiery breath from the surrounding volcanic heights, 'stinking with despair and endless decay'. In due course they pass away, just as an authoritarian government will in due course pass on and away. (And the national curriculum will go packing with it.) What remains are stories, 'made from those people's wonder at their own survival'. In time the stories become, says Antonia Byatt, 'charms against boredom for their children and grandchildren, riddling hints of the true relations between peace and beauty and terror'.

At the end of this evening I joined my daughter and son-in-law to watch Victoria Wood on TV. She talked a lot about pregnancy and childbirth, there was some stuff about epidurals, it was all very robust and physical, and so the three of us were even more aware than we might otherwise have been of a fourth person in the sitting room — the one inside my daughter, whose nativity is due in early February. The stand-up comic as storyteller. As if sitting and chatting in a familiar cafe, canteen, bar, kitchen or bedroom she conjures stories from that random world of Tesco's and labour wards which she has in common with the audience and she makes the familiar world shine, gives it a sense of specialness, reduces its randomness. Eventually she comes home. Safely but provisionally. Predictably but surprisingly. To be very grand, indeed over the top, but seasonal: the stand-up comic deals in epiphanies. 'The most delicate and evanescent of moments,' said Joyce, 'when the soul or whatness of a thing leaps to us from the vestment of its appearance. The soul of the commonest object ... seems to us radiant. The object achieves its epiphany.'

The stand-up comic is an archetypal storyteller in other ways too. She wraps and unwraps, maintains a sense of suspense, turns the audience on, teases, breaks interdictions, makes probes into holy and forbidden space, delays the climax, uses throwaway material, promises, and deliciously uncovers 'riddling hints of the true relations between peace and beauty and terror'. For the audience, she is like a bare page. The bareness is beautiful because it seeks, invites, holds. And it is terrifying for the same reasons. Danger and burden as well as gift. And it's the same the other way round: for her, the audience is like a bare page, beautiful because it seeks, invites, holds. And terrifying for the same reasons. Danger and burden as well as gift. Receive it, move into it. Beauty, terror. Gift, burden. Bareness, prints. The choice is between both or neither. We take, we are given, both or neither, that is the present. Scheherazade and the tyrant, true and false love, night after night, this is the present.

Monday 26 December — Two
Most important things

In an essay entitled *Blood, Bread and Poetry*, published a few years ago, Adrienne Rich recalled her teenage self, and what she read for in those days. She turned to books, she said, in order to ask and find answers to questions: 'What is possible in this life? What does 'love' mean, this thing that is so important? What is this other thing called 'freedom' or 'liberty' — is it like love, a feeling? What have human beings lived and suffered in the past? How am I going to live my life?'[2] This seems a very satisfactory summary of why children should write as well as read — to dis-cover two most important things, love and liberty. The personal and the political: two most important things.

News today that John Osborne died on Christmas Eve. Arnold Wesker on the radio recalls something Osborne once said to him about autobiographical writing: 'Feeling is more important than facts'. It's all right to be economical with historicity and the facts, even a bit spendthrift and inventive with non-facts, providing the feeling is correctly expressed. In evening I watched Dennis Potter's *Midnight Movie*. Indeed, economical with factual accuracy and cavalierly prodigal with fantasy, in order to probe differences between true love and false love. Leitmotif and *déjà vu*, prefiguring and reprise, layer on layer and layer off layer, wrapping and unwrapping, probing onto forbidden ground, probing into the rag and bone shop of the heart. A friend has given me, as a Christmas present this year, a book entitled *Potter on Potter*, a mix of biography and autobiography, woven from a series of interviews. 'Part of me,' said Potter once, 'is the wistful youth, the other part is the dirty old man. We're a mix of ape and angel.' On politics he said: 'Obviously I could never bring myself to vote Conservative, and I suppose it would be accurate to say that I am on the left, but many of my feelings are what would commonly and crudely be called right-wing. Emotionally, I believe the greatest danger to the human race is lack of order. That doesn't necessarily imply a sanctioning of hierarchies, but it does imply a belief in law.' On religion: 'I remain sufficiently a Christian to know that despair is, in the old words, a very great sin.' And this is what he said once about writing: 'No matter how corrupt, wicked, cruel, disastrous the world is, some little tributary of feeling says it's all right. That is where the writing comes from.'[3]

Tuesday 27 December — Three
Defiant writers

Roy Hattersley in today's *Guardian*: 'If the Angel of the Lord came down and promised peace on earth and goodwill to men, why is Michael Howard Home Secretary?' Hugo Young writes about MI5 and MI6, and his attitude towards them as a professional journalist: 'They're not a national enemy, like the KGB, but they are a professional enemy. They want to twist our words and steer our pens.' Will Hutton reports that throughout the industrialised world there is a rise in clinical depression, and attributes this to the destruction and undermining of friendships and support systems by consumerism and market relationships. The feel-good factor cannot be provided, he says, *pace* John Major and his advisers, by economic means alone. Antonia Byatt's dragons, 'stinking with despair and endless decay', are inside us as well as around and above us. They are both backdrop and subject-matter of writer, speaker, storyteller, as they search and probe for a lasting feel-good factor. 'No matter how corrupt, wicked, cruel, disastrous the world is,' said Dennis Potter, 'some little tributary of feeling says it's all right. That is where the writing comes from.' Here follow four vignettes about writing, respectively by Anne Tyler, Jill Tweedie, Grace Nichols and R S Thomas.

Ian Bledloe is a school student aged 17, and is the main character in Ann Tyler's novel *Saint Maybe*. In his own words, he is 'a medium kind of guy, all in all' but 'even so,' adds Anne Tyler, 'there were moments when he believed that someday, somehow, he was going to end up famous'. Near the start of the novel she has a brief passage describing him as he arrives home one day from school, and meeting his mother in the kitchen:

> Famous for what, he couldn't quite say; but he'd be walking up the back steps or something and all at once he would imagine a camera zooming in on him, filming his life story. He imagined the level, cultured voice of his biographer saying, 'Ian climbed the steps. He opened the door. He entered the kitchen.
>
> 'Have a good day, hon?' his mother asked, passing through with a laundry basket.
>
> 'Oh,' he said, 'the usual run of scholastic triumphs and athletic glories.' And he set his books on the table.
>
> His biographer said, 'He set his books on the table.'[4]

It's a beautiful passage to cite at a conference on children and young people as writers. For it recalls that each of us is a fabulist, we picture our lives as narratives and ourselves as protagonists. Either directly or (more usually) indirectly, all important writing is in this sense autobiographical: the search for pattern and significance, and for the feel-good factor ('oh, the usual run of scholastic triumphs and athletic glories') which experiences of pattern and significance provide. It's also worth noting that the passage contains one of the great questions which all of us in education should be continually putting to ourselves and each other: 'Have a good day, hon?' We need to concentrate, yes, on daily minutiae: but daily wholes, not daily fragments, and we need to be asking about their quality — were they good? Good-enough parents ask this question of their children every day, and also good-enough teachers and inspectors ask it, though not usually so explicitly, of themselves. The sad truth is that in the 1990s all too many children and young people do not have a daily good day at school, and this is because, amongst other reasons, they do all too little real writing, based on real fabling, real narrativising. And teachers and inspectors too: however prone we may be to adolescent exaggeration and self-dramatisation, it's rare to be able to observe, looking back on a day's work, that it was, oh, the usual run of scholastic triumphs and athletic glories. We too do not write, really write, enough.

In her autobiography *Eating Children,* Jill Tweedie recalls herself as a teenage writer. One day she won a prize and waited eagerly with her mother for her father to come home so that she could tell him. He was late and in a bad temper. 'Idiots,' Jill Tweedie recalls him saying as he came into the house. 'What a bunch of idiots I have in the Department. Half of them, I swear, are barely literate. If I want a decent report I have to write it myself. And the train was late again. *And* standing all the way. Pity we didn't lose the war. Hitler would have had them running on time.' Proudly, she told him that she had won a prize at school for writing. 'Fine,' he replied, 'you've won a prize. Just don't go thinking what you win at school has anything to do with the real world out there. You think you're clever? Let me tell you, you haven't half my brains, never will have so don't give yourself airs. And I'll tell you something else. It's not clever that counts, it's hard work and character ... Work on your character, that's my advice, and never mind the scribbling. I'm telling you this for your own good, so you can take that look off your face and listen for once.'[5]

Jill Tweedie adds, bringing the episode to a close: 'With that look on my face I looked at Mother, but she was looking up at my father and there wasn't any room for me.' It is a desperately poignant vignette of exclusion, rejection, aloneness. But somehow, we must remind ourselves that she did become a glorious writer, defiant to the end. 'No matter how corrupt, wicked, cruel, disastrous the world is, some little tributary of feeling says it's all right. That is where the writing comes from.'

In her poem entitled 'Holding My Beads' Grace Nichols is defiant too, and you feel that for her the threading of words together into a poem is part of the threading of events together into a life-story, and that this in its turn is inseparable from her assertion of herself as distinct, and of her strong strenuous rejection of other people's attempts to define her as subordinate or subaltern.[6] 'I am here, ' she says, 'with all my lives strung out like beads before me.' She doesn't want privileges, doesn't seek pity, isn't after quick fixes. As both writer and person (the two being barely if at all distinguishable) she wants 'the power to be what I am ... a woman holding my beads in my hand.'

Love and liberty, Adrienne Rich said, these two most important things. An opposite of both is loneliness. But both are reached *through* loneliness not apart from it — or so, any way, R S Thomas seems to suggest, in his meditation entitled 'The Word' on the loneliness of writing.[7] He imagines being instructed by a god to write down what it is like to be a human being. 'My hand hovered long,' he says, 'over the bare page'. He compares then the bare page to an expanse of land, perhaps to an expanse of snow, and the marks he sets down on the page are like footprints of a lost traveller on the bare earth, the bare snow. They spell the one word 'lonely'. He is inclined to erase this and start again, but all the world's marginalised and excluded people — all those, as he puts it, 'waiting at life's window' — seem at this point to cry out that it is true. The human condition is a bare page. This is known by writers, Thomas seems to say, quintessentially.

Late evening today I watched Jasper Carrott, this time with my son and his partner. Again, the stand-up comic as storyteller, as every person. He tells a gently blasphemous epiphany story, probing onto forbidden ground. It's about a nativity play at an infants school which he visited, so he said, the other day. The innkeeper was shy and tongue-tied but Joseph was a bold ad-libber. 'Have you any room at the inn? ... Please, it's desperate, we need a bed. Do you know who's in there?' Joseph pointed at the cushion inside Mary's dress. 'Inside there we've got, we've got, you're not going to believe this, but we've got God Almighty himself.' — 'Jesus Christ!' said the innkeeper, his tongue loosened. 'That's right,' said Joseph, congratulating the innkeeper that he'd at last said something, and something true into the bargain. The joke's on the naive, unknowing children, and to this extent the story is merely cute. (Another story in the same genre appeared in a paper last week. A primary school class had been asked to write imaginary letters from the Magi to Mary. 'I hope you liked the gold I gave you,' wrote one child. 'If you would like some more do please let me know.') But also the joke's on the school, failing to keep up respectable appearances, and on Christianity, for its preposterous myth. And it's also on the worldly stand-up comic, reminding himself and his audience that blasphemy only has power if it's dangerous, and that it's dangerous only if the beliefs it mocks may in some sense be true. 'I remain sufficiently a Christian,' said Dennis Potter, 'to know that despair is, in the old words, a very great sin.' Face it and engage with it, Thomas's god said to him, face and engage with the bare page.

Wednesday 28 December — Four Enumerations of the enemy

Rich, Tyler, Tweedie, Nichols and Thomas remind us what writing by children should ideally be about, and that even at the best of times writing doesn't come easy. In British education in the mid 1990s it's not the best of times. To get our bearings we need, amongst other things, to enumerate the enemy — and the enemy's enemies. Our enemy's attack on writing in schools is part and parcel of a wide-ranging attack on many other things also. It follows that we need to see it in context, and to be in alliance with many other places of resistance and struggle too.

For both enumerations we can use a seasonal device. First, our enemy's enemies, homing in finally on the subject area of this conference, writing: twelve single mothers, eleven welfare scroungers, ten trendy teachers, nine Brussels bureaucrats, eight multiculturalists, seven muslim mullahs, six new age travellers, five *Guardian* readers, four bogus refugees, three p.c. zealots, two loony socialists, and a writer with a probing pen. And then the enemy itself. My false love sent to me — my seducing, manipulating, dominating, self-preening, possessing, posing, invading, devouring love sent to me — twelve security officers, eleven racist patriots, ten gerrymanderers, nine preachers preaching, eight testers testing, seven customer-orientated quality-controllers, six opted out individualists, five bottom lines, four internal markets, three part-time drudges, two sleazy quangocrats, and a canon-ful of sacred texts.

Enumerations such as these are useful for signalling that the enemy seems to come at us with one damn random and unhelpful thing after another, and from a range of different directions. The various things are joined together by context and common ownership, and by their cumulative effects, rather than by logic or bonds of affiliation. To use a military analogy, we are up against several different armies, currently in coalition, collusion and alliance with each other, scratching each other's backs but not necessarily very committed to each other with ties of deep loyalty. The enemy we are up against is not a single monolith with no internal contradictions. That is why we not only can, but also must, enumerate.

Later in the week I shall re-visit this matter of enumerating the enemy, trying to be more systematic, and to be geared to practical resistance and opposition.

At the end of the evening today, yet another stand-up comedian, this time Lenny Henry. Amid glee from his audience he contrasts festivals in England with festivals in Jamaica. It's in vibrant Jamaica not pale grey England that people know how to celebrate, how to put away the current season's cakes and ale. He sings: 'On the hundredth day of Christmas my true love sent to me ...', and the audience cheers in delight. Malvolio in these twelve days is the archetypal white male, virtuous but morose, and hopeless.

Thursday 29 December — Five
Myths of hope

Today sketched out the daily titles for the rest of this meditation for Hereford. After today's myths of hope there will be: rational arguments; storytelling animals; hybrid identities; practical plans of action; contrite confessions; epiphanies; and true loves.

Today, then, myths of hope. The grand narrative of hope was succinctly summarised by Dennis Potter. 'No matter how corrupt, wicked, cruel, disastrous the world is, some little tributary of feeling says it's all right.' — 'That is where,' he continued, 'the writing comes from.' He might have said, where the myths come from. That is what myths are for. Hope that 'it's all right' is kept alive in story and imagery: 'The wolf shall dwell with the lamb, and the leopard shall lie down with the kid. The calf and the lion cub together, with a little child to lead them. They shall not hurt or destroy ...': the myth that peace is possible, or if not possible any way worth fighting for. Inner peace between, in Potter's terms, ape and angel. Peace with those we can see and touch: true love as distinct from false love. Peace, as distinct from direct or structural violence, in the social order. These two most important things, said Adrienne Rich, love and liberty: the myth that they exist, or any way are worth looking for. The myth that Isaiah wasn't just talking, writing, sentimental tosh.

Alarming to consider that what is required in British education and British society at the present time is perhaps not defeat of the enemy, enumerated here yesterday, but peace with the enemy, a peace process. Sounds like sentimental tosh, indeed. But worth looking at again later during this season. In the meanwhile, worth reminding ourselves that we go into 1995 with two amazing stories about the peace process from 1994, two amazing strengthenings of myths of hope. A friend has given me for

Christmas the currently definitive book about one of them, *Long Walk to Freedom*. 'I never lost hope,' writes the author towards the end, 'that this great transformation would occur. Not only because of the great heroes ... but because of the ordinary men and women of my country. I always knew that deep down in every human heart there was mercy and generosity ... Even in the grimmest times in prison, when my comrades and I were pushed to our limits, I would see a glimmer of humanity in one of the guards, perhaps just for a second, but it was enough to reassure me and keep me going.'[8]

The other great 1994 story of a peace process is described as follows in abstract terms — but with hard-nosed, hard-faced knowing, grim hands-on, physicality-on experience of bombs, of bullets — by the Opsahl Commission on Northern Ireland: 'Negotiation should involve the inherent risk of compromise. Each compromise is a building block, and as the parties grow to trust each other, they move from one compromise to the next, with concessions, though difficult, being made on all sides. Each party becomes invested in the process, each develops a stake in seeing the other succeed, and a sum of mutual investment develops which provides the cushion when it comes to the crunch.'[9]

Friday 30 December — Six
Rational arguments

The argument developing here these days is that we're up against a deadly enemy but that, horrifyingly, the task is to negotiate a settlement rather than to win a victory. This could be, though, sentimental and treacherous tosh. A first stage, if the argument has any merit, is to enumerate the enemy with greater precision than earlier in the week. Something like this. We are faced with several different tendencies, trends, voices, sets of concerns, ideological constellations. These interact with each other, yes, and act as proxies for each other through coded language, but all the same they are separable — and must be separated out if we are to take them on. (And taking them on is, yes, part of the peace process, part of the negotiation.) They include the following, in no particular order:

1. Racism and xenophobia, within and between countries.

2. Uncritical commitments to the market, managerialism, efficiency, 'quality', etc.

3. Acceptance of widening inequalities of income, wealth, status and well-being.

4. Fear of change, and lack of trust in the next generation.

5. Insecurity, and loss of confidence and purpose — loss of the 'feel-good factor'.

6. Rejection of traditional structures of democracy and accountability.

7. A psychological preference for purity as distinct from complexity and ambiguity.

8. A generally mechanistic, technocratic approach to problems of all kinds.

9. A belief that 'intelligence' is hereditary.

10. In literature and all the other arts as well, championing of the past ('the canon') over the present.

The composite title for this set of voices is 'the new right'. The term is useful for the sake of a quick summary. But it is crucial to separate out the various strands, not least in order to loosen the holds which they have on each other. So far as possible, we need to develop rational arguments against each of these, patiently countering every point and objection in turn. Of course, it's not entirely reasonable to be entirely rational — there are vested interests and emotional attachments which cannot be removed simply through intellectual argument. But that is a reason for complementing intellectual argument, not for rejecting it. One of the principal complements is storytelling, the theme of tomorrow's thoughts. Another is political action of various kinds, the theme of Monday's.

There has been coverage in the *Guardian* these last few days of controversies in the field of mathematics education. A *Guardian* columnist remarks that it is well known that there are three kinds of mathematician: those who can count and those who can't. Is this delightful self-criticism or an example of the very kind of anti-intellectualism I'm trying to inveigh against? Don't know. Do feel fairly sure, though, that I cannot cope with Rory Bremner's macabre bad taste on TV at the end of the evening: the Royal Family's story in 1995, he says, will probably be titled Two Divorces and a Funeral.

Saturday 31 December — Seven
Storytelling animals

Not a great deal to say about this, since it's been implicit throughout, and is an entirely well-known to all members of the conference at Hereford. Human beings are, distinctively, storytelling animals. In an article in the *Financial Times* this time last week, on Christmas Eve, Ian McEwan referred to the twentieth century as one great novel. At one time it looked as if the novel would have a happy ending, he says. But we realise as we embark on the last chapter that key characters are still racism, nationalism, xenophobia and antisemitism; and unemployment, homelessness and recession; and 'everywhere that deep pessimism and ungenerosity of spirit known as the far right'. And also, he adds, there are 'anti-rational cults and religions of all kinds, with their attendant consolations and intolerance'. The conclusion of his article is very beautiful:

> According to literary fashion, it is for every reader to deconstruct this text. As we begin to turn to the final chapters we had better start thinking about the reviews we will prepare, not for newspapers and journals, but for bars, cafes, kitchens and bedrooms. Our chosen literary form is democratic: the more we listen to the reckonings of others, hear how they shuffle the priorities and try to see the different shapes of plots they discern, the better we will understand for ourselves this gigantic sprawling novel that no one can put down.[10]

Children as writers are children as fabulists, narrating and deconstructing their own lives, and narrating and deconstructing their times, and the times of humanity. All around them, in McEwan's phrase, there is 'that deep pessimism and ungenerosity of spirit known as the far right'. But they cannot put down the gigantic sprawling novel, they have to read it, and more especially have to help write it. This is true of their teachers too, of course, and all other educationists. Teachers as writers, teachers as fabulists. A modest proposal: at least once every year every teacher should attend an inservice course designed to help them be better fabulists, better able to narrate their struggles against 'that deep pessimism and ungenerosity of spirit known as the far right'.

Many people at Hereford, no doubt, will know Harold Rosen's story *Not Yet,* a wonderful example of an educationist acting as fabulist. In an article which referred to the making of this story he wrote: 'Sentences end with full stops. Stories do not. That is the guarantee that not only do we learn from the making but that the process continues beyond the end as the seed of another story readies itself for germination.'[11] And no doubt many will know another remarkable story of recent years, Anne Fine's *Goggle Eyes*, whose central theme is child as fabulist, possessing incidentally many of the skills of a Victoria Wood-style stand-up comic. Here too there is weak closure — there isn't much of a full stop at the end — but this absolutely does not matter since the whole point of the book is that it's a celebration of the art and craft of story-telling, and also incidentally a most wonderful celebration of good teaching. Well it would be, wouldn't it. 'Living your life is a long and doggy business,' the teacher Mrs Lupey is quoted as saying. 'And stories and books help. Some help you with the living itself. Some help you just take a break. The best do both at the same time.'[12]

Sunday 1 January — Eight
Hybrid identities

One of the strands in 'that deep pessimism and ungenerosity of spirit known as the far right' is a desire for purity and tight impermeable boundaries. It has to be countered by a celebration of hybridity and unboundedness, of many kinds. One kind is the hybrid sexuality in true love; to cite a seasonal summary during these days of Christmas: 'You are betrothed both to a maid and man,' says Sebastian to Olivia on, as it were, the twelfth night. There is the lack of purity and of tight boundaries in all real story-telling and fabling, touched on in this meditation yesterday. Narrator and audience in an endless unwrapping. Around them there is the unbounded expanse of the bare page on which the storyteller treads and leaves prints, the still air in which words hover for a while then fall. There is a text, yes, but if the sacred is here it's in the context, the space between speaker and audience, not on the page.

And of course there is cultural hybridity in the formation of identities. This is vitally important in the present times and struggles. We are all of us torn, like the narrator in Salman Rushdie's story *East, West* in two or more directions. Children and teachers as fabulists need the strength of the Rushdie character, who observes that to be tugged between different cultural loyalties is like being 'roped by two different loves ... whinnying and rearing, like those movie horses being yanked this way by Clark Gable and that way by Montgomery Cliff.' The narrator concludes: 'I buck, I snort,

I whinny, I rear, I kick. Ropes, I do not choose between you. Lassoes, lariats, I choose neither of you, and both. Do you hear? I refuse to choose.'[13] And there is the strength of the wonderfully ironic purity at the story's end: no, says the new caretaker, with one of the most beautiful weak closures of 1994's literary heritage, no-one round here knows anything about a mix-up.

Michael Billington in the *Guardian* this week saluted two great 1994 productions at the Barbican, the *Romeo and Juliet* from Dusseldorf and *The Merchant of Venice* from Chicago. For me too these were two high-points of the year, glorious and gloriously generous celebrations of hybridity, in so many ways, and of the human spirit. Adrienne Rich's two most important things, love and liberty. And Shakespeare's two most important things in the *Merchant,* mercy and justice. The brave and defiant message of those productions in 1994 from Chicago and Dusseldorf: 'I choose neither of you, and both. Do you hear? I refuse to choose.'

Monday 2 January — Nine
Practical plans of action

In today's *Guardian* there is an article which purports to be by David Blunkett. But it's difficult to believe that a practising politician would really write, as distinct from give their name to, something so lifeless, decaying and grey. The genre to which the piece belongs is all too recognisable: it is written by a hack research assistant, reasonably literate of course but also deadeningly unimaginative and uninspiring, and keen on long words and long sentences. It's the sort of thing which civil servants write for ministers to read out at conferences, very measured and prudent, with boring references backwards and forwards in time to other things the minister has said or will say, and giving the minimum possible hostages to fortune. Civil servants, when they write this sort of stuff, know that the minister will not inwardly digest it, but simply bark it out without bothering to understand what it means; they know all too well that their minister isn't really interested, and they're not very interested either. It is sad and indeed alarming to find that David Blunkett's private office apparently works like this as well.

How extremely uncomradely and ungenerous these comments are. It would be comradely and generous to see the article as part of the negotiation, trust-building and peacebuilding which Blunkett has to take part in, and indeed in some important respects to lead, over the next few years. Be that as it may, it's important to re-emphasise the notion that practical plans of action at this time may be better conceptualised as a process of peacebuilding rather than as a process of war with the intention of victory and surrender.

Any way, a few further modest proposals. First, every teacher, inspector and adviser in the country should read and reflect on the report of the Commission on Social Justice, chaired by Sir Gordon Borrie[14]; should massively improve and enrich the sections and proposals on education, drawing on other parts of the report; and should energetically lobby David Blunkett and his counterparts in other parties, in partnership with thousands of bus-loads of parents and governors (Trafalgar Square over-flowing with them), to take the new proposals on board. Second, academics specialising in education should ensure that there's at least one major article about education in the *London Review of Books* every month. There wasn't a single article on education in the LRB in 1994, nor in 1993 either.

Third, we have to break down the barriers between teachers and inspectors. This will be a relative doddle compared with the work involved in implementing the fourth modest proposal: breaking down the barriers between inspectors and education officers. Fifth, there is the small matter of re-writing the whole national curriculum — though this could perhaps be delayed for a few days, if we have too many other things to do just at present. Sixth, particularly important, there must be a really serious effort, at long last, to reverse and reduce inequalities of (a) resourcing and (b) gains and benefits. Seventh, a small matter of which Frankie Howerd reminded us in a clip on television last night: 'I am not,' he said, in an address to the Oxford Union, 'an intellectual. No really, I'm not, I'm not what you'd call an academic, really, no. Which is why I feel so at home here.' Starting with Oxford, we have to reform the universities.

This is a ragbag of measures. Yes, of course.

Tuesday 3 January — Ten
Contrite confessions

Another modest proposal: we should ruefully admit a few of our own faults. There are two main constellations. First, the fact that we did make it terribly easy, in the sixties and seventies, for the new right — 'that deep pessimism and ungenerosity of spirit' — in due course to gain the ascendancy. True, they would probably have gained the ascendancy any way, however strong and skilled we might have been. But we must do better next time. Second, we're still rather disorganised, to put it mildly, and rather distracted.

This meditation, how disorganised and distracted is it going to turn out? This evening I listen again to the Dawn Upshaw CD which my daughter gave me for Christmas. It includes a setting by Kurt Weill of some verses by Ogden Nash describing the excellence for which we all have modestly to strive:

> He is as simple as a swim in summer,
> Not arty, not actory.
> He's like a plumber when you need a plumber —
> He's satisfactory.

Wednesday 4 January — Eleven Epiphanies

On the train to Hereford re-read two Christmas stories. Both end with snow. Both come at the end of compilations of short stories. The one is James Joyce's *The Dead*. Gabriel Conroy seeks the feel-good factor. Achingly, it's nowhere here, the party is dead, his paralysis is complete. 'I'm sick of my own country, sick of it,' he says at one point. As if A S Byatt's dragons, 'stinking with despair and endless decay', stalk all Dublin, all the world. They could be here, slithering amongst us at the Green Dragon, too. But the story ends not with despair but with solace. 'Generous tears filled Gabriel's eyes ... His soul swooned slowly as he heard the snow falling faintly through the universe and faintly falling, like the descent of their last end, upon all the living and the dead.'[15]

Most of Italo Calvino's *Santa's Children* could provide material for Victoria Wood, or Jasper Carrott, or Lenny Henry, or Frankie Howerd. They'd love, and make their audiences love, the revelations, the manifestations, of crazy absurdity underlying Christmas commercialism. But then the situation in the story suddenly changes. There's snow over the city, like the snow over Joyce's Dublin, and also there's snow out there in the countryside, like the snow over Joyce's Ireland, and like the whiteness of R S Thomas's bare page. Also there's this wolf, and this hare, and we're up to our neck in the absurdity known as postmodernism. In folktales wolves are like dragons, they devour you. It's a white hare, and the wolf can't see it very well against the snow. So the wolf watches and follows the hare's footprints. 'At the point where the prints ended there should be the hare, and the wolf came out of the black, opened wide his red maw and his sharp teeth, and bit the wind.' And the story ends thus:

> The hare was a bit further on, invisible; he scratched one ear with his paw, and escaped, hopping away.

> Is he here? There? Is he a bit further on?

> Only the expanse of snow could be seen, white as this page.[16]

Thursday 5 January — Twelve True loves

Twelve true loves, eleven epiphanies, ten contrite confessions, nine practical plans of action, eight hybrid identities, seven storytelling animals, six rational arguments, five myths of hope, four enumerations of the enemy, three defiant writers, two most important things, and a bare page.

5

Review of the Decade

a period piece, perhaps

'In this speech now in December 1999, I propose to look
back over our principal achievements of the decade which
is drawing to a close and to highlight the main
components of our success. I hope and intend in this way
to clarify and to consolidate the policy priorities for our
race and for our nation in the century, or rather — to
speak more frankly and less modestly — in the
millennium, which stretches before us.'

*Part of a lecture in 1991, for a conference entitled 'Race,
Gender and the Education Reform Act', held at the
University of Warwick.*

5. Review of the Decade
a period piece, perhaps

The 1990s began, before the end of their first year, with an event which at the time had all the appearance of being the most momentous setback, perhaps indeed the most devastating tragedy, which our nation had ever had the misfortune to experience. I refer to the departure from our shores, through barely believable cowardice, treachery and shortsightedness, of leadership and inspiration, and — it appeared — of order and decency, vigour and purpose. It seemed for a while, with the departure of the prime minister who had made Great Britain great again, that we no longer had any national vision.

And yet the genius of our nation — of our race — is such that men in this great land did quite swiftly recover from the tragic loss of leadership in November 1990 and in the course of the ensuing decade did continue steadfast, vigorous and faithful in the new pathways which had been so boldly planned and so bravely pioneered in the 1980s. In this speech now in December 1999, I propose to look back over our principal achievements of the decade which is drawing to a close and to highlight the main components of our success. I hope and intend in this way to clarify and to consolidate the policy priorities for our race and for our nation in the century, or rather — to speak more frankly and less modestly — in the millennium, which stretches before us.

The first essential component of our success lies in a piece of legislation which has been quite remarkably effective, perhaps more so than even its own architects were able fully to predict, in moulding the thoughts and behaviour of the men of this land. It is a sign of its extraordinary success that most people do not even recall any longer that the legislation exists. I refer to the Policy Discourse and Semantics Act 1992. It had, you may recall, two main aspects. On the one hand there was PONST, the Prohibition of Non-Sanctioned Terminology. This enabled us to introduce the Relaxation of Restraints on Crime and Subversion Detection (RRCSD), for example, without irresponsible, mischievous and unpatriotic critics and opponents being able to claim that we were introducing what they themselves would no doubt have called 'torture'. Similarly we were able to introduce Accommodation and Enterprise Units (AEUs) to support unemployed people without incurring the unhelpful allegation that these were similar to 'workhouses', and Key Stage Three Identification of Non-Academic Citizens (KS3INAC) without anyone being permitted to call this 'LOSLA', lowering of the school leaving age.

The other main aspect of the Policy Discourse and Semantics Act was the prohibition of certain words and phrases which had had a certain vogue in the 1980s amongst self-styled and self-appointed intellectuals but which would only foster discontent in the population at large if we permitted them to remain any longer in daily use in policy-making and decision-making. Thus we finally rid the public vocabulary of 'anti-racism' and 'anti-sexism', also of all other unpatriotic and un-English words beginning with the prefix 'anti', and ludicrous and unhelpful phrases such as 'sex discrimination', 'positive action', 'equal opportunities', 'multicultural' and 'chairperson'. Further, we successfully defended the English language against various nonsensical words coined by European bureaucrats, for example 'harmonisation', 'asylum-seeker' and, the worst of all, as older people here may remember, 'xenophobia'.

Other achievements of the decade include the abolition of the Race Relations Act and the Sex Discrimination Act in 1993, the creation of the Guestworker and Immigrant Redefinition Act 1994, the Guestworker and Immigrant Dispersal and Assimilation Act 1995, the Guestworker and Immigrant Humane Repatriation Act 1996, the Women as Homemakers Act 1997, and the Christianity and Morality Act 1998.

In the field of education the decade saw the abolition of teacher training institutions in 1992, Her Majesty's Inspectorate in 1993, local education authorities in 1994 and the National Union of Teachers in 1995. We were remarkably fortunate, from 1994 onwards, to able to put all teacher training and re-education, and all monitoring and inspection of schools, into the hands of the former British Army of the Rhine, which took on a new name with the old acronym, the Benchmarks, Appraisal, Observation and Rationalisation service. In the writing and dissemination of inspection reports BAOR has been much helped in relation to good schools by its partnership with Saatchi and Saatchi. With regard to bad schools, at the same time, the partnership with the *Daily Mail* has been most invaluable.

I am proud to announce today that just over 60 per cent of the population is now being educated at good schools. Twenty-five per cent are at independent schools, and 35 per cent at grant-maintained schools. This is a remarkable achievement. Teachers at these schools are so well paid and fulfilled that they do not feel any need to join a so-called union. Barely 40 per cent of the pupils in our schools are so lacking in innate ability that they are affected by KS3INAC (Key Stage Three Identification of Non-Academic Citizens) to the point that they need to leave school. This too is a remarkable achievement.

In the course of the decade we have magnificently succeeded in removing from positions of power and influence all people with 'progressive' or 'caring' ideas about education. I can illustrate this achievement with an interesting statistic. Near the start of the decade there was a conference at, as it was in those days called, the University of Warwick. The title, if you please, was 'Race, Gender and the Education Reform Act'. Before coming here today I consulted the National Subversives and Undesirables Computer Index, and I can tell you this. Of the people who were at that conference, five per cent are now, sadly, dead; ten per cent are in detention or psychiatric hospitals; thirty per cent are unemployed. Of the remaining 55 per cent, 25 per cent no longer have any connection with education. Of those who do still work in education in some way, only five per cent have higher status and greater influence than they had ten years ago. I am happy to reassure everyone here today that those persons are, of course, kept under very strict surveillance indeed.

There is still, we should confess, both in education and in society, some unfinished business. We still need to expand the police force, for example, and to build more prisons and psychiatric hospitals. We still need to ensure the rigorous implementation of the Eugenics Act 1997, for it is alas still the case that intelligent people are not breeding enough children and that non-academic people are breeding too many. It remains the case that women, bless them, are still allowed to vote in local elections.

But basically matters such as these are entirely straightforward. There are no grounds for pessimism, concern or anxiety. On the contrary, the future for our race and for our nation is — is it not? — gloriously hopeful.

6

A Great White Paper

musings for a vision statement

'The Government is firmly wedded to quality excellence for absolutely every single child. The greater the excellence of the quality, the greater the quality of the excellence, and the more absolute the singleness. The more absolute the singleness, the more wedded the firmness. But let there be no confusion.'

Imaginary jottings for a speech given by a government minister, shortly after the publication of the White Paper on Choice and Diversity, summer 1992.

6. A Great White Paper
musings for a vision statement

Jottings for a speech shortly after the publication of the White Paper On Choice and Diversity, summer 1992.

The Funding Agency

The proposed Funding Agency has been very warmly received. Even people you might have expected to be critical have been heard to refer to it as the 'sweet' F.A.

Progression

Evil habits start young. Give a girl a meccano set when she's at primary school, and you'll find before long that she wants to be assessed through coursework. As sure as tadpoles turn into wrinkled ugly toads she'll be a man-hating feminist before she's 30, and she won't believe in hell either. This has got to be stopped.

Inspection training

The new national inspectorate will report on children's beliefs in the afterlife. That is why inspectors must understand the afterlife themselves. So the initial training courses for inspectors must give potential inspectors the skills and understandings which they need. Therefore we shall check them for this. The more we check, the more they will understand. I am pleased to hear the first reports. All who have so far attended an inspection training course have been unanimous in reporting that it gave them, to quote their own words on the evaluation sheets, 'a shared vision of hell'.

Phenomenal

In the first month after the publication of the White Paper I received a letter from a headmaster saying he thought it contained a good idea. In the second month I received two such letters. That is twice as many. If the White Paper continues to be praised at this rate, then in only 16 months from now the success rate will be phenomenal. I shall have received letters praising the White Paper from no fewer than 131,072 headmasters — more than five times as many as there are at present headmasters in the country. This is just one of the Government's many very remarkable achievements.

Morality

We are amending the criteria for awarding Grant Maintained status. Schools will not be allowed to opt out unless they can show how successful they are in moral and spiritual development. This means at least 75% of the pupils must believe in hell. The beliefs must be held categorically and sincerely. The more categorical, the more sincere, and the greater the spiritual and moral roundedness. Her Majesty's Catechetical Investigator (HMCI) will supervise the writing of what we are rightly calling a Doomsday Book about this.

Bureaucracy

When a school reaches the 75% belief-in-hell cut-off point, opting out will take place retrospectively. That is why it be will back-dated. It will be back-dated to whenever the headmaster first felt that his local council was sometimes perhaps inclined on occasions to be a trifle bureaucratic. In cases of lack of clarity about this the Secretary of State will determine the exact date. We have got to stamp out insensitive bureaucracy. That is why we are stamping it out.

Misuse of terms

We believe firmly that every child in the country should receive an excellent education. Let there be no doubt about this. The Government is firmly wedded to quality excellence for absolutely every single child. The greater the excellence of the quality, the greater the quality of the excellence, and the more absolute the singleness. The more absolute the singleness, the more wedded the firmness. But let there be no confusion. It is a regrettable fact that the word 'child' has been much misused in recent years by educational theorists and administrators with ideological axes to grind. The Government cannot let this continue. That is why we shall bring forward legislation to explain exactly what a child actually is. We shall also define what a parent is. These simple words have been misused for too long. It cannot be allowed. Most teachers, most of whom are excellent, already do know what a real child is. This is very fortunate. It is why most teachers are mostly excellent. Teachers who have been indoctrinated by educational theorists, however, and in consequence do not recognise real children or real parents, must be stamped out. That is why we are putting a stop to this.

Democracy

We are totally committed to local democracy, accountability, partnership, autonomy and diversity, with the highest possible quality specialisation for every rounded citizen. Let there be no doubt about this. Good local authorities are already in sight of having an Education Committee which is invisible. It would never, I wish to emphasise, in no circumstances not be incorrect to deny that a non-existent Education Committee is not undemocratic. This must be completely clear.

The Government's vision

The SCAA is to be re-titled the Schools Catechism and Attendance Authority. It will be a pillar and a landmark under the lifeblood overarching the mechanisms inside the benchmarks beside the foundations next to the frontiers before every vibrant thread — opening doors and demystifying horizons beneath our national heritage cascading down the generations through the 21st century. It will be regular and rigorous, robust and rounded. That is why we shall be the best in Europe. If we are the best in Europe we shall be the best in the world. *Choice and Diversity* will be recognised as the Great White Paper of all time. This is the Government's vision for education in this country.

7

Returning Home

tribute to a tireless comrade

How are we to use our rage and anger — the rage and anger which we feel when we suffer defeat, failure or rejection, or when those whom we love and care for are crushed and broken? The task is to avoid demonising our opponents, and on the contrary — so to speak — to humanise ourselves. So the energy of rage has to be directed against defeat and defeatism, not against opponents. Also, the energy of rage has to be directing into making things, and into the building and maintaining of hope.

Lecture in memory of David Ruddell, who was one of the principal pioneers of antiracist education in Britain, given on 25 September 1991 in the Library Theatre, Birmingham.

7. Returning Home
tribute to a tireless comrade

Through the gone years, across the now years, in and out the maybe years, it was all the same: her life was relentless, soul-crushing toil.

Washing, scouring, sweeping, scrubbing, patching; hoeing, hacking, digging, pruning, chopping; dragging and pressing, never getting, never reaping; exiled, robbed, emptied, tangled, shackled; never enough knowing, never fully seeing.

This was Miriam's life-world. She had dwelt in it for 16 years, since her birth — though no-one knew for certain where or when she had been born. That was true of all the slaves, they were not allowed to know when exactly and where their mothers had given birth to them. And now Miriam had a baby in the world with her.

This is the beginning of a story entitled *Daring to Fly*.[1] It's a tale about injustice and oppression, therefore also about anger and rage, and about the need for, and the nature of, hope. And it is about the roles of imagination and narrative in shaping and maintaining hope. This lecture will recall and reflect some of the setbacks and difficulties which have been experienced in recent years by people working against racial injustice in this country, and it will reflect their consequent anger. But also it will be about the wellsprings of determination and hope, and therefore about the making and setting of practical agendas. From time to time I shall return to the story entitled *Daring to Fly* and the ending of the lecture will coincide with the ending of the story.

'We need to haunt the halls of history,' Maya Angelou has said, 'and listen to our ancestors' wisdom. We must ask questions and find answers that will help us to avoid falling into the maw of history. How were our forefathers able to support their weakest when they themselves were at their weakest? ... How were they, lonely, bought separately and sold apart, able to conceive of the deep, ponderous wisdom found in 'walk together, children ... don't you get weary'.'[2] *Daring to Fly* is a story which, in Maya Angelou's phrase, helps us to haunt the halls of history. In it we meet, to quote her further, 'a people who had the courage to be when being was dangerous, who had the courage to dare when daring was dangerous and, most important, had the courage to hope.'

David Ruddell was a person who in his life and work over many years in this city, and also further afield, was a source and resource of courage and hope for large numbers of people. There are three particular aspects of his being which I should like to recall at the onset here, and which I shall then try to weave into the subject-matter and format of this lecture in his memory.

First, David was a brave pioneer. He was one of the first white people in this country to take into his own thinking and understanding what black people were saying about structural and institutionalised racism: that is, about the ways in which racist beliefs and attitudes are the product as well as the reinforcement of unequal structures and relations of power, and of discriminatory, excluding rules and customs. He gave form to his insights through his many writings and educational materials — outside Birmingham, the best known of these are the *Race Relations Teaching Pack*, the *Recognising Racism* audio-visual pack, and the *Multicultural Education Review* — but also through the workshops and training events which designed and organised, and through the nationally known and respected support service, the Multicultural Development Unit, which he helped to create and of which he was the leader. The clarity of his insights and the force of his analysis inevitably meant that he caused discomfort amongst white people, for he found much fault with schools and other mainstream institutions, and he strenuously confronted and resisted the deficit assumptions which many schools have about black and ethnic minority people. But he doggedly and courageously persevered, committed considerably more to justice and to truth, as he saw and spoke them, than to a quiet and easy life for himself.

Second, David was a loyal and listening friend. He gave practical assistance and moral support to a wide range of people, and there are now many people, in Birmingham and elsewhere, whose personal and professional lives would have been very different — much narrower and much poorer — had it not been for David's influence and inspiration. Many of the staff whom he appointed, supervised, supported and developed in the Multicultural Development Unit are now in positions of responsibility in schools throughout the city, and indeed beyond. He lives on through his friends and comrades: those to whom he used to listen, those whose growth he cared for and cherished, those whose courage and hopefulness he nurtured and strengthened. An obituary by his friend and former colleague Mal Leicester[3] contained many beautiful reminders of the person we knew:

... His funeral filled a large church in Edgbaston. From Birmingham, London, Ireland and Ghana we came with grief and respect. That large and multiracial congregation was a testimony to David's life; to his character and actions; and to his anti-racist work.

... As a young man he became a CND activist, and joined Voluntary Service Overseas and went off to Ghana. There he taught, worked on his PhD, and became head of a school. Being an excellent teacher and a good man, his work benefited many young Ghanaians, and David developed strong links with a country which he came to love.

... David Ruddell was a man of integrity. He spoke as he thought to whomever he spoke. His straight dealings and lack of ruthlessness meant that his abilities and his contribution to education were never professionally rewarded at a commensurate level. He practised his convictions in his personal and his professional life. David expected from people according to their abilities and their role, and criticised when they failed to measure up.

To the less powerful and less able he was warm and non- patronising. My own daughter, despite considerable learning difficulties, was able, as a result of a conversation with David, to reprimand me years later for laughing at an Irish joke and to explain coherently why it was racist, hurtful and wrong. ('David explained it to me.') David was firm in his convictions and strong in facing attack. He was brave in the face of death.

David was a big person — the world is smaller and meaner without him.

Third, David was a committed and caring traveller. By traveller, I mean someone who had many homes, and who was known and welcomed in many places; who had sufficient inner strength to cross and criss-cross boundaries, and to encounter and live with newness, dislocation and uncertainty; and who stood and worked at the edges of institutions and organisations, as distinct from being swallowed and absorbed by them. I do not, of course, mean someone who was casual, aloof, touristy, lonesome: on the contrary, David was caring and committed.

David travelled: from Ireland to Handsworth in his childhood; to Ghana from Birmingham for several years at the onset of his professional career, and to Nigeria for a year in the late 1970s; within this city between the LEA and the University, and between schools and the support service; and of course in and with his business, Zip Travel. It takes great strength and courage to be a traveller not a tourist, a migrant not a stay-at-home, a visitor not a yesperson. The Multicultural Development Unit was and is a reminder of the importance of work on the boundaries between inside and outside. Work for justice requires that certain people, certain especially strong and caring people, will stand and work and live at those boundaries. David Ruddell was such a person.

It is a great honour to be invited to Birmingham to give this lecture in David's memory. I am always, may I say, glad to come to this city. The first time I came was on the day my mother gave birth to me. Also my mother herself was born in Birmingham and so was my father; also my wife, and the mother of my wife. Six of our children's eight great-grandparents were living in Birmingham from about 1900 onwards, most of them having been born here themselves. This city is inside me. Yet I have not always, I confess with shame, been proud to belong here: at the age of about 19 I tried hard, with a success which I am relieved now was only partial, to rid myself of something which I had just discovered I possessed, a Birmingham accent. But nowadays this place is a symbol of energy and continuity for me, both professionally and personally. For so many reasons, I am delighted and grateful to be here this evening.

The lecture has two main parts and these are evoked by two main words, accounts and agendas. First, I shall present a pessimistic account of race equality in education in the 1990s, and in this connection shall look in particular at the new Section 11 arrangements which are being introduced. Second, I shall suggest five main sets of ideas which might be useful to us as we construct agendas. Before starting on the first part, about accounts, I wish to return for a while to Miriam in the story *Daring to Fly*:

> Her baby slept on her back as she worked in the plantation, hoeing, chopping, pruning, planting. The sun beat down, the same sun which in Africa had warmed and softened and delighted Miriam's foremothers and forefathers, but which now, in the slavery-land of America, was hard and ferocious; cruel, pitiless and implacable; savage in its casual, unthinking, careless brutality.

> Tiny babies do not slumber long, least of all when they are empty and thirsting, and when their mothers are stretched with pain and worry. Miriam's baby awoke on her back, and began to cry. He cried out in rage at the sun, at the plantation, at his whole life-world. He cried for softness, for tender love spaciously given. 'Stop that!. Strangle that thing's noise!. Stop it, put an end to it, I say!' The plantation overseer rode up to Miriam, cracking his whip. She looked up wearily at his white face, towering on his horse high above her, and her baby son continued to cry.

> Crack, the overseer lashed both Miriam and her baby deep into their skin. She fell sobbing to her knees as her baby screamed, and the overseer rode on, forgetting Miriam and her life-world in less time than it takes to crack a whip.

Accounts

I am going to present a pessimistic account of what is happening to race equality in British education in the 1990s, and to do so by offering a satire on the current arrangements relating to Section 11.[4] Satire is a dangerous weapon for the person who uses it, for at least four separate reasons. First, since its tools are exaggeration and distortion it may misfire, and may then hit targets which were not being aimed at. Second, it may involve poking fun at realities which are no laughing matter, and its misfires will then be backfires, showing up starkly the satirist's own sick and superficial sense of humour. Third, the satire may go grotesquely over the top, and totally fail then to make its point. Fourth, satire can so infuriate those who are attacked, not only in its content but also because it is difficult for them to respond directly without appearing ridiculous, that they resort to indirect and perhaps immoral, but efficient and deadly, means of retaliation.

I am not anxious, here this evening, about the fourth of these dangers. (Though if and when the lecture is in due course published, the danger may become real. Watch, as it were, this space.) But the first three dangers are serious, and I present this piece therefore with trepidation. I re-emphasise before starting that the purpose is to recall and reflect some angry and despairing feelings about how things are going in our society at the present time so far as race equality is concerned. The new Section 11 arrangements are a sign of what is happening, not the cause — and are therefore not the real target of the satire which follows.

I assume, by the way, that most people here are broadly familiar with the new Section 11 arrangements, and with the fact that the kind of antiracist work for which David Ruddell stood, and which he so strongly and remarkably developed, is no longer fundable in the way in which it was, and is no longer officially encouraged by central government. And I daresay many people here are familiar with the kind of correspondence which has been plodding its wearisome way between LEAs and schools, and between LEAs and the Home Office, during the summer of 1991. Familiarity with the correspondence involves being familiar also with the language, Seckelevenspeak, in which the correspondence is conducted. There isn't room here to provide a complete glossary of Seckelevenspeak, but I will just mention one word which it continually uses, pronounced Unkwa. This is spelt NCW, which is short for New Commonwealth — yes, three letters stand for two words, Seckelevenspeak being illiterate and innumerate as well as ugly and crude in a large number of other ways as well. In Seckelevenspeak Unkwa people (often, incidentally, known as Unkwa clients) suffer from a double disadvantage. It's not their fault, as Seckelevenspeak sees the issues, just their misfortune, that (a) they are not really British and (b) they don't really look British, either.

From the Chief Education Officer
Somewhere Education Authority

September 1991

Section 11/EMG Team Coordinator
HOME OFFICE
Queen Anne's Gate
London SW1H 9AT

Dear Colleague

SECTION 11 OF THE LOCAL GOVERNMENT ACT 1966:
PERFORMANCE INDICATORS, SIGNS AND STATISTICS (PISS)

I am writing to provide additional information about the Section 11 project applications of this Authority, as requested, and specifically to describe how we are intending to monitor progress and evaluate success. Also I wish to make a number of requests. I should be grateful if you please pass this letter in its entirety to your Ministers.

CAREERS GUIDANCE PROJECT
1.1 You request clarification on performance indicators. Our goal with this project, you will recall, is that NCW clients should have more realistic career expectations, such that they are less likely to experience disaffection and alienation in British society. The principal performance indicator to measure the success of this project will therefore be whether there is a decline in the number of complaints from NCW clients about their inability to gain employment, other than in manual occupations.

1.2 Our target is that there should be a 15% decline in complaints each year, year on year, in the period 1992-1995, and that by 1995 all NCW youngsters in this Authority will be entirely content with their, admittedly lowly, station in life.

2 LANGUAGE ISSUES PROJECT
2.1 I confirm that we are re-structuring and re-titling our language service. In future it will be known as the Comprehension and Elocution Support Service (CESS).

2.2 With regard to comprehension, we are developing Graded Assessment Strategies (GAS) to monitor the progress of NCW language learners. Successful completion of Stage One of language acquisition will be deemed to have occurred when learners are able to comprehend instructions by their class teachers. Stage Two will be complete when learners can comprehend their headteachers. With regard to so-called Stage Three of language acquisition, we have decided to abolish it.

2.3 With regard to elocution, we appreciate that material resources for elocution lessons and assessment are not Section 11 fundable. However, we should be grateful if your Ministers could please use their good offices with the Prime Minister, and if he in his turn could please approach Her Majesty the Queen, and respectfully request her to make available some tape-recordings of her grandchildren's conversations. Such tape-recordings would enable us then to design some truly innovative learning and assessment materials. These would clearly show, at children's own attainment levels, proper and correct standards of articulation and grammar, and they would be, we believe, truly inspiring.

3 ACCESS TO THE NATIONAL CURRICULUM
3.1 *Literacy*
We are introducing ethnic fingerprinting in all of the Authority's schools, in order to monitor usage of school library books. Our target is that there should be a 20% decline each year in the number of NCW fingerprints on books published in languages other than English, and a 30% decline in NCW fingerprints on books by authors who are not British.

3.2 *Outreach*
We are taking expert advice, from a higher Authority than ourselves, on appropriate performance indicators for the workers whom we wish to appoint in accordance with our mission statement on the Decade of Evangelism. I will of course give you further information on this matter as soon as it is disclosed to us.

3.3 *Standards*
Our team of peripatetic UJWAs (Union Jack Welfare Assistants) will deliver a maintenance service for the flags which we are installing in all classrooms in the Authority. Our performance target is that there should be a 10% decline, year on year, in the number of flags requiring repair, and a 15% decline in those requiring replacement.

3.4 *Harmony*
There will be a 5% increase each year in the number of NCW clients able to sing, respectively at the ends of Keystages 1, 2, 3, and 4, Rudolf the Red-Nosed Reindeer, All Things

Bright and Beautiful, You'll Never Walk Alone, and Land of Hope and Glory.

3.5 *Assessment*

We have devised a series of Standardised Cricket Tests, and believe your Ministers will be particularly interested in these. Our target is that by 1993 all NCW clients in the Authority's schools will be supporting England in cricket matches against NCW countries; by 1994 all will also support Australia and New Zealand in such matches; and by 1995 all will support, in any match it happens to play against an NCW country, the Republic of South Africa.

4 PASTORAL CARE AND SCHOOL ETHOS PROJECT

4.1 As you are aware, our plan is to appoint peripatetic squads of pastoral care and school ethos officers, who will deliver a service targeted on facilitating conditions conducive to learning in the Authority's schools.

4.2 We entirely appreciate that material resources for these post-holders will not be Section 11 fundable. It is a mark of the Authority's serious commitment to this project that we are ourselves budgeting to provide finance for the purchase of skin-lightening creams, and for uniforms, helmets, shields and truncheons. With regard to dogs and horses for these post-holders, however, I should like respectfully to point out that such items are of course not – strictly speaking - 'material' resources, and I am hoping therefore that your Ministers will accept that dogs and horses should be Section 11 fundable.

5 EVALUATION

We have, I emphasise, a full commitment to inspection, monitoring and evaluation, and to value for money. The unit for Section 11 Teacher Appraisal and Surveillance and Inspection (STASI) which we are setting up will therefore aim to make 33% of present post-holders redundant by the end of 1992, and a further 33% redundant by the end of 1993. Our overall ethnic minorities strategy, to conclude and summarise, is (a) to implement as fully as possible what we understand to be the spirit of the new Section 11 arrangements, and (b) to secure therefore for this Authority as large a grant as possible.

In closing, I should like to take this opportunity to wish you and your colleagues well in your important work.

There are seven targets at which the satire is directed. I will name each of them briefly in turn, but wish first to comment on the connections and relationships amongst them. The seven sets of realities are separate from each other in the sense that each can be named and described on its own, and in that each is logically distinct from each of the others. In practice, however, they are like cogwheels in a machine or like organs in a body — they are interdependent parts of a whole, each affecting and being affected by each of the others. Further, and this is why it is particularly difficult to keep them apart, they can act as proxies for each other, such that statements about one may rightfully be understood as coded or disguised utterances about another. For example, when people talk about the need to protect traditional British culture what they may really mean is that they wish to protect the British class system, and its inequalities of wealth and power. The fact that these realities can be used as codes for each other means that they require — as the terms are — not only structural analysis but also discourse analysis.

Be that as it may, here are very brief namings of the seven realities targeted by the satire. First, and most obviously, there is racism: the beliefs (a) that the human species can be divided into so-called races (b) that white people are superior to people whom white people think are not white, and (c) that material and structural inequalities reflecting this superiority are both inevitable and right. Second, there is cultural nationalism: the belief that Britain is, and ought to be, culturally pure, and that the hegemony of elite British (more accurately, elite English) culture is right and proper. Third, there is acceptance and indeed defence of major inequalities in the division of labour, and in wealth, income and power. Fourth, there is a concern for stability and social order as values in themselves. Fifth, there is reductionism: a concern with performance indicators and so forth, that is to say with outward behaviour, and with trivial uniformity and simplification.

Reductionism makes much use of mechanistic, militaristic and (so to speak) marketistic terminology — not only performance indicators (a term originally derived from hydraulic engineering) but also 'strategy', 'client', 'targeting service delivery', and so on. Also, a sinister aspect of reductionism is the debasing of language, such that terms such as pastoral care, school ethos, evaluation and literacy are twisted into almost unrecognisable new meanings. Sixth, subliminally through some of the allusions and through the sheer absence of any explicit references, there is an acceptance of gender inequality. Seventh, there is routinism and conformism: the chief education officer is simply accepting central government's requirements, as he or she understands them, without even a trace of critique, let alone opposition and resistance.

Racism, nationalism, inequality, social control, reductionism, gender inequality, business as usual: these seven are separate from each other, but also interact with and strengthen each other. Both singly and collectively they are what we are up against, they are what make us angry.

> An old slave, Moses, happened to see. He came over to Miriam. 'You must go, little mother, it is time for you to go. You can fly, you know, my daughter, you can fly to Africa. Kum yali, kum buba tambe, fly, little sister, fly. You shall be the first, the mother of us all.'

> She stepped up on to the air. First with one foot, then with the other. Next she was gliding, and her whip wound was healed, and her baby's wound was healed, and she was floating, soaring into the breeze, free as an eagle, and she was on her way now, on her way home. The overseer on the land beneath her caught sight of her, and he roared with fury, and he began to pursue her. But on she flew, over the fields, over the fences, over the cabins, over the streams, over the woods, and out of sight.

> The next day four young slaves dropped exhausted where they were working, and were lashed without mercy by the overseer, and left for dead. 'Kum yali, kum buba tambe,' whispered Moses approaching them. 'Fly, my young brothers, fly away home, fly to your Africa.'

> The overseer boiled with fury as he saw the young men, beautiful now, stepping up on to the air, first with one foot and then with the other, and floating and gliding over the fields, over the fences, over the cabins, over the streams, over the woods, and out of sight. He called the slave-owner himself, and the slave-owner arrived with a posse of his aides.

Agendas

As we take account of what we're up against we need some general principles to help us draw up detailed agendas. I am going to mention five clusters of ideas which seem to me, just at the moment, to be important. They're definitely a hotch-potch, these five ideas, not logically tidy and not comprehensive. If I were sitting down with you to create an agenda these are some of the main things I would bring. You would bring your things. Together we would construct an agenda for discussion and a plan of action, and these would emerge out of our encounter and exchange. We cannot in advance predict what the agenda would be. But any way, I am not sitting down with you but standing before you. I regret that the occasion cannot be more participatory, yet nevertheless am accepting the role, that of lecturer, which I have been requested for a brief while to take.

First, the importance of narrative. What we are up against is a body of narrative. For example, racism and nationalism are kept alive through narratives as well as through structures, and we need — amongst other things — our own oppositional narratives in order to deal with them. Racism has a grand narrative, or myth, and then countless small episodes and anecdotes which both embody the main myth and also help to vivify and perpetuate it. (Similarly a religion, for example, has a grand narrative, and then a mass of history, biography, fable, parable, legend, wisdom tale, chronicle, and so on.) One of our minimal duties is to tell stories and accounts about antiracism, and about both its successes and defeats. Some of our stories need to be about our own faults, failings, weaknesses and internal quarrels — though we need to be careful, of course, as to where exactly we tell these, and who exactly may be eavesdropping.

We need true stories (though bearing in mind that marvellous Russian saying: 'he lied like an eye-witness'), and also tales of the imagination. Our stories should not only foster opposition to the myths of racism but should also be strengthening and illumining as we each of us tell and construct our own life-story. Just as a religion has a grand narrative and then lots of much smaller episodes which fit into it, so too does each of us have a single story into which we try to fit all the smaller happenings of our lives. The single story has a beginning in birth to that one mother, in that one household and family tradition, to that one constellation of language and accent, in that one place, at that one historical moment. It has its own distinctive and unique middle in our work and loves. On a day such as today, as we meet to salute and cherish David who is no longer with us, we forcefully remember that each life story has an end. We need stories — myths and folktales as well as true accounts — to help us hold the beginnings, middles and ends of our lives together. Without them we shall not have hope: yes, to lose stories is to lose hope, but conversely to construct and cherish stories is to maintain hope.

'Human beings,' writes Gabriel Garcia Marquez, 'are not born once and for all on the day their mothers give birth to them, but life obliges them over and over again to give birth to themselves.'[5] The construction and sharing of stories helps us, daily, to give birth to ourselves. And Italo Calvino says, with words which have special poignancy and resonance for us here this evening, as we remember one particular friend whom we knew: 'The ultimate meaning to which all stories refer has two faces: the continuity of life, the inevitability of death.'[6]

Second, there is the importance of religious education, as both a site and a stake of the struggle. RE is important in itself, but also focuses and illustrates a number of threats and possibilities which it shares with the field of arts education. Briefly, the struggle in RE is between (a) a view of the subject which places its main emphasis on pupils' spiritual development — that is, on the construction and understanding of personal life-stories, with their unique beginnings, middles and ends — and then on humankind's religious traditions as resources or storehouses to assist such development and understanding[7] and (b) the sort of view which is implicit in the following news item, which appeared in the *Daily Star* in spring 1991. 'Praise ye!' proclaimed the *Star,* commending the campaign of someone in a London borough who had been 'horrified when her local council — then Labour-controlled — adopted a 'multi-ethnic' approach to religious teaching.' 'They weren't even going to mention God, the Bible or Jesus Christ,' continued the report. But it had been found that 'the loony Lefties were breaking the law. So now education authorities throughout Britain — whatever their feelings about Jesus — will HAVE to teach our kids about Him. It is a famous victory for parents, for Christians — and for common sense. Britain may now be a multicultural country. But that doesn't mean British culture should be banned from the classroom.'

The *Daily Star's* comments and cautions about breaking the law, and about what education authorities 'now . . . HAVE' to do, were in relation to a letter sent by a civil servant at the DES to all chief education officers on 18 March. The letter was described in *The Times* under the heading 'Clarke urges emphasis on Christian education' and in the *Guardian* under 'Schools told to focus on Bible'.

What was striking about the press coverage of the letter was not the diversity of style but the uniformity of disinformation. The *Daily Star, Times* and *Guardian* had in common that they were all, quite simply, wrong.[8] The letter did not say what they said it said. In certain respects, it said the exact opposite. Way back in the 1960s the young Bob Dylan sang a bitter song about the role of religion in conflicts and injustices of various kinds. In the light of, for example, the *Daily Star* coverage quoted above, and of the disinformation which appeared in many other papers, it does not seem over-melodramatic to construct a further verse for Dylan's song:

> Multi-faith is a mish-mash,
> It leads our nation astray.
> We must maintain purity,
> There is only one Way:
> So make our schools Christian
> The whole nation wide,
> And keep Britain for the British,
> With God on our side.

It may be that the struggle in Religious Education will spread in the next few years to the whole field of arts education. Here too there is a profound tension between the reductionist tendencies of the Education Reform Act and the main values of certain cultural traditions. The arts have in common with religion that they contribute to spiritual development, the construction and understanding of life-stories. It would not be surprising if the right-wing forces in our society trying to co-opt and contain RE were to turn their attention in due course to the arts, perhaps particularly theatre, drama, film and dance. Unceasing vigilance is required of us.

Third, the reference to religious education is a reminder that the struggle is happening in a myriad of different places: inside each curricular subject, also inside each classroom, each school, each LEA. Everyone has an important role to play, wherever they happen to be. The frontline runs everywhere, not in distant foreign fields.

Fourth, we need to re-visit the whole question of Section 11. Broadly speaking, there are two possible approaches to implementing the government's objective that Asian and black people, the victims of racism, should be able 'to participate fully and freely in the economic, social and public life of the nation'. (I quote here the phrasing in the official documentation — it's rather impressive, though the term 'nation' here, as so often, sounds rather ominous and disturbing.) The one approach involves assuming that Asian and black people have special needs internal to themselves, and that these should be met. The satire presented here earlier illustrates what can happen to our thinking when this approach is adopted without first, in the phrase which David Ruddell made famous, recognising racism.

The second possible approach is to adopt what may be called, paradoxically, a colour-blind race equality perspective. Such a perspective has four main features. One, it arises from a passionate concern to remove racism and to build race equality. Two, the practical implementation of social policy is therefore monitored, evaluated and modified with regard to possibly differential impacts on Asian and black households and communities. But three, all or most practical measures are to do with identifying *all* members of society who do not, to quote again the official Section 11 documentation, participate fully and freely in the social, economic and public life of the nation, and therefore with addressing and removing poverty and disadvantage in housing, employment and education, not with addressing the so-called special needs of ethnic minority people; such measures are likely therefore to benefit all people at the margins of society, not Asian and black people only. Four, it provides the policy context for specific measures to combat racial harassment; to remove discrimination in employment and service delivery, and create equal opportunities; and to address the distinctive special needs which indeed some communities do have.

In practice, as the satire tried to recall, the Home Office has guided local authorities forcefully away from designing and implementing projects based on this second type of approach — even though there is nothing in the legislation itself which requires that such guidance should be given, and even though, prima facie, the government's objectives would be more efficiently and more cost-effectively met through the second approach. At present there is no prospect of the second approach being adopted at national level. It is, however, a policy option at LEA level, and in individual schools.

Fifth, there is a question about our inner lives. How are we to use our rage and anger — the rage and anger which we feel when we suffer defeat, failure or rejection, or when those whom we love and care for are crushed and broken? The task is to avoid demonising our opponents, and on the contrary — so to speak — to humanise ourselves. So the energy of rage has to be directed against defeat and defeatism, not against opponents. Also, the energy of rage has to be directing into making things, and into the building and maintaining of hope.

Energy is needed for the making of art, including the making and sharing of narrative, for political action at many levels to fight injustice; and for the unheroic and unsung, but absolutely essential, tasks of maintaining social fabric in good repair: keeping and cherishing the weft and warp of common decency and courtesy, the web and custom of fairness and integrity. In a poem entitled *Integrity*[9] Adrienne Rich begins with some definitions of her title from the Webster Dictionary: 'the quality or state of being complete; unbroken condition; entirety'. She then imagines herself in a frail vessel, voyaging towards, and with, integrity. 'Really,' she says, 'I have nothing but myself to go by'. But then she reflects immediately on what she has just said: *'Nothing but myself? ... My selves.'* And a few lines later, pondering the energy which underlies her tenderness as well as her anger, she explains:

> Anger and tenderness: my selves.
> And now I can believe they breathe in me
> as angels, not polarities.
> Anger and tenderness: the spider's genius
> to spin and weave in the same action
> from her own body, anywhere —
> even from a broken web.

David had strong links with West Africa throughout all his working life, and it is therefore appropriate here this evening if we turn finally to some West African writers as we consider the themes of suffering, rage, hope and making. Chinua Achebe has said that 'suffering should also give rise to something beautiful'. And Ben Okri, in a meditation[10] on Achebe's words, writes: 'The dreams of the oppressed are planted in the earth and watered through all the bitter seasons. Their suffering could make them farmers of dreams. Their harvest could make the world more just and more beautiful. It is only the oppressed who have this sort of difficult and paradoxical responsibility.'

Okri adds that this requires 'the humility and the silence to transcend their rage, distil it into the highest creativity and use it to reveal greater truths'. He ends his meditation by dreaming and rejoicing that the oppressed 'can teach us all how to live again and how to love again and could well make it possible for us all to create the beginnings of the first true universal civilisation in the history of recorded and unrecorded time'.

'It's time for us all to go,' murmured Moses. 'Kum yali, kum buba tambe.' And he moved swiftly through the plantation, partly running and partly flying, speaking to everyone. And each and every slave, every woman and every man, every girl and every boy, stepped up on the air, first with one foot and then with the other, and they all hovered in the air above the slave-owner and the overseer on their horses, and then they turned and rose higher, like eagles, free in the bright air.

Soaring, rising, floating, gliding; hoping, willing, dreaming, trusting; cherishing, dancing, singing, praising; pulsing with beauty, rejoicing in their own strength and grace; firm and determined, with their love and their tenderness flying to freedom; and on their way home now, to give birth to new life.

The story soon began to spread around, about how the people had dared to fly. Oh they tried to suppress it, the slave-owners, but there was no way now the story could be suppressed. All over slavery-land the story was told, and year after year. Even after the slavery-time people still told the story.

And even outside of slavery-land the story is known.

In prisons and war zones everywhere, on treadmills and conveyor belts in all lands, in homes and workplaces, markets and arenas, parks and fields, in Africa, Europe, Asia, the Americas, in our hearts and in our memories, we cherish that special day, and those special words, kum yali, kum buba tambe. And here today also, with affection and gratitude for David Frederick Ruddell, 11 August 1944 to 23 June 1990, we cherish that it has happened, and that it has been learned, that people dare fly.

Turning Inwards

8

All the World's a Keystage

schools and the politics of spirituality

What do we do, as teachers, for and with learners? What stories, pictures, music, games, tasks, activities, do we use? What groupings? What balances of exploration and information, finding and telling? And how do we make these choices in ways which really do lead to children learning, as distinct from merely adding to our own power and pride?

Reflections on one of the key terms in the Education Reform Act, 'spiritual development', and on practical, political, philosophical and personal tasks which arise.

8. All the World's a Keystage
schools and the politics of spirituality

Henderson Dores, says William Boyd, is just like you or me. Look at him, adds Boyd, as he walks up Park Avenue in New York City:

> ... he seems as composed and unconcerned as, well, as you or me. But Henderson has a complaint, a grudge, a grumble of a deep and insidious kind. He doesn't like himself any more; isn't happy with the personality he's been provided with, thank you very much. Something about him isn't up to scratch, won't do. He'll keep the flesh, but he'd like to do a deal on the spirit, if nobody minds. He wants to change — he wants to be different from what he is. And that, really, is why he is here.[1]

'That, really, is why he is here': because he wants to change his spirit. He is here at the start of this chapter about spirituality in education because the word spirit is used about him in an accessible, ordinary, unassuming way. We can most of us relate to it, whatever our religious beliefs and disbeliefs happen to be. There is a first rough sketching here, in this extract from a recent novel, of how that term in the Education Reform Act, 'spiritual development', may be used: spiritual development is what Henderson Dores ('as composed and unconcerned as, well, as you or me') is looking for, wanting, needing.

Dores is 40 years old, an archetypally critical, pivotal and representative age in the human life-cycle. It is appropriate to listen, before this chapter goes any further, to some people at a different age and stage, a different season in their lives. Here are the voices of two children.[2] They do not use the word 'spirit', but here too, surely, the term 'spiritual development' is being given a first rough sketching. Their names are Rachel and Yusuf, and they are both eight years old. Their teacher has asked them to write acrostic portraits of themselves, using the letters of their names as basic building blocks or seeds. Rachel writes:

> Rather good at maths
> Always working hard
> Charming in all my ways
> Happy all the time
> Excited by parties
> Learning to be strong.

And Yusuf:

> Young and interesting
> Understanding the unusual
> Space is my destiny
> Ugly I'm not
> Fountain of the future.

What was Henderson Dores like when he was the age of Rachel and Yusuf? What will they be like, when they are 40? To speculate about such questions, it will be argued in this chapter, is to speculate about spiritual development. The chapter refers frequently to the role of story in spiritual development, for traditional tales, passed by word of mouth over the centuries, frequently start with someone wanting and needing, as William Boyd put it, 'to do a deal on the spirit'. The Scheherazade tale, for example, begins, as does William Boyd's novel, with an evocation of spiritual withering and wilderness:

> The king hated life. His food had no taste or zest. There was no spring in his stride or light in his eyes; no newness in his mornings, no contentment or rest in his nights. He was disgusted by women, and incapable of love.[3]

The king's feelings about life are entirely different, then, from those of young Rachel and Yusuf. By the end of the tale, however, after 1001 nights of storylistening and storytelling, and of the bonds these create and strengthen, there will be glorious pattern in his life, and wisdom and justice, and love. He will have grown young again ('when I grow up,' someone once said, 'I want to be a child'), grown to be like Rachel, like Yusuf:

> He no longer hated life. Food was delightful to him, he loved walking and seeing, everything in the world seemed to fit together for him in a glorious pattern. He respected and admired, and he cared for, all the people whom he knew. He ruled his country with wisdom and justice. He loved Scheherazade.

The king's transformation is personal within himself, but also has political consequences in the outer world: 'he ruled his country with wisdom and justice'. The arts of storytelling which bring about his transformation are speculative and inventive, but also truthful. They are seductive and teasing, but also caring and affectionate. 'The Baal Shem Tov,' wrote Rabbi Nachman of Bratslav, 'when he saw the lines of communication with heaven were broken and it was impossible to mend them with prayer ... used to mend them and restore them by telling a tale'.[4]

'You can teach meditation,' says a character in Iris Murdoch's novel A *Good Apprentice,* musing about pupils in schools, 'what used to be called prayer, and give them an idea of what goodness is, and how to love it'. The novel runs to 522 pages in its paperback edition. On page 520 there is a conversation which contains resonance and texture from all that has gone before, and indeed the whole story has been leading up to, we now realise, this exchange. It is a summation and consummation of the narrative artfully constructed over the previous 519 pages. It is nevertheless accessible out of context, and can usefully help us to reflect on spirituality in education, and on various tasks before us. The novel's main character, Stuart, has decided to become a primary school teacher:

> 'What's this place you're going to?'
> 'It's a teachers' training college, I can do a short course. I have to have a diploma.'
> 'I suppose you'll teach sixth-formers?'
> 'No, little children.'

'You mean ten, eleven?'

'No, eight, six, four.'

'You must be mad!'

'You see, things must be got right at the start —'

'You mean computers? I thought you hated them!'

'No, I mean thinking and morality —'

'You sound like a Jesuit, indoctrinate them when they're young —'

'Computers, OK, but that's just mechanical. You can teach language and literature and how to use words so as to think. And you can teach moral values, you can teach meditation, what used to be called prayer, and give them an idea of what goodness is, and how to love it —'

'Stuart, you've opted for power after all! I thought good men were powerless. You're a power maniac, just like I said!'

'Of course the problem is how to do it, it's all in that, the whole problem is in that — I'll have to learn ...'

The conversation suggests that as we consider spirituality in education we have to engage in four separate but inter-related tasks: separate in the sense that each can be described on its own, but inter-related in the sense that how each is addressed and tackled affects, qualifies and contextualises how we can address and tackle each of the others. We cannot, in practice, get them sorted neatly one at a time. The four tasks conveniently allow themselves to be named with words which all begin with the letter P:

- philosophical

- political and presentational

- practical and pedagogical

- private and personal

Philosophy is to do with the clarification of meanings, both big and small. The philosophical tasks in the present instance are to do with describing spiritual development clearly, so that we know reasonably clearly what we are talking about, and are reasonably confident that everyone is using key terms and concepts in much the same way.

It is entirely plain in Iris Murdoch's *A Good Apprentice* that her character Stuart does not believe in God and has no religious affiliation. He does, however, wish to teach children to meditate and pray, and to know and to love goodness. In her major book *Metaphysics as a Guide to Morals,* which can be read as a kind of commentary or gloss on *A Good Apprentice* (and also on most or all of her other novels, for that matter), Iris Murdoch is passionately interested in the concept of spirituality. At no stage, however, does she use traditional religious language to describe it. 'The loss of prayer', she says, 'through the loss of belief in God, is a great loss. However, a general answer is a practice of meditation: a withdrawal, through some disciplined quietness, into the great chamber of the soul. Just sitting quiet will help. Teach it to children.' Throughout the book she emphasises the importance of art, though is anxious, she says, not 'to suggest that religious experience is merely aesthetic or any nonsense of that sort'. At one stage she writes, referring to St Paul and the authors of the New Testament gospels:

> Christianity was indeed fortunate (if one may put it so) to find available, at the crucial moment, five geniuses including two great thinkers. Five artists of genius one might also say; Christianity, providing us with a mythology, a story, images, pictures, a dominant and attractive central character, is itself like a vast work of art.[5]

It is difficult enough to define and talk about spirituality with theistic language, and within the established and agreed meanings of a faith tradition. It is even more difficult — but even more necessary — to define our key terms if we are proposing to talk about spirituality after, as Iris Murdoch uses the terms, 'the loss of belief in God'. Do we agree with Iris Murdoch and her character Stuart that spiritual development happens regardless of whether or not a person belongs to a specific religious tradition and regardless of whether they are reasonably comfortable with the language and concepts of a religious faith? Do we assent to the proposal that 'a general answer is a practice of meditation: a withdrawal, through some disciplined quietness, into the great chamber of the soul. Just sitting quiet will help. Teach it to children.'? Do we agree that 'Christianity ... is like a vast work of art'? And that other religions are, too? Whether we do or we don't, how do we talk with each other about spirituality with sufficient precision to be able to plan a curriculum together, and teach it together, and evaluate it, and be accountable to each other? These are the key philosophical questions, and they require a lot of hard work. There is nothing so practical, it has been said, as a good theory.

Also, there is nothing so political as a good theory. The presentational and political tasks are different, however, from the philosophical ones. They are to do with tailoring and trimming (adding an embellishment here, cutting away an awkward part there) our arguments and ideas according to the audiences and constituencies whom we have to address, and for whose material and moral support and approval we need to negotiate. (Also, of course, there are audiences whose moral and material opposition we are prudent to reduce, and indeed minimise.) Iris Murdoch, in the passage quoted above, beautifully shows that her character Stuart needs to be not only philosophically rigorous but also politically astute, for he is continually having to riposte to scepticism and criticism. You have to find the right arguments for the right occasion, the nimblest defence and footwork for each specific bid or lunge against you.

One advantage of distinguishing between philosophical and political or presentational tasks, incidentally, is that it enables us to contextualise specific publications and events more accurately than we might otherwise do, and therefore respond to them not only more effectively and energy-efficiently but also, perhaps, more humbly and more generously. Consider, for example, discussion papers on spiritual development issued by the National Curriculum Council and the Office for Standards in Education.[6] Insofar as these are seen as contributions to the philosophical tasks before us, they are inadequate and disappointing. But as political texts, seen in the context of negotiations currently raging about the nature of British society and about the role and purposes of education, they reflect achievements and small victories (as well as, though, some worrying threats) and have their values and uses.

The pedagogic and practical tasks are to do with how we plan and fashion, and lead and teach and respond, in those places called classrooms. What do we do, as teachers, for and with learners? What stories, pictures, music, games, tasks, activities, do we use? What groupings? What balances of exploration and information, finding and telling? And how do we make these choices in ways which really do lead to children learning, as distinct from merely adding to our own power and pride? 'Of course,' says Iris Murdoch's Stuart, 'the problem is how to do it, it's all in that, the whole problem is in that — I'll have to learn ...'

As teachers engage with practical questions of methodology they may find it valuable to recall the story of a sheep which escaped from the fold through a broken fence and was chased by dogs. The shepherd went out looking for the sheep, and found it. She fought off the dogs, and carried the sheep lovingly back to the fold. 'You must repair the hedge,' people said to the shepherd. 'No,' she said. 'I cannot fence them in. I love my sheep too much.'

The private and personal tasks are about ourselves. How do we, inside our selves, cope and grow? So that we are learning too — our own spiritual development creatively affected by, and creatively affecting, our day-to-day work as educators? So that we are not dehumanised in our struggles against dehumanisation? So that there is no ugly mismatch between what we say and what we are? So that we are not overwhelmed or embittered by the bargainings and manoeuvrings in which we spend all too much nowadays of our professional lives, and so that we are not power-hungry in our dealings not only with each other but also, most seriously of all, with children? ('Stuart, you've opted for power after all! I thought good men were powerless. You're a power maniac, just like I said!') And so, in short, that spirituality is caught as well as taught?

Philosophical, political, pedagogic, personal: the four tasks are about what we think, what we say, what we do and what we are — about conceptualising, operating, instructing and being. They are separable for the sake of preliminary description, but need also to be addressed all at once, in a single package or bundle, or in the way that — for example — a juggler handles four objects at once, or the composer of a quartet four sources of sound. In order to begin approaching them more closely, let us recall that famous speech by Jaques in *As You Like It,* designated in the 1990s by the curriculum authorities as a text with which all young teenagers in England and Wales should be thoroughly familiar. In a reworked version for our times, these times of tests, charters and customers, it goes as follows:

All the world's a keystage

And all the men and women mere examinees.
They have their outcomes and their entrances,
And each one in their time takes many tests,
Our trials having seven levels. As, first, the infant
Schooled to note, mark, inwardly digest — not puke.
And then in streams and sets and bands
Creeping like tube trains to the final stations
Of our destined routes. And then the lover,
Seeking sublimation in trends and charts,
And dark satanic mills and boons. Next on terraces,

Full of strange oaths, yes, and strange jeers and chants,
Jealous in the colours of their club,
Worshipping league tables for the measurement of man,
And as mirror of our nature. And then the customer,
Getting and spending as the market needs,
And consuming goodies from its hidden hand.
As parent, patient, passenger and paying taxes
Humbly fain to dwell with charters and their gentle rule.
And so we take our tests. The sixth age reaffirms
The wills and the affections of our earlier lives:
Obedient peasant slaves, ever uncomplaining drones,
Batting for this scepter'd isle, attending church on time,
Loyal and proportion'd, rocking ne'er a boat,
Knowing right from wrong, and on quinquennial occasions
Thinking, choosing, voting right. Last test of all,
That ends this flat and uneventful tale,
Is gracefully to accept our final end-of-keystage grade:
No face, no flesh, no spirit — nought.

This re-working of Jaques' speech raises four main sets of points relating to spirituality in education. First, a point which was present also in Shakespeare's original: the central importance in this context of the concept of life-cycle. Our lives unfold in time, and our fundamental life-experience is of sequence and consequence: one thing happening before and after, and therefore seeming to lead to and from, another. Within the overall narratives of our lives there are certain stages and ages, or seasons or crises, in each of which there are distinctive struggles, needs, opportunities and tasks. Jaques' speech on this theme, incidentally, is highly sexist, misanthropic, cynical and biophobic (life-fearing, life-hating): it portrays and celebrates spiritual maldevelopment or spiritual underdevelopment, that is to say, not spiritual growth, and is a horrifically and outrageously inappropriate text to present to children and young people, unless contextualised, placed and corrected.

A seminal account of the human life-cycle in the twentieth century has suggested that we are faced as our lives unfold by a sequence of eight successive tasks, each consisting of a tension between opposites which we have to live with and, to an extent, settle with and resolve.[7] The eight struggles in this scheme are respectively between trust and mistrust, autonomy and shame, initiative and guilt, industry and inferiority, identity and confusion, intimacy and isolation, generativity and stagnation, and integrity and despair. Inspired and informed by this scheme, workers in the field of adult religious education have suggested six main stages of spiritual development.[8] Their not-really self-explanatory terms for these are (a) intuitive/projective (b) mythical/literal (c) synthetic/conventional (d) individuating/reflexive (e) paradoxical/consolidative and (f) universalising.

The various stages or seasons in the human life-cycle relate to each other not like the successive links in a chain, or like the successive stations on a train journey, but like the strands in a braid or plait, or like the motifs in a piece of music. In a braid or plait, all the strands are present at the same time — all are here and now in every cross-section, the reality is holistic not linear. In a piece of music, motifs come and go and come again, there are reprises and prefigurings, and for any one motif there are times of relative assertion and relative recession. 'Spiritual development,' it has been observed, 'is no steady, regular advance, but is punctuated by crises in which growth appears to have come to a stop for a time; old battles have to be refought and old experiences relived at a deeper level'.[9]

The concept of human life-cycle provides a convenient framework for the structuring of content and subject-matter. A recent anthology of stories of schools about spiritual development, for example, is divided up according to the spiritual tasks of emerging, seeking, loving, struggling, organising, reflecting and transforming.[10] Also, this concept can help with the planning of process as well as content. At the start of a course or unit or module there are distinctive tasks to do with beginnings; in the mid-life of a course the distinctive tasks are different, including those of 'storming', it is sometimes said, as distinct from 'forming' and 'norming' earlier and 'performing' later; towards the ending and end there are again special tasks. In all teaching and learning we need to be aware of, as the term might be, seasonality. Particularly we need to be sensitive to this fact of life whenever we are attending to the concept of spiritual development.

Another important point which the notion of human life-cycle points up is that we ourselves, we teachers and educators, are engaged in a spiritual journey. We are not people who have arrived and know it all, functionaries whose task is simply to pass on chunks of what we know, or chunks of what the government and the School Assessment and Curriculum Authority know. Rather, we are travelling companions, soul friends, pilgrims who learn as much from children as, in any conventional sense, we are likely to teach to them. (Recall again, for example, Rachel and Yusuf, introduced at the start of this chapter.)

Third, Jaques' speech reminds us of some the main features of the inner world. It recalls in particular the human yearning for significance, the feeling that the changes and the chances of our lives can be held together in wholes, and that our life-story as a whole makes sense and is worthwhile. To recall young Yusuf's words, we all need and want to feel that we are fountains of the future. Experiences of finitude, loss and bereavement raise questions about pattern and purpose but also the desire for significance may surface through absence and absurdity. Jaques himself sees life as ODTAA, one damn thing after another, and basically one unappealing and pointless thing after another at that. His speech is an expression of fatalism not of faith. Similarly the modern re-working is about a flat and uneventful tale, and is suggesting that there is nothing which is not flat and uneventful in our public lives and discourse in the 1990s. Our dominant images are of greyness and dullness: the Citizen's Charter and its offshoots for parents, patients, passengers, etc; numbers, quantities, league tables, reductionism everywhere, reduction of the human spirit; the market as measure of all things, everything material and instrumental. The reworking recalls subliminally that there is growing poverty, inequality and injustice in our society, and that the education system is being used to cement and normalise this, not in any way to challenge or correct it. In this context discourse of spiritual development in education is a sick joke if all it means is that children should be schooled to accept inequality and injustice as inevitable, ordained by gods and fate.

A further point arising from the re-working of Jaques' speech, then, is the suggestion that the Government's concern with spiritual development in the 1990s cannot be welcomed as something which is unambiguously or unproblematically benign. 'Spirituality', declared an international conference of Third World theologians a few years ago, 'involves people's resistance to dehumanisation and fills the quest for self-discovery, self-affirmation and self- inclusion, for in each of us as in the whole human community is the urge to live and to live fully as human beings.'[11] Spirituality itself, therefore, may involve resistance to the Government's current plans and proposals for spiritual development in schools. We need — putting the point in entirely traditional language — to watch as well as to pray.

It is appropriate now to draw some threads together from the earlier parts of this chapter in order to refer to four main themes requiring further thought and work. First, there is the issue of definition, or rather of succinct description. We need a brief statement, the kind which might appear in a dictionary which provides explanations of contexts as well as of meanings, with which we can work: something which delimits and demarcates, gives us boundaries within which we can be free. Such a definition can be arrived at only collaboratively: it cannot be promulgated. It requires, in Britain at the present time, the involvement of secular people as well as religious. It is sad and ominous that there is little or no consultation about spiritual development with the world of artists, philosophers, novelists, musicians and poets. 'The non-human and spiritual fascinated me,' reflects a dramatist and theatre director, as he recalls his experiences and achievements of the last twenty years, 'as much as the human.'[12] Commenting on the character of K, in Kafka's *The Trial,* he writes:

> K's guilt, for which he must die, is the guilt of betrayal: the guilt of betraying his inner spirit to the safety of mediocrity ... Guilt is the difference between what your spirit sings out for and what your courage permits you to take.

Work on a definition of spiritual development will need to draw a distinction between the inner life of people on the one hand and their outer life on the other: between feelings, orientations and imaginings and actual, material, historical, visible behaviour in relationships, work, politics, religious observance, lifestyle, and so on. Of course, there are links between these two worlds, and each affects the other. The inner world is the ground or seed-bed, but also the consequence and fruit, of the outer. But the value of the preliminary distinction between inner and outer is that it enables us to begin to demarcate the area named as spiritual: spirituality is essentially about the inner world, surely, what the re-working of Jaques' speech, echoing a phrase in the Book of Common Prayer, referred to as wills and affections. 'The aim of our worship,' observed Samson Raphael Hirsch, a great Jewish writer on the spiritual life, 'is the purification, enlightenment and uplifting of our inner selves ... Its aim is ... the cleansing of heart and mind.' St John of the Cross once said, 'I am not made or unmade by the things which happen to me but by my reaction to them. That is all God cares about.'[13] A contemporary specialist compares and contrasts religious and secular language:

It is our inner life which affects our perception of the world and determines our actions and reactions to it. We tend to ignore this inner life, but it refuses to be ignored either in individual or in national life. If ignored, the inner life will erupt in some form of violence. In religious language, this inner life is called 'the soul', and the art of knowing it, healing it and harmonising its forces is called spirituality.[14]

People who are comfortable with traditional theistic language define spiritual development along lines such as the following:

An individual's spiritual development means growth towards a fuller union with God through prayer and a growing conformity to God's will in life.[15]

Spirituality ... focuses upon the communion we have with God ... and the ways in which that communion is initiated, maintained and improved. [16]

Spirituality ... has to with the sense of the divine presence and living in the light of that presence ... Spirituality has to do with life under God.[17]

The word 'spiritual' refers to that dimension, capacity, relationship which our whole self can have with God.[18]

The goal of spiritual guidance is openness and responsiveness to God's presence in our lives.[19]

Theistic language of the kind used by these five writers is not readily available in the public debating chambers of modern secular society. It would be a great pity, surely, if we were to permit discussion of spirituality to be monopolised by theists of various kinds, and therefore also, almost certainly, by members of religious organisations. We need nontheistic texts such as Iris Murdoch's *Metaphysics as a Guide to Morals* as well as texts written in traditional religious language. Here is a reminder of how Iris Murdoch uses the word spiritual, and of the way in which theistic language is for her metaphorical:

The energy of the attentive scholar or artist is spiritual energy. The energy of the bereaved person trying to survive in the best way, or of the mother thinking about her delinquent son (and so on and so on) is spiritual. One uses this word with a certain purpose, to set up certain pictures, to draw attention to similarities and to explain and clarify the obscure by the familiar. Plato calls such energy Eros, love. Zeus became Eros to create the world.[20]

It is in addition relevant to recall how the word 'spirit' is used in everyday conversation within, for example, the words 'spirited' and 'spiritless'. Here are quotations from the Collins Thesaurus:

Spiritless
Apathetic, dejected, depressed, despondent, dispirited, droopy, dull, lacklustre, listless, low, melancholic, mopy, torpid, unenthusiastic, unmoved.

Spirited
Active, animated, ardent, bold, courageous, energetic, game, high spirited, lively, mettlesome, plucky, sparkling, sprightly, vigorous, vivacious.

Well, recalling the words of the theatre director cited above, it would be a kind of betrayal, a choosing of mediocrity, not to contribute a specimen definition of spirituality here — even though the task of working out a definition has to be collaborative, not individualistic. So here is something to play with and knock about, and to go back from to the drawing board. It is written in a secular, not theistic, frame of reference:

Spirituality is to do with the inner world of feeling, orientation and imagining. In particular it refers to feelings, orientations and imaginings to do with trust and anxiety, humility and self-importance, determination and self-pity, self-esteem and self-rejection, relatedness and isolation, purpose and nihilism, acceptance or denial of boundaries and finitude, meaning and fragmentation, courage and despair.

It is different from, but affects and is affected by, the outer world of behaviour, lifestyle, relationships, arts, recreation, employment and politics.

It is frequently expressed through terminology of human beings having 'souls' or 'spirits' and being in contact with supersensible, 'spiritual' realities or reality: gods or God.

For some people but definitely by no means for all it is expressed and nourished by the beliefs, stories, practices and rituals of a religious faith.

Probably the first thing we need to do is not merely scrap that definition but use it instead to discuss and decide the kind of definition we need — its formal properties rather than its content. Agreement on content may come fairly easily once we have agreed about form.

A second concluding reflection is to do with tradition. A fundamental precept of spiritual teachers and leaders has always been that people in the present need to see themselves not only as rebels and pioneers but also as heirs, with treasures to hold in trust — and to be formed, fashioned, disciplined and corrected by. 'Avoid,' wrote the Muslim teacher Ibn Abbad at Fez in the fourteenth century, 'those who esteem only what is established; their minds are little cells of ice.'[21] But avoid also, he said, 'those who esteem only innovations, for their opinions are aimless, without meaning.' We should see the past as innocent, it has been said, until proved guilty. From the past we learn the skills of discernment, humility and objectivity, essential skills in the field if we are to avoid, to recall that character cited earlier in Iris Murdoch's novel, being obsessed by personal power.

Third, a brief note on the relationship between inner world and outer, and specifically on the relationship between spirituality and politics. Reflecting on the psalms of ancient Israel a commentator in the 1990s observes that 'we are required to struggle against the enemies of God in His world, and against that same enemy in ourselves. Our struggle against injustice is an extension of the struggle against the same distortion of the love of God within ourselves.'[22] In non-theistic language, the inner world of spirituality is on the same continuum as the outer world of politics: each leads to, and each leads from, the other. Question, how shall we sing the Lord's song in a strange land? Answer, with difficulty: but there is on earth no other land to sing it in, and for coping with strangeness (and strangerness) there is no other song.

It is probably true to say that all great writings and teachings on spirituality over the centuries, in all traditions, have arisen from — to return to theistic language — *either* 'the struggle against the enemies of God in His world' *or* the struggle 'against that same enemy in ourselves'; or else, of course, and most typically of all, from both at the same time. 'The inner and outer struggles,' writes a theologian, 'may look different, but they are both struggles for the triumph of love over hatred and hope over despair.'[23] Here are those famous words about action and contemplation from the *Bhagavad Gita*, as presented in a modern play:

Victory and defeat, pleasure and pain are all the same. Act, but don't reflect on the fruits of the act. Forget desire; seek detachment. Renunciation is not enough. You must not withdraw into solitude. You must not stay without action, for we are here to serve the world. Matter changes but I am all that you say, all that you think. Everything rests on me like pearls on a thread. I am the earth's scent and the fire's heat. I am appearance and disappearance. I am the trickster's hoax ...[24]

'Our language about spirituality,' say the Third World theologians in the statement cited earlier, ' ... directs us not to the next world but to justice here and now. Spirituality is not a call away from life but the life-force that urges us on to do justice and to resist evil.'

Fourth and finally, a word about the central importance, in the context of a discussion of the spiritual in education, of story and stories. Spiritual development is about the development of each person's life-story, with its distinctive beginning, middle and end, and about how each of us narrativises the big and small crises of daily living and working. As resources for these twin tasks of story-telling and myth-making, we need to draw on and be nourished by the stories and myths which we inherit from the past, both written and oral. An attempt to summarise the teachings in traditional stories for pupils in schools goes as follows:

Have faith in the past. Don't walk away. You can't take it with you. Love one another. Use your head. Love life. Keep going. Look with new eyes. Let go. And never stop telling stories.[25]

The function of stories, says a contemporary theologian, is to cure us of belief and trust in 'an impossible Beyond':

We dream of an impossible Beyond in which we will find certain Truth, eternal happiness, absolute reality. The task of religion is not to gratify this incoherent yearning, but to cure us of it by telling us stories. The moral of all Christian stories is: 'Give up those illusory mystical yearnings, accept the human condition, love your neighbour, pour your own life out into the common life of all humanity. In a word, give up God and be content with Christ.' However, if it is put as bluntly as that people will of course not accept it. So the story-teller's art is needed.[26]

Henderson Dores, the archetypal 40-year-old in mid-life crisis, sought 'to do a deal on the spirit'. It could be said (though he himself, probably, would not put it quite like this) that he dreamed 'of an impossible Beyond in which we will find certain Truth, eternal happiness, absolute reality'. The same could be said of Scheherazade's king, he who at the beginning 'hated life ... There was no spring in his stride or light in his eyes; no newness in his mornings, no contentment or rest in his nights. He was disgusted by women, and incapable of love.' Scheherazade did not gratify his incoherent yearning but cured him of it by telling stories:

> By now, after one thousand nights and one thousand mornings, both Scheherazade and the king had changed. He no longer hated life. Food was delightful to him, he loved walking and seeing, everything in the world seemed to fit together for him in a glorious pattern. He respected and admired, and he cared for, all the people whom he knew. He ruled his country with wisdom and justice. He loved Scheherazade. On that last night she told the story through to the end.

9

Paradise Postponed

in the meanwhile, hell of an in-tray

'I absolutely hate my work,' explained the headteacher. 'I feel I'd like to dig up old Father Adam's grave and dance on the blighter's bones.' — 'Mm,' said the angel, 'that wouldn't really help, you know. But I can arrange, if you like, for you to go and live in a wonderful place which I know, and you'll have there a life of complete leisure. You'll never have to do a stroke of work if you decide to live there.' — 'It sounds wonderful,' replied the headteacher. 'When can I start?' — 'Straightaway,' said the angel.

An Arab folktale. The setting has been modernised but the imagery (and philosophy) are unchanged.

9. Paradise Postponed
in the meanwhile, hell of an in-tray

She sat at her desk, and looked with disgust and nausea at the piles of paperwork in front of her. Her work as a headteacher was a treadmill of one dreary and pointless chore after another. She felt like a key on a keyboard, a scrap of paper in a file, a misprint on a spreadsheet from her LEA.

She mentioned her feelings one day to a colleague she met at a conference. 'We all feel like that, though, don't we,' said this other person. 'We're all condemned to pointless and dreary drudgery. It all goes back to Adam in the Garden of Eden. He disobeyed instructions, and ever since then human beings have had to slave away at pointless chores. It's tough, but there's nothing anyone can do about it, we live in a tough world.'

'If only,' said the headteacher, 'I could get my hands on old Father Adam. I — I feel I'd like to dig up his grave and dance on the blighter's bones, or find his files, and shred the lot, or burn all the books he ever wrote, if he did write any. I really hate that man.'

Now it so happened that God was listening to this conversation. So God sent an angel, disguised as an ordinary human being, to have a word with the headteacher.

'I absolutely hate my work,' explained the headteacher. 'I feel I'd like to dig up old Father Adam's grave and dance on the blighter's bones.'

'Mm,' said the angel, 'that wouldn't really help, you know. But I can arrange, if you like, for you to go and live in a wonderful place which I know, and you'll have there a life of complete leisure. You'll never have to do a stroke of work if you decide to live there.'

'It sounds wonderful,' replied the headteacher. 'When can I start?'

'Straightaway,' said the angel. 'The place is called the Paradise Gardens Theme Park. You can live there in complete luxury and leisure, but on one condition: you mustn't speak to anyone else whom you happen to meet there.'

'Well that's perfectly all right by me,' commented the headteacher. 'To be frank, I don't much care for other people any way. Let's start.'

And immediately the headteacher found herself in the Paradise Gardens Theme Park. She lived in wonderful leisure. But one day, after she had been there for about a week, she saw a gardener pruning rose bushes. The gardener was cutting out the fresh green shoots bearing buds, and throwing these away; and he was leaving all the dead wood from previous years. The headteacher wondered what to do. 'Do I speak, or do I keep silent?' she asked herself. She was silent for a while, but eventually was seized with impatience. 'Hey,' she said to the gardener. 'Don't you realise that that's not the way to prune roses?' The gardener looked at her, and said, 'How long have you been here?' and at that moment the headteacher was transported suddenly back to her office. The angel was waiting for her there.

'Oh please,' begged the headteacher, 'give me another chance.'

'Very well,' said the angel, 'one more chance.' And immediately the headteacher found herself back in the Paradise Gardens Theme Park. Again she lived in wonderful leisure. But one day, after she had been there for about a week, she saw two old age pensioners chasing after a beautiful white horse. The horse was very swift as well as very graceful, and there was absolutely no chance that the pensioners could catch it. The headteacher wondered what to do. 'Do I speak, or do I keep silent?' she asked herself. She was silent for a while, but eventually was seized with impatience. 'Hey,' she said to the two old age pensioners. 'Don't you realise that you don't stand the slightest chance of catching that horse?' The old people looked at her, and said, 'How long have you been here?' and at that moment the headteacher was transported suddenly back to her office. The angel was waiting for her there.

'Oh please,' begged the headteacher, 'give me another chance.'

'All right,' said the angel, though very reluctantly, 'one more chance.' And immediately the headteacher found herself once more in the Paradise Gardens Theme Park. Again she lived in wonderful leisure. But one day, after she had been there for about a week, she saw four strong young men trying to lift a large heavy wheel, of the kind used in the roundabouts at a fairground. They were all standing very close to each other, and there was absolutely no possibility of lifting the wheel off the ground unless they spaced themselves out all round it. The headteacher wondered what to do. 'Do I speak, or do I keep silent?' she asked herself. She was silent for a while, but eventually was seized with impatience. 'Hey,' she said to the four strong young men. 'Don't you realise that you don't stand the slightest chance of lifting that wheel, unless you space yourselves evenly all round it?' The four men looked at her, and one of them said, 'How long have you been here?' At that moment the headteacher was transported suddenly back to her office. The angel was waiting for her there.

'Oh please,' begged the headteacher, 'give me — .'

'No,' interrupted the angel. 'No more chances. Adam was only given one chance, you know, and you've had three. Three times now you have disobeyed instructions. There's nothing more I can do for you. It's tough, I know, but good-bye.'

The headteacher looked sadly at the papers on the desk before her. Pruning roses, chasing after horses, lifting a wheel … she had these strange memories. She sighed, and reaching forward picked up a paper from her desk.

10

The Monarch and the Inner Life

seasons and the spirituality of politics

Stories make the inner world real, show us what transformations look and feel like. They are distinctively capable of exploring the difference between fact and fiction, faith and superstition, miracle and magic. To explore and discern this difference is a formidable but inescapable task in all phases and seasons of our lives. A recurring character in stories is the holy fool, the prince of jesters, the clown ...

Lecture for a Standing Advisory Council on Religious Education, exploring the nature of spirituality at different stages and ages of life.

10. The Monarch and the Inner Life
seasons and the spirituality of politics

It's about this king. This king is a character, as kings frequently are, in a folktale. At the start of the tale he is spiritually weary, but by the end he has changed, he has been transformed. So it's a pretty normal sort of folktale. When monarchs suffer from spiritual weariness, as frequently they do at the start of folktales, an awful lot of other people are likely to suffer too. That's one obvious reason why we need to be interested in stories about monarchs. In their process of transformation it often happens that monarchs are influenced, inspired and supported by non-monarchs, people such as ourselves. That's a second obvious reason why we non-monarchs are interested in, indeed fascinated by, stories about monarchs.

A third reason is to do with the nature of monarchy in its extended sense. A wise if rather eccentric modern thesaurus would give the following synonyms for the word monarch: governor, boss, chief, principal, captain, ruler, superintendent, leader, line manager and chairperson. Also bishop, elder, guru, imam, minister, pastor, priest, rabbi, sister and swami; performer, actor, storyteller and fabulist; parent; teacher; headteacher. Oh yes, and lecturer.

It's relevant to recall, before the lecture this evening gets any further, that most monarchs belong to, as the term might be, key stage six.

Spirituality at this key stage is in significant respects different from spirituality at key stages one, two, three, four, five, seven and eight: it has its own distinctive contours and colours, themes and scenes. But also it is based on, and follows rhythmically from, spiritual development in the five key stages which precede it; and it prepares the way and the ground for spiritual development in the two key stages which follow. We need to be alert both to its distinctiveness and to its relatedness.

This evening's lecture has four main subjects. They are like themes in a piece of music, or threads in an embroidery, sub-plots in a drama, objects in a juggler's hands. I shall move from one to another and back again rather than try to sort them out tidily one at a time. First, there's this king in the folktale I mentioned. I shall be telling his tale and shall be commenting on it as I go. Second, there's this business of eight key stages, the notion that spiritual development is something which happens over a lifetime, and is therefore something which we are all of us, teachers as well as pupils, adults as well as children, inescapably involved in, all the time. I shall be suggesting that key stage one runs from birth to age seven; that stages two, three and four conveniently correspond to junior school, lower secondary and upper secondary; that five is young adulthood, say from 17 to 36; that six is the age of monarchs, roughly 36 to 60 (though some monarchs, of course, take early retirement); that seven is what our society calls retirement; and that eight is, er, is when you're really, like, old.

The third subject is to do with spiritual qualities. I shall refer to eight main qualities and shall suggest that these eight qualities roughly correspond to the eight key stages of living. I shall suggest that the quality of confidence is associated with key stage one, curiosity with two, cunning with three, commitment with four, congratulations with five, care with six, contrition with seven and contentment with eight. It is of course not a happy coincidence, rather it is a slightly heavy-handed contrivance, that all eight qualities begin with the same letter. I shall hope to say and show that the qualities are related to each other not only like links in a chain but also like themes in a piece of music, or threads in an embroidery, sub-plots in a drama, objects in a juggler's hands. The fourth subject is a question: what then do we do in schools, and how do we do it, to promote and support spiritual development at key stages one, two, three and four? I shall be suggesting that we ourselves need all eight of the spiritual qualities — confidence, curiosity, cunning, commitment, congratulations, care, contrition and contentment — and also that we should be aiming to nurture all eight of these in children and young people. I shall make eight modest proposals to guide us.

So, eight key stages, eight spiritual qualities, eight modest proposals. And oh, I should have mentioned this earlier, the story about the king has eight episodes. The first episode introduces him:

Episode One: in which we meet the weary king
The king was weary. His hands and his feet, he felt, were withered, and his bones and limbs were unconnected. The words of his mouth were jagged and dry, like the shards and fragments of a broken pot, and his eyes were dull and unseeking. The land he ruled was waste and barren, and the ceremonies he performed were forsaken and vain. The people of his realm seemed to dwell in darkness, as if among graves. In the beats of his heart he met dragons and vipers, and monsters and witchcraft in the breaths of his lungs. He was missing confidence and curiosity, lacked cunning and commitment, had neither congratulations nor care. He wanted contrition and contentment.

The story comes to us from Afghanistan through oral tradition in seventeenth century Poland. It is a fairy tale about magical transformation and appears in a book of such tales first published in America.[1] The compiler of the book remarks that just as the outer garments of religious ritual signify for devout religious believers much more than mere custom so does 'the safe and familiar format of the fairy tale encompass some of humanity's most elemental drives and emotions'. In particular the traditional fairy tale at its best describes, within the framework of telling a tale about magical transformation, the drives and emotions associated with what may be called spiritual development. The imagery I have used to describe the weary monarch is not only from the world of Grimm, Anderson and Walt Disney — the tales with which we adults make and maintain contact with infant children in our arms and in our classrooms, and with the infant voices, wonderings, phobias and yearnings which are still active inside our own deep hearts and minds — but also biblical: there are echoes from Psalm 22, and the dereliction of crucifixion. Further, there are echoes here from medieval romance — the sick monarch and the waste land, with both monarch and land waiting for fertility, springtime and renewal.

From whence cometh the monarch's help? What magic and miracles shall restore this person to wholeness of life, and restore also his surrounding society and community? How do the eight spiritual qualities which he seeks and needs come about? These are the questions in this story, and in all stories which are about, as this one is, the nature of spiritual development. And about the connections between the spiritual development of individuals, for example monarchs in medieval folklore, and the spiritual development of societies and communities, for example schools in Britain in the 1990s. Let us continue for a brief while with the story. Something in the king prompts him do something unusual — unusual from his own point of view, though fairly predictable for people such as ourselves, who know our traditions of story-telling. He dresses himself as a commoner and goes out into the highways and byways of the city around his palace. Here is the second episode of his eight-part story:

Episode Two: the king meets the shoemender
Wondering how he might restore himself and his people to wholeness of life, he one evening discarded his royal garments and went out, disguised, into the backstreets and alleys of the town near his palace. He found himself in an area where the most rejected and despised of his subjects lived, and came then to a house with a lighted window and the curtains undrawn. He looked inside. A family sat around the supper table and he watched them spellbound. They were clearly quite poor, but were laughing and talking, full of life. At the end of the meal the mother and the father spoke some solemn words together: 'O Lord our governor, how exalted is your name in all the world! Out of the mouths of infants and children your majesty is praised above the heavens.' The king in his disguise went inside the house. 'You all seem so very happy,' he said. 'Tell me, what is the secret of your contentment?' — 'I repair shoes for a living,' replied the father of the family. 'And God, may his name be blessed and praised for ever,' added the mother, 'provides sufficient wages for us each week.' The king went away, thoughtful. The next day he issued a decree that in future no-one in his realm should receive wages for mending shoes.

Let us consider briefly what the king sees and what happens to him. He sees confidence — the family's confidence in their God. He sees commitment — the family's relatedness to a religious tradition. And he sees congratulations — the family rejoices in the goodness and greatness of their God. Seeing these three spiritual qualities in the family, the king feels curious: his own spiritual development, we notice, starts with curiosity. That is often the way. Frequently in schools we should be aiming to awaken curiosity. One very simple way to do this is to tell stories. A good story, by definition, awakens curiosity. The listener wants to know what's going to happen next, and how a problem situation is going to be resolved. At a deeper and perhaps less conscious level the listener wants to know how, if at all, spiritual development is going to take place. The third episode of the story about the king goes like this:

> **Episode Three: the king meets the water carrier**
> At the end of the following week, in the evening, the king again went out in disguise into the alleys and backstreets of the town near his palace. He came to the house of the poor shoemender and looked in at the lighted window. The family was eating and laughing and talking, full of life. At the end of the meal the mother and the father spoke some solemn words together: 'O Lord our governor, how exalted is your name in all the world! Out of the mouths of infants and children your majesty is praised above the heavens.' The king in his disguise went inside the house. 'Again you all seem so very happy,' he said. 'Tell me, what is the secret of your contentment?' — 'I used to repair shoes for a living,' replied the father of the family. 'But a few days ago the king issued a decree saying that no-one may receive wages for mending shoes. So now I carry water for people.' 'And God, may his name be blessed and praised for ever,' added the mother, 'provides sufficient wages for us each week.' The king went away, thoughtful. The next day he issued a decree that from henceforth no-one in his realm should receive wages for carrying water.

The king continues curious. Also, though not at all in an admirable way, he is cunning — he is using ruses, tricks and ingenuity to find the answers to his questions. But with regard to all the other spiritual qualities which are our concern here this evening, we see them here through their absence. The king does have not confidence in himself, or in other people, or in life and living. He is not committed to any tradition. He is not disposed to praise or celebrate — there are no congratulations in him. He does not care for others or for himself or for the future. There is no contrition in him — no repentance, no conscious sense of himself as imperfect, as in need of forgiveness. He is not content. He is still the same in the fourth part of his story and also for that matter in the fifth. This is how the fourth part goes:

Episode Four: the king meets the wood gatherer

At the end of the following week, in the evening, he again went out in disguise into the alleys and backstreets of the town near his palace. He came to the house of the poor family and looked in at the lighted window. The parents and children were eating and laughing and talking, full of life. At the end of the meal the mother and the father spoke some solemn words together: 'O Lord our governor, how exalted is your name in all the world! Out of the mouths of infants and children your majesty is praised above the heavens.' The king in his disguise went inside the house. 'Again you all seem so very happy,' he said. 'Tell me, what is the secret of your contentment?' — 'I used to carry water for a living,' replied the father of the family. 'But a few days ago the king issued a decree saying that no-one may receive wages for carrying water. So now I gather firewood.' 'And God, may his name be blessed and praised for ever,' added the mother, 'provides sufficient wages for us each week.' The king went away, thoughtful. The next day he issued a decree that all wood-gatherers in his land should be forced to become soldiers in the palace guard. He knew that soldiers in his palace guard were paid monthly, not weekly.

It's relevant to pause here for a moment and to reflect on the importance and significance, in any discussion of spirituality and the inner life, of stories. I should like to recall a wonderful story on the nature of narrative by John Updike, entitled *Should Wizard Hit Mommy?*[4] Joanne aged three loves stories. Her father Jack tells Joanne stories each evening to help her go to sleep. This is not the most noble of motives for telling someone stories, admittedly, but all parents with young children would say it's not entirely unreasonable. In the recurring plot in the stories which Jack tells little Jo there is a creature called Roger. Sometimes it is Roger Squirrel, other times Roger Frog, or Roger Chipmunk. This Roger creature always has, at the outset of the story, a problem. Roger goes with his problem to the wise owl in the forest for advice. The wise owl always says: 'Go to the wizard, and the wizard will sell you a magic spell, and the magic spell will solve your problem.' The plot then continues. In today's story Jo has asked, much to Jack's surprise and initial dismay, that the story should be about a wholly new character, Roger Skunk. We pick up the story where Roger Skunk goes to see the wise owl in the forest in order to outline what Jack imagines to be his problem:

'Mr Owl,' Roger Skunk said, 'all the other little animals run away from me because I smell so bad.' 'So you do,' the owl said. 'Very, very bad.' 'What can I do?' Roger Skunk said, and he cried very hard.

'The wizard, the wizard,' Jo shouted, and sat right up ...

'Now, Jo, Daddy's telling the story. Do you want to tell Daddy the story?'

'No. You me.'

'Then lie down and be sleepy.'

Her head relapsed on to the pillow and she said, 'Out of your head.'

'Well. The owl thought and thought. At last he said, 'Why don't you go see the wizard?'

'Daddy?'

'What?'

'Are magic spells *real?*' This was a new phase, just this last month, a reality phase. When he told her spiders eat bugs, she turned to her mother and asked, 'Do they *really?*' and when her mother told her God was in the sky and all around them, she turned to her father and insisted, with a sly yet eager smile, 'Is He *really?*'

'They're real in stories,' Jack answered curtly. She had made him miss a beat in the narrative.

Roger Skunk is not real. But for Joanne he represents a real problem in her real life with other children. Updike beautifully recalls that bedtime stories can help children to cope with real things in their real lives. Also, and even more importantly, and even more consolingly, he recalls that within the framework of a story you can believe both in God and (this is perhaps the same thing?) in the possibility of magical transformations. Speaking of magical transformations, let us continue with our main story:

Episode Five: the king meets the soldier

At the end of the following week, in the evening, the king again went out in disguise into the alleys and backstreets of the town near his palace. He came to the house of the poor family and looked in at the lighted window. The parents and children were eating and laughing and talking, full of life. At the end of the meal the mother and the father spoke some solemn words together: 'O Lord our governor, how exalted is your name in all the world! Out of the mouths of infants and children your majesty is praised above the heavens.' The king in his disguise went inside the house. 'Again you all seem so very happy,' he said. 'Tell me, what is the secret of your contentment?' — 'I used together firewood for a living,' replied the father of the family. 'But a few days ago the king issued a decree saying that all wood-gatherers should be forced to join the palace guard. We were issued with swords, but a sword is useless to me, since I would never harm a fellow human being. So I sold my new sword, and put a harmless length of wood in my scabbard instead.' 'And God, may his name be blessed and praised for ever,' added the mother, 'provided sufficient money for the sword for us to eat for many more weeks.' The king went away, thoughtful.

It would be relevant at this stage to consider this evening's eight spiritual qualities in slightly greater detail, and relate them to eight key stages of development. The underlying assumption is that spirituality is concerned in the first instance, to put the point in religious language, with an individual's or a community's relationship with God or with divine reality, as distinct from the outer world of morality, behaviour, politics and society. Secular definitions of spirituality do not refer to God or to a divine reality, but do emphasise that the focus of attention is the inner world as distinct from outer behaviour. Both religious and secular discourse acknowledge and emphasise that individual development takes place within the context of a community, and that the inner life and the outer are in reality inseparable. In religious language, for example, there are 'fruits of the spirit' made manifest in the outer world, and the inner, invisible world of prayer is judged with reference to what it leads to in fields of practical and visible action: 'by their fruits shall ye know them'.

The basic idea that there are eight main stages of inner development, and that in each there is a kind of spiritual struggle, was first suggested about 50 years ago by the psychologist Erik Erikson.[2] The scheme which I am suggesting is not in all respects the same as Erikson's, but at many points it is similar and the first and the last stages are identical in both schemes, even though they have different titles. A hand-out accompanying this evening's lecture (reproduced in this book as chapter 11) meditates on the eight key words which I have chosen, noting the richness of their nuances and etymologies. In our inner lives, the theory goes, each of us is developing over time, through the changing phases and seasons of our life. The inner life or spirituality of a child or teenager is different from that of a 35-year-old, and for a 55-year-old it is different again. An older person is not necessarily more advanced spiritually than a younger one. On the contrary, a seven-year-old child could be coping much better with the tasks of being a seven-year-old than a 70-year-old is coping with the tasks of being a 70-year-old. Although each phase or season has its particular tasks, these are linked to each other like the strands in a rope rather than like the links in a chain; or like the instruments in an orchestra rather than like stations strung out along a railway line. All are always present: as Psalm 8 famously said, babes and sucklings are as able to praise God, to congratulate, as well as anyone much older. The front page of *BBC Music Magazine* in March 1995 has a photograph of Pierre Boulez at the age of 70 and quotes him on the subject of curiosity, a quality more usually associated with human beings aged seven than 70: 'Curiosity is life. If you're not curious you're in your coffin.' Scientists as well as parents know that babies are 'born curious'.[3] All the eight qualities are always present. Let us return to our story, for its sixth episode:

Episode Six: preparations for a public execution
The next day the king announced that there would be a public execution and summoned all his courtiers, and many hundreds of his subjects, to attend. And of course he called the palace guard out on parade. A young man had been caught trying to steal a marrow from the palace garden. The king spoke to the soldier who had previously been a wood-gatherer, water-carrier and shoe-repairer. 'Draw your sword,' he ordered him. 'And behead this young man who has stolen a marrow from my palace garden.' The soldier asked if he might speak in private to his wife, who was amongst the crowd of onlookers. The king agreed. The couple spoke briefly together and the soldier then returned and stood before the king.

Stories require the willing suspension of disbelief. This is not the same as religious faith. But it's not entirely dissimilar, and not entirely irrelevant. 'Are God and miracles *real*?' asked the little child in the short story by John Updike. 'They're real in stories,' her father replied. Stories show us people of faith, people who believe they are in contact with God, people who are exploring their inner lives. Stories make the inner world real, show us what transformations look and feel like. They are distinctively capable of exploring the difference between fact and fiction, faith and superstition, miracle and magic. To explore and discern this difference is a formidable but inescapable task in all phases and seasons of our lives. A recurring character in stories is the holy fool, the prince of jesters, the clown who with trickery, cunning, resourcefulness and high spirits pokes cheerful fun at the human comedy, and joyfully celebrates a God who playfully loves and makes and re-makes the world.

Human beings are storytelling and storylistening animals. It's how we make sense of events. Little events — the myriad of things which happen to us, and which we make happen, every day. And also, our life-stories, the big things which determine who and what we are. Stories give tips, guidance, warnings and suggestions. About the inner life. Also about the outer life of behaviour, relationships and politics. And about the connections between inner and outer, each the ground and the consequence of the other, and the nature in both of transformation.

Episode Seven: a transformation

He prayed out loud so that all the crowds could hear: 'Blessed are you, God of compassion and mercy! To you be praise and glory for ever. If it is Your will that I should sever this man's head from his body, then give me strength to kill him cleanly with cruel and vengeful force. But if (as I suspect, O Lord) You do not delight in inhumanity, and do not desire this beloved creature of Yours to die, least of all for the trivial offence of stealing a marrow from the palace garden, then perform here a miracle, and transform this steel sword of mine into a harmless length of wood.' So saying, he unsheathed his harmless length of wood, held it aloft, and dropped it softly to the ground.

There is one episode to go. We'll be there very soon. First, extremely briefly, here are eight invitations or suggestions, to guide us as teachers and educators. Someone once said that the Ten Commandments don't tell you what to do but they do put ideas into your head. It's the same with these eight guiding suggestions. They don't set out a curriculum, but do sketch the headings for an agenda. They are very, very brief:

Let us return and repeat.
Let us trust the past.
Let us wonder.
Let us revel in metaphor.
Let us trust the young.
Let us sing.
Let us tell stories.
Let us start again.

Each of those is a lecture on its own. I hope I have given quite a lot of hints to show what each lecture would be about. Let us go back one more time to our story, to its last episode. You remember, I trust, where we were. The soldier, formerly a water-carrier and a wood-gatherer and before that a shoemender, has just prayed for a miracle, a magical transformation; has unsheathed his wooden sword; has held it aloft; has dropped it to the ground:

Episode Eight: and a further transformation

He looked into the king's eyes and the king looked into his. The king spoke very quietly, almost under his breath: 'O Lord our governor, how exalted is your name in all the world! Out of the mouths of infants and children your majesty is praised above the heavens.' The ranks of courtiers and crowds did not hear the king's whispered words but they did see the length of harmless wood and they had heard the soldier's prayer. They clapped and cheered and roared with delight. They had witnessed, they were sure, a miracle, pure magic. From that day forth, in the light and warmth of the miracle, the king ruled his land with confidence and curiosity, cunning and commitment, congratulations and care, contrition and contentment.

Let us return and repeat. Let us trust the past. Let us wonder. Let us revel in metaphor. Let us trust the young. Let us sing. Let us tell stories. Let us start again.

Please note: A hand-out accompanying this lecture, summarising key ideas in the eight stages or seasons of life, is reprinted as chapter 11.

11

Roots and Routes

journeys of a lifetime

Care

From Old English *caru,* grief, lament, burdened state of
mind. Later: serious attention, charge, oversight, concern.
An inclination to look after, take care of, see to, mind, be
prudent, be a steward. Something has been entrusted to
you, and you look after it, and in due course you pass it on.
Traditions, customs and structures. Ideals, dreams.
People. Developing care: a key task throughout
the middle years of life.

*Hand-out provided to accompany the lecture entitled 'The
Monarch and the Inner Life' (chapter 10), providing notes on
eight main stages or seasons of life.*

11. Roots and Routes
journeys of a lifetime

1. Confidence

From the verb confide, to put faith in. Latin *confidere* — *con* (intensive, but with implications of *cum*, 'together, in combination or union') + *fidere*, to trust. Trusting, self-assured, trusted, trusty. Being confident in yourself, feeling you are yourself trusted by others — they believe in you. Trusting others — parents, tradition, life. Developing confidence: a key task in the first few years of life.

2. Curiosity

From Latin *curiosus*, careful, assiduous, studious, ingenious, skilled, eager to know or learn, from *cura*, care. Being interested, asking questions, speculating, probing, being discontented with the untested. Nuances of exciting attention, being interesting: finding oneself interesting. Developing curiosity: a key task in childhood, particularly when you're aged 7-11.

3. Cunning

From Old Norse *kunna*, to know. Original meanings: learning, wisdom, ability, skill. (So cunning was the fruit or product of curiosity.) Later: skilful deceit, craftiness. In folktales, cunning is the opposite of fatalism or infantile belief in magic and miracles, it involves taking your fate into your own hands. Trickery and deceitfulness are means of self-assertion and self-rescue. Developing cunning in these senses: a key task in late childhood and early adolescence.

4. Commitment

From Latin *committere,* to join, practise, perpetrate, place with another for safety, entrust, consign to custody. *Com + mittere,* to send, nuances of sending forth on a service (mission, missionary). Entrusting yourself to, saying yes to, being knowingly confident in (so, with curiosity and cunning) a tradition, the faith, ways, customs of (certain of) your forebears. Choosing to be you. Developing commitment: a key task in late adolescence and early adulthood.

5. Congratulations

From Latin *congratulari* — *con* (intensive, but with implications of *cum,* being together with others) + *gratulari,* manifest one's joy. Express sympathetic joy, address with expressions of satisfaction. Connected with Latin *gratus,* pleasing, and Sanskrit *gurtas,* welcome, agreeable, thankful, and family of Indo-Iranian words denoting praise. Feeling and expressing joy — in self, lover, partner, nature, the arts. Developing the capacity to praise, celebrate, congratulate: a key task in the first decade or so of adulthood.

6. Care

From Old English *caru,* grief, lament, burdened state of mind. Later: serious attention, charge, oversight, concern. An inclination to look after, take care of, see to, mind, be prudent, be a steward. Something has been entrusted to you, and you look after it, and in due course you pass it on. Traditions, customs and structures. Ideals, dreams. Developing care: a key task throughout the middle years of life.

7. Contrition

From Latin *contritus,* past participle of *con + terere,* to rub or grind ('trite' originally meant 'worn out by use'). Being broken in spirit. Cf the Lenten prayer: 'create and make in us new and contrite hearts'. Being penitent, knowing one's faults and weaknesses, knowing oneself in need of forgiveness, of mercy. Developing contrition: a key task in the later years of life.

8. Contentment

From Latin *contentus,* satisfied, gratified; past participle of *con* + *tenere,* to hold, keep within limits, contain. Being quietly happy with, accepting of, one's lot. The lot which is completed with death. Developing contentment: a key task before the end.

Projects

12

They Struggled Here

bearing witness and telling tales

It's a story, is this, of defeat and destruction. Such stories
can be, of course, merely depressing, demoralising. But
also they can recall the dignity and importance of
struggling for certain values, certain ideals, and they
can portray, commend and celebrate the values and ideals
themselves. They recall thus the dignity of recollection,
of storytelling: the dignity of bearing witness,
of telling the tale.

*Account of a specific project aiming to create greater
equality in the curriculum and organisation of schools, and
of the project's destruction by politicians and the media.*

12. They Struggled Here
bearing witness and telling tales

One day, perhaps, the full story will be told. Warts and all, blow by blow. There will be multiple viewpoints and broad perspectives. Secrets will be told. There will be generous and frank self-criticism, and indeed humble confession and contrition, from everyone involved, whether as combatants or as onlookers. Every intricate complexity will be unpicked, there will be no more economising with the truth, and there will be judicious apportionments of responsibility and blame. The respective roles of deliberateness and coincidence, intentionality and sheer bloody luck, will be gravely weighed. Demons and villains will be redeemed. All passion and anger will be spent. In the meanwhile, there is this account.

It's a story, is this, of defeat and destruction. Such stories can be, of course, merely depressing, demoralising. But also they can recall the dignity and importance of struggling for certain values, certain ideals, and they can portray, commend and celebrate the values and ideals themselves. They recall thus the dignity of recollection, of storytelling, the dignity of bearing witness, of telling the tale. In many African countries and cultures a tale is told of defeat and dignity involving a tortoise, or a similarly weak and slow creature, and a fierce predator, for example a lion or a leopard. This particular version is from a novel by Chinua Achebe:

Once upon a time the leopard who had been trying for a long time to catch the tortoise finally chanced upon him on a solitary road. 'Aha,' he said. 'At last! Prepare to die.' And the tortoise said: 'Can I ask one favour before you kill me?' The leopard saw no harm in that and agreed. 'Give me a few moments to prepare my mind,' the tortoise said. Again the leopard saw no harm in that and granted it. But instead of standing still as the leopard had expected the tortoise went into strange actions on the road, scratching with hands and feet and throwing sand in all directions. 'Why are you doing that?' asked the puzzled leopard. The tortoise replied: 'Because even after I am dead I would want anyone passing this spot to say, yes, a fellow and his match struggled here.'[1]

Achebe's novel was one of the texts used by teachers in the 1980s in a project known as the Development Programme for Race Equality (DPRE). They used it in particular to explore the conventions and purposes of storytelling, both oral and written, and the role of story in situations of unequal power, for example in situations of colonialism in Africa in the past, and in situations known by the students and pupils here and now, in their lived experience at school and in society, and the lived experience of their families and communities. This account is about that project, its values and ideals, and about its defeat and destruction by sections of the press and by right-wing politicians, both locally and nationally. Early working papers about the project included the word Schools at the end: it was the Development Programme for Race Equality in Schools. But the acronym would then have been DPRES, readily but inauspiciously pronounced as Depress, hence the name that was actually chosen. Opponents and critics called it the Race Spies project. This latter term, coined from within an unholy alliance between the local branch of the National Union of Teachers and the local Conservative Party, and then given enthusiastic currency by the tabloid press and government ministers, passed into folklore, particularly locally.

Some of the media attacks mentioned my own name, as one of the officers involved in the DPRE's planning and design. Shortly after the attacks started, in autumn 1986, I received an anonymous letter. The handwriting was ill-formed and the lined paper was of poor quality. It was unusual, of course, to receive such a communication in one's in-tray. But there was so much fear and anger around at the time that it arrived, in people far more literate and, in conventional terms, better educated than the author of this letter, that I did not find it particularly surprising or disturbing. Quoted now here, in a different surrounding atmosphere, the letter may seem much more obscene than it did in the first instance. Be that as it may, it recalls with savage clarity the hysteria and fury which the DPRE aroused and — even more strikingly and relevantly — the attitudes and world-views which the designers, supporters and defenders of the DPRE believed themselves to be up against:

> ... you must be out of your tiny little mind you silly bastard if you are going to send niggers round to my kids school to scare them, you are in for a lot of trouble. Is this scheme to spy on our kids, my two kids hate the black bastards so do their Mum and Dad and you and your spies will not alter that you cunt, So our rates are being used to keep a bunch of niggers in Luxury send them back to Bongo Bongo Land, which is their real home. and let our country start smelling sweet again, We did not know what muggings, rapes, drugs, looting of shops etc were until the golliwogs arrived here, by the way my kids are reading all about Uncle Toms Cabin and all the other childrens books you call racist.

Five main points, I suggest, may be drawn from this letter. First, it portrays the racist views and feelings which are present in the formation of the minds and hearts of very many white people, and which are latent (though in polite society, of course, never thus expressed) in a great deal of daily interactions amongst white people and in their commonsense culture. For example, some of the press reporting about the DPRE was consonant with, and did nothing to distance itself from, the sentiments expressed in that anonymous letter.

Second, the letter shows the nature of the fear and anger which the DPRE encountered: the fear that the endemic racism in British culture and institutions would indeed be uncovered and documented by the 'spies', and that this would lead to intolerable pressures for fundamental change in national self-consciousness and in institutions such as schools, and in the understandings and self-images of white individuals. Third, the letter is a succinct and dramatic introduction to what the DPRE was all about: it was a project to create new procedures and structures in schools, for the underlying view was that existing procedures and structures all too often have the effect of obstructing and excluding black and ethnic minority children and young people in their learning, and in this way are in tacit collusion with, as distinct from being (as they should be) in energetic opposition to, the kinds of racist ideas and feeling which were expressed in the letter. It is entirely appropriate to set up schemes such as the DPRE which seek to identify and uncover aspects of schools which generally are invisible or unscrutinised — feelings, attitudes and prejudices of individual teachers; private-ish conversations and actions amongst staff and between staff and pupils; various exchanges and events behind classrooms' closed doors; and a plethora of taken-for-granted customs and routines which have the effect, even when this is not the intention or the wish of the staff who uphold them, of excluding or rejecting black and ethnic minority pupils, and their families and communities. Uncovering secret or barely visible matters is a necessary preliminary to combating and removing them. If a spy is a reporter or whistle-blower in situations where damage is being prepared and done, yet where no-one apart from spies will bear witness, then indeed the world needs spies. It is a brave and dignified profession though also, of course, one which is unusually hazardous and stressful. If race spies did not exist, in other words, it would be necessary to invent them.

Fifth, there is a further sense in which this is the case: that if race spies did not exist, it would be necessary to invent them. In this second sense, the creation of the spies is required by racism's own inner world, and the spies are figments or bogeys of the racist's paranoid imagination. The racist fears to be found out and therefore imagines that there are people out there, spies, who are seeking out shameful secrets. The spies use underhand, undercover tricks or surveillance and reporting, it is assumed, and they are therefore disloyal and deceitful. The behaviour of the spy, thus constructed by paranoid imaginations, is considered to be far more reprehensible than racism itself and it therefore provides a comforting justification for it. 'I may have,' goes the reasoning, 'well, I admit it, I do have, a mote in my own eye. I'm a bit of a racist. But the speck in my eye is of trivial significance compared with the great block of wood in the eyes of these so-called and self-styled anti-racists — these disloyal, unpatriotic, untrustworthy, deceiving and scheming race spies, blowing things up out of all proportion and stirring up all sorts of trouble wherever they go They actually cause racism, come to think of it. They're much worse than me.'

Certainly, of course, not all criticisms of the DPRE were unprincipled, unwarranted and paranoid, as distinct from thoughtful and well-founded, nor were all motivated or fed by racism. Legitimate criticisms and misgivings will be acknowledged here in due course. First, it is appropriate to describe the prolonged attacks made on the DPRE which were anything but principled and warranted. These were at best carelessly indifferent to their effects and implications and at worst were entirely consistent with (though more politely expressed than) the virulent and obscene anonymous letter cited above. In February 1995, several years after the DPRE had finished, a leaflet from the local Conservative Party was put through letterboxes in the borough with the following prominent message. It was clear that the Race Spies demonology was still alive and well, and that the local alliance with the National Union of Teachers and teacher opinion still had sufficient strength to be worth mentioning:

> Labour have recently been defending their record on education in Wemsden. Remember when they last controlled Wemsden [1986 — 1990] and their policies caused thousands of parents to send their children outside the borough? Wemsden's schools were the butt of merriment in newspapers throughout the land and teachers were frightened to blow their nose in case they offended the race spies. Don't ask a Conservative for proof of that — ask the teachers' own union and ask the teachers themselves!

('Wemsden': a fictitious but transparent name is used in this account, in order to help recall that the account is partial and a construct, not the whole and impartial truth, and in order to reduce the echoes, assumptions and expectations which would be around if the borough's real name were continually to be used here. But the real name is no secret, and can readily be seen in the notes and references on a later page.)

The account which follows is presented under six main headings: chronological summary; principles of management; press hysteria; independent reports; contexts and problems; continuing to hope.

Chronological summary

Early 1980s   There is much concern amongst parents and in community organisations in the borough about the poor educational achievements of black and ethnic minority pupils, particularly those of Afro-Caribbean background, and growing hostility to schools and the LEA (though the LEA does develop and publish a fine document entitled *Education for a Multicultural*

Democracy). In this context there is bitter criticism of what is seen as an irresponsible and wasteful use of Section 11 funds. The LEA sets up an independent enquiry into the education of black and ethnic minority pupils (who incidentally make up about two thirds of the total school population). This is boycotted by schools, led by the National Union of Teachers. Political control in the borough is not clear-cut.

Mid 1980s   The concern locally about misuse of Section 11 funds is reinforced by concern from central government. It is in consequence clear that it will no longer be possible to use Section 11 funds merely to enhance teacher-pupil ratios. Staff will have to be clearly identified and have precise job descriptions. Various alternative schemes are considered by officers and councillors, but there is still much inertia and there is still no clear political control.

Summer 1986   The municipal elections produce, for the first time in many years, a Labour Party administration with a large majority. About a half of the Labour councillors are themselves black or Asian and all are aware that the borough's black and ethnic minority communities have high expectations of them. By the end of July the DPRE has been planned in detail on paper and during August it is approved for Section 11 funding by the Home Office.

Autumn 1986   Advertisements for DPRE staff appear in the press and about 50 teachers are appointed. The 'Race Spies' hysteria, led by the *Mail* newspapers on Sunday 19 October, starts. Within days central government freezes the Section 11 funds which had been promised.

January 1987   The DPRE starts.

Spring 1987   A report on the borough by Her Majesty's Inspectorate (HMI), compiled in response to the press hysteria, is critical of the borough itself though not of the DPRE, since the latter has only just begun.

Summer 1987 The LEA conducts a consultation with schools and in the light of it publishes a policy framework for all further developments, entitled *Equality and Excellence.*

Spring 1988 Central government publishes two independent reports on the DPRE, the one by Sir David Lane, a former cabinet minister, and the other by HMI. Both praise the DPRE and recommend that the Section 11 funding earmarked for it should be released. But central government sets up yet another independent enquiry, this time led by Baroness Cox, and continues to withhold funding. The continuing uncertainty about the programme's future means that staff begin leaving for other, more secure posts.

1988/89 The programme is increasingly welcomed in schools as valuable and effective. But more and more staff leave, and virtually none are replaced.

Summer 1990 Municipal elections produce a substantial Conservative Party majority. In August, without a proper report from officers, the Education Committee resolves that the DPRE should close at the end of the year. In the summer Baroness Cox publishes a report broadly similar in its conclusions to those of Sir David Lane and HMI, commending the DPRE for its valuable work, and similarly recommends that Section 11 funds should be released. At long last the earmarked funds are indeed released, but by now there are very few staff left.

December 1990 The programme finally closes, though at the last moment two or three staff are permitted to stay on till March 1991.

Principles of management

The programme's formal aim was 'to enable schools to develop metho-
dologies, structures and curricula which will improve the attainment and
life-chances of black pupils, and thereby create greater race equality'. The
Programme was designed according to a number of fundamental principles
reflecting national and international experience over the years of how
changes and improvements in schools are most effectively implemented.
There were eight such principles, as follows. They are set out here with
almost exactly the same terminology that was used in formal
documentation at the time. As will be seen, there was nothing particularly
radical about them. On the contrary, they were sensible and unexceptionable. Yet quoted here almost ten years after they were written,
they may seem almost quaint. For it is not only antiracism which has been
massively criticised and delegitimised by central government and its
supporters in the media in recent years, but also the professional skills and
dignity of teachers, support structures and change agents, and holistic
approaches to management.

First, the programme was based on the fundamental assumption that
the responsibility for raising attainment, and for introducing and managing
change aimed at raising attainment, lies with headteachers. The role of
DPRE staff was to assist headteachers, and other senior staff. Headteachers
for their part are accountable for raising attainment to their governing
bodies, and there was explicit reference in DPRE job descriptions to regular
reports on progress to governing bodies. It was considered essential that
the programme should be embedded in existing management and
accountability structures, and in already well established procedures and
practices for the management of organisational and curricular change.

Second, most DPRE staff were members of the senior management
structure of the schools where they were based. This enabled them to have
an overview of the schools as wholes, and to contribute to decision-making
on important cross-curricular and organisational matters. Their salary
scales reflected their senior status, and this seniority was in its turn a
reflection of the view that effective change in schools needs to be
institutionalised from the top, and must be organised and legitimised at
the highest possible level. In this respect they were different from Section
11 staff in most other local authorities, who typically are on low salary scales
and can make very little impact on whole-school policies and decision-

making. In order that they could assist headteachers with management and coordination tasks DPRE staff did not at the outset of the Programme have direct contact with pupils for more than about 40% of their time. This proportion was similar to that of other staff of comparable seniority and responsibility. Later, they had considerably more contact time.

Third, the DPRE reflected the conclusions of school effectiveness research, which has shown that raising educational attainment requires, simultaneously, three main kinds of development: curriculum development, teacher development and organisational development. These three separate but overlapping and interacting dimensions of change were expressed formally in various early documents as follows:

(1) The development of new subject-matter, topics and materials, and of new practical classroom methods and approaches.

(2) The development of new perspectives, skills and expectations amongst teachers, both as individuals and also as teams, groups, departments and whole staffs.

(3) The development of new practices, procedures and customs, for example in decision-making, and in relationships between schools and the wider community.

Fourth, there was an emphasis on collaborative or tandem teaching. This mechanism of curriculum change has been shown throughout Britain in recent years, and indeed in many other countries also, to be extremely valuable in promoting and supporting improvements aimed at raising attainment. In addition, DPRE staff taught on their own as well as collaboratively. Their role in this respect was not only to have an immediate impact on pupils' learning but also to develop modules, materials and examples which could be adopted by other staff.

Fifth, there was an emphasis on pedagogy and methodology, for one of the main conclusions to be drawn from the last 30 years of curriculum development and improvement is that we do not change what pupils learn merely by changing what teachers teach. What really makes a difference is not the 'what' of teaching, the content, but the 'how', the pedagogy and process. The key practical tasks are do with enabling each individual pupil to engage successfully and perseveringly with the concepts and principles which are to be learnt. This means paying close attention to the relationships between teachers and pupils, and the quality of the interaction between them. Also, and just as importantly, it involves attending to the quality of relationships between pupils. The DPRE put a great deal of emphasis, both in its actual work and also in the intensive training which its members received, on issues of classroom interaction and pedagogy.

Sixth, a distinctive feature of the DPRE was the pattern of close relationships which it was expected to develop with advisers (later known in the borough as inspectors), advisory teachers and other support services. The overarching policy framework for all work by these groupings, as for all the borough's schools and colleges, was outlined in the major document entitled *Equality and Excellence,* published in summer 1987. The fundamental intention was that the Programme should not be marginalised within the LEA as whole, as so often happens with Section 11 services in other parts of the country, but on the contrary that it should be strongly integrated with all other services and agencies working from outside schools to promote and support change.

Seventh, particular care was taken to support the learning and professional development of DPRE staff. An assistant head of the programme had responsibility for overseeing this aspect of DPRE activities, and there were three inservice tutors. The immediate purpose was to provide moral and professional support, and in this way to benefit the schools where DPRE staff were working. The longer-term purpose was to help staff return, in due course, to mainstream posts. In this latter respect, incidentally, the Programme was extremely successful: more than nine in ten of the DPRE staff subsequently gained promotion to more senior and responsible posts, virtually all in the mainstream of education (as distinct, that is, from Section 11 posts), and are now working as headteachers, deputy heads, inspectors, advisers, senior lecturers, and so on.

Eighth, DPRE staff were to be catalysts and agents of change, but also were of course expected to respect, and to adapt to, the specific circumstances, history, traditions and personalities of the schools where they worked. In order that they could take on successfully these two complementary, but at times perhaps contradictory, sets of tasks, it was essential that they should be able to receive guidance and support from outside the school where they were based. Amongst other things, such external support and guidance enabled there to be consistency between projects and initiatives in different schools. Thus staff had a dual accountability — both to headteachers for their day-to-day work and also to the head of the programme for overall policy issues. Such dual accountability in the case of the DPRE was precisely analogous, incidentally, to that which exists in all other support services.

Press hysteria

RACE SPIES SHOCK ran the front page banner headline in the *Mail on Sunday,* and the front page story beneath it began as follows:

> Race commissars in a Left-wing borough are recruiting 180 Thought Police to patrol schools for prejudice ... Wemsden plans to put a race adviser in every school from January. They will be backed by project teams who will move in at the first hint of prejudice. The 180 advisers will have the power to interfere in every aspect of school life, from discipline to the curriculum.[2]

This was the essential storyline which all other newspapers recycled the following day, and which continued dominant throughout the body of public mythology and demonology which developed in the ensuing months and years. Some of the language in the initial story — 'patrol', 'move in', 'commissar', 'thought police', 'interfere' — was clearly emotive and typical of tabloid journalism at its most economical with factual accuracy. But also some of the other language, apparently neutral, had been invented or chosen by the newspaper: it was not present, that is to say, in any of extensive documentation about the DPRE which was already by then widely available. In particular the term 'race adviser' to describe DPRE teachers was an invention of the *Mail on Sunday,* and, incidentally, there had been absolutely no implication in any of the documentation that the DPRE teachers would be concerned at all centrally with something called 'prejudice'. The term 'project team' did, however, appear. The preliminary disinformation thus had a mix of three main ingredients: (a) hysteria (spies, thought police, move in) (b) apparently innocuous terms which in context were inventions (adviser, prejudice) and (c) terms which indeed were in use but which were now given a new and sinister meaning (project team). On the basis of disinformation such as this the paper was able to obtain a formal statement from the general secretary of the National Association of Head Teachers:

> We have trouble with a number of Left-wing councils — but none as extreme as Wemsden. Heads are 'guilty' of racism until proved innocent. It's dreadful. The appointment of more race advisers and

officers is totally objectionable. Heads will be constantly looking over their shoulders and be forced to submit their professional judgement to people who really have no business interfering in the curriculum. But when the new Education Bill becomes law, we'll really launch ourselves at Wemsden.

The following day, Monday 20 October 1986, the rest of the national press re-ran the story and material which had appeared the previous day in the *Mail on Sunday*. The *Sun* provided the rhythmic and alliterative headline SPIES IN CLASS TO SNOOP ON SIR; the *Express* pleaded SAVE US FROM THIS EPIDEMIC OF NITWITS; and the headline in the London *Evening Standard* was RACE SPIES LIKE THE DAYS OF HITLER. These and several other papers referred to Orwellian thought-police, and most used the term evil. The recurrent subliminal imagery was of East European authoritarianism, an evil and alien empire taking form in Britain only a taxi ride from Fleet Street. What was particularly sinister about Wemsden, the papers implied, was that many of its political leaders, and some of its senior officers, were Asian or black: in some boroughs, it was said, the appropriate term of criticism is merely 'loony', but since the leadership in Wemsden contained black and Asian people the more apposite term was evil.

A cartoon in the *Daily Mirror,* for example, showed clearly some of the real battle-lines. Wemsden has proportionately more black and ethnic minority people living within its borders than any other local authority in Europe, and in 1986 had more black and ethnic minority people involved in the political leadership. The *Daily Mirror* portrayed the Town Hall as a Native American tepee, and borough councillors as half-naked savages brandishing tomahawks, and dancing in heathen ecstasy round a white sacrificial victim. Several officers and councillors received obscene anonymous letters and death threats (for example there was the letter cited at the start of this chapter), and these too showed totally clearly that one of the forces expressed and released by the media scare was a most virulent and primitive kind of racism. The borough was demonised by right-wing politicians and the press, to the point of becoming a kind of Bonaparte figure. 'Eat up your greens,' said a parent to a child in a cartoon in the *Guardian,* apropos of this demonising process, 'or Wemsden Council will get you.'

Independent reports

Subsequently, in spring 1988, a Home Office report written by Sir David Lane concluded formally that the press coverage in the early days had been 'grossly inaccurate' and 'disgracefully distorted'.[3] In addition Lane described the behaviour of certain individual newspapers as 'deplorable'. Not a single newspaper quoted any of these phrases from his report. Further, Lane praised the Programme as 'a bold and innovative approach' to raising attainment and to creating greater race equality, and his report contained observations such as the following: 'I was able to see many examples of devoted effort and fine achievement'; 'much good goes on in Wemsden all the time'; 'Wemsden Council, to its credit, was one of the first local authorities to take seriously its duty under Section 71 of the Race Relations Act'; 'Wemsden deserves praise for giving high priority, more than most local authorities, to tackling racism and discrimination'; 'More local authorities should join Wemsden in giving higher priority to this aspect of their educational provision, and the Wemsden scheme, if it proves itself, could well be a model for application elsewhere'. No newspaper report about Lane's report carried any of these quotations. Nor did any cite the following categorical and totally unambiguous statement:

> The DPRE teachers are in no sense 'spies' but are seeking to play their proper role as catalysts and stimulators of new ideas and practices.

The day after Sir David Lane's report was published the *Daily Mail* carried a front page story claiming that he had strongly criticised Wemsden for appointing race spies — even though the objective truth, as the quotations above show, was that he had praised Wemsden for introducing the scheme, and had categorically declared that the DPRE teachers, to quote him verbatim again, 'are in no sense spies'. Two years later, in summer 1990, a further report was written for the Home Office about the Programme, this time by a monitoring panel chaired by Baroness Cox. The *Daily Mail* gave it the following coverage:

> A Labour plan to place 'race spies' in schools to give black youngsters a better deal may now be scrapped. The scheme at Wemsden, North London, employed 'blinkered and insensitive zealots' according to a Government-backed inquiry led by educationist Baroness Cox. (2 July 1991)

This item drew a personal letter from Baroness Cox to Sir David English, the *Mail's* editor, parts of which ran as follows:

> I was deeply disturbed by the grossly inaccurate account ... about the work of the Monitoring Panel ... of which I am Chairman. The *Daily Mail* attributes the phrase 'blinkered and insensitive zealots' to this Monitoring Panel. The Report that we have made makes no such statement or anything resembling it ... The Report ... nowhere contains the words quoted or anything like them.

This letter reflected well on the fair-mindedness and objectivity of its author, and of the monitoring panel which she had been chairing. The DPRE was never afraid or slow to listen to criticisms when these were made within a context of objectivity and respect for accuracy and truth. We found it impossible, however, to cope against sheer malice and deceit.

Both Sir David Lane and Her Majesty's Inspectorate[4] formally concluded that the Programme was entirely eligible for Section 11 funding, and eventually, in autumn 1989, the Home Office conceded that it would pay its 75% share of the costs. It made, however, a number of requirements and conditions. A report by the University of Warwick commented as follows on the Home Office's treatment of Sir David Lane's supportive report, and on its overall behaviour in the affair:

> What is truly extraordinary ... is the role of the Home Office. To have a major department of state agree to fund a new and exciting programme, but then back off as soon as some of the ideas are subject to nonsensical reporting, is bad enough. To institute a thorough independent enquiry and subsequently treat its supportive conclusions as if they justified a wholly negative and punitive stance against the authority, is a major reason why morale, direction and purpose have been so thoroughly undermined.[5]

Contexts and problems

The malicious allegation that the DPRE staff would act as spies needs to be contextualised and understood within a range of tensions and disputes, partly local and partly national, of the late 1980s. Locally within Wemsden, for example, there were five main sets of quarrels or conflicts in the background.

First, there was a major tension between, on the one hand, the leadership of the Labour Party which had come to power in the local elections of May 1986 and, on the other, the leadership of the local branch of the National Union of Teachers, the Wemsden Teachers Association (WTA). Earlier in the decade these two groups had worked in close alliance and indeed harmony with each other, and each had seen the other as a useful and trusted friend and supporter in their various specific agendas. By summer and autumn 1986, however, the relationship had become very strained indeed, not least since the politicians were now under pressure from the electorate much more, proportionately, than from their employees. Second, and to an extent related to the first point, there was longstanding mutual enmity between the leadership of the WTA and a number of influential black community leaders. This had been particularly evident at the time of the Barrow Enquiry into standards in Wemsden schools, with which the WTA had refused to cooperate. It was exacerbated by profound disagreements about the appropriate use of Section 11 funding, with the WTA favouring the use of additional staff to create smaller classes and the black community arguing for a much more targeted, and for an explicitly antiracist, approach. The tensions in these regards were clearly set out in an internal memorandum in the Labour Party in 1985.[6] The memorandum began by asserting that 'it is now clear that our policy of bolstering school establishments by using Section 11 money has been useless in furthering the education of Black children'. It then went on to itemise the reasons why the previous policy of reducing pupil/teacher ratios had failed:

1) The deeply embedded racism, classism and sexism of society reflected in the teaching profession.

2) The dominance of white senior teachers who set the ethos of a school and who believe in a deficit theory of educational failure which puts the blame on parents, society and therefore the children themselves for inadequacies of the education system.

3) The inability of dedicated junior teachers who have the right attitudes to change the ethos of a school because of their lack of power and influence.

4) The resulting poor child/teacher relationship due to the above attitudes and the inability of staff to change the curriculum or disciplinary framework brought about by such attitudes.

The memorandum also said that the answer to such problems was to 'by-pass heads and senior staff by the creation of a central team of teachers answerable to borough staff'. Remarks such as this did nothing, of course, to help develop trust and partnership in the education service as a whole, however well-founded they may have been.

A third local conflict in 1986 in which the DPRE got caught up was an episode involving a high-profile campaign by the WTA to defend one of its members against whom, it genuinely believed, false and unfair accusations of racial discrimination had been made. The campaign was legitimate in itself but it meant also that the WTA acquired some remarkably unsavoury allies. There was in consequence massive pressure on the Labour leadership, both from within Wemsden and from other parts of London, to stand firm against the latent or explicit racism evident in much of the press coverage of this case, and in much of the support which the WTA attracted.

Fourth, there were debates and arguments throughout the Council about the roles and styles of departmental race equality advisers. It suited people who were critical of the ways these posts were functioning to claim that the DPRE staff would be 'advisers' rather than teachers, and to claim that DPRE staff would be treacherously unaccountable to headteachers. Fifth, there was of course the local conflict between the two main political parties. At the time that the DPRE was first conceived, and still when it was submitted to the Home Office for Section 11 funding, it had all-party support. But by autumn 1986 the political consensus in Wemsden had collapsed, and both parties perceived the collapse to be to their own electoral advantage. The inevitable consequence of this party-politicisation was that the Conservative Party became formally committed to abolishing the Programme as soon as possible if it ever had the power to do so. Sixth, there was a split in the Education Department between inspectors and officers. Such splits are alas quite frequent, throughout the country. But definitely it was a major disadvantage that the officers, as distinct from the inspectors, were never more than lukewarm about the project and never seemed to make much effort to understand it let alone to defend it. It is sadly relevant in this respect to note that the Warwick report, mentioned above, documented much incomprehension amongst senior officers in relation to the Programme, and quite high levels of dissatisfaction and hostility.

Nationally, the DPRE was caught up in preparations for a general election, and with the criticisms in this regard which the Conservative

Party nationally wished to make of Labour-controlled local authorities; with the preparations which were being made within the Conservative Party for major new legislation on education; with conflicts and tensions between central and local government; with a view taking shape at the Department of Education and Science that moral issues are separate from and less important than curriculum issues; and — very obviously — with the government's desire to review and reform arrangements relating to Section 11 of the Local Government Act. Also, as already emphasised and highlighted, the DPRE has of course to be contextualised within the very circumstances which it had been set up to criticise and confront, those of institutionalised racism. Some of its opponents simply did not want racism in the education system and in society to be exposed and confronted.

There was, to summarise, a massive alliance of separate interests and forces operating against the Programme. It was extremely difficult, and in the long run impossible, to resist them. Specific difficulties flowing directly from, to quote Sir David Lane again, the 'grossly inaccurate' and 'disgracefully distorted' press reporting, or from the uncertainties about future funding to which it gave rise, were our inability to recruit and appoint someone to be head of the Programme other than in an acting capacity; our inability to recruit an assistant head to take on the task of leading rigorous monitoring and evaluation; our inability to persuade schools to set up adequate data bases for monitoring and evaluating the Programme's effectiveness; and our inability to retain staff long enough to document fully what they had achieved. These were all serious and regrettable weaknesses. Further, the fact that we were under continual hostile scrutiny from outside made it very difficult indeed for us, psychologically, to look at our work with genuine and open-minded self-criticism, and according to the normal procedures and practices of rigorous self-evaluation.

By summer 1990 the single most significant factor affecting the DPRE was that the Wemsden Conservative Party was on occasions now able to have a majority on the Education Committee. At a meeting in August 1990 the Committee resolved formally to end the Programme in December. The Committee did not receive a report recommending or even discussing this, and — contrary to the requirements of the Council's own standing orders — there was no reference in the Committee's minutes to the reasons why the Programme was ended.

The final destruction of the DPRE in summer 1990 without the existence of a formal report on the matter, and without a public record of debate and rationale, was a shock to many people. Yet also it was entirely predictable, in view of the way that the programme had been treated by its critics and opponents from the very first days. The programme had been all but strangled at birth by the Race Spies hysteria, and it was perhaps inevitable that it would be one day killed off in a casual and brutal way, with scant regard for the normal rules and customs of informed debate and rational decision-making.

Continuing to hope

The values, concepts and ideals underlying the programme are not, however, so easily killed off. The key ideas and ideals were expressed clearly at the start of the borough's 1987 Curriculum Statement, *Equality and Excellence,* reprinted and redistributed in 1994. The opening words were and are a succinct and bold reminder of what the DPRE was all about, and why it was inevitably met in some quarters by hostility and opposition:

> All learners are of equal value and have unlimited potential for development. There is inequality and injustice in wider society. The education service has a vital role to play in helping to combat, reduce and eliminate inequality and unjust discrimination, and in improving the opportunities, achievements and life-chances of all learners.[7]

Amongst many other things, the DPRE involved enabling pupils and students to describe their own experiences of living in multicultural, multiracial Britain, and their own individual and collective endeavours to create a strong and dignified personal identity. As part of a unit of work organised by the DPRE at a secondary school, an Asian-British young woman wrote a poem which began as follows:

> Oi! Paki! Wotcha doin' in our country?
> Go back to where you belong.
> I hold my head up high and proud
> And walk on with dignity.
> How long can I walk on?
> How long can I ignore?
> The anger inside me burns red, dark red.
> How I'd like to tear them apart ...
> But instead I hold my anger.[8]

The attacks on the DPRE were similar, in their effects and motivation, to the attacks made on that young woman. The long term task is to educate against, and to eradicate, racial harassment and abuse, and the wider political task is to create and maintain a society in which all people can — as the poem puts it — hold their heads up high and proud, and walk with dignity. These are tasks in the outer world. In the immediate short term, one task amongst others is in the inner world. It is to 'hold the anger': to acknowledge and name one's feelings ('how I'd like to tear them apart'), but not to be broken by them. And to walk, describe and narrate — bear witness, tell tales — with dignity. I want it to be known, said the tortoise in the folktale, that people struggled here.

Remembering and marking the struggle is one side, but only one side, of the coin. The other is hope. The sense of boundless possibilities and confidence reflected at the start of *Equality and Excellence* — 'All learners are of equal value and have unlimited potential for development' — was expressed well in a brief poem written by a child at a local primary school in summer 1990:

> I am rich and pure and full of fresh thoughts
> Ready to take on the world.
> I'm full of action,
> Smart as anything,
> And full of quality.
> I am an egg ready to hatch.
> I bring with me life.[9]

That, yes, was what it was all about. It was for the sake of unlimited potential — hope, fresh thoughts, action, life — that they struggled here.

13

The Answer Lies in the School

contexts and conditions of change

'We are very keen to have light thrown on this matter, if at all possible. We wonder, therefore, whether any of you here today have any comments or suggestions? Have you ever heard a story which was at all similar?'

A parable about — is it? — ethos, climate and relationships.

13. The Answer Lies in the School
contexts and conditions of change

Colleagues, I begin my report at this year's sales conference by giving an account of a project concerning our major new software package, the SEED desktop publishing system. We donated a free copy to each of four different schools.

For the sake of convenience, I shall call these four schools Appatheaton, Brashbury, Cooloffham and Deapchangeley. They are extremely similar to each other, for example in terms of size, catchment area, attainment levels of the pupils, ethnic composition, range of occupations amongst the parents, qualifications of the teachers, the actual architecture and age of the buildings, and so on. You would think that if SEED were to succeed in one of these schools then it would be bound to succeed in all the others also. However, each school reacted to SEED in its own very distinctive way. This is what I wish to tell you about:

(A) Appatheaton

At Appatheaton, to put the matter bluntly, our project was a disaster. Virtually no-one at the school took the slightest interest. SEED, as I am sure everyone here today knows, is a very versatile publishing package indeed, and has the potential for being able to transform people's lives, in a whole range of fascinating and creative ways, and particularly by enabling people to share their stories. At Appatheaton, however, we were totally unable to make any reasonable progress.

(B) Brashbury

In Brashbury we were more successful. Indeed, progress at the start was very satisfactory indeed. Many teachers took our product to their classrooms. The sad and disturbing fact, however, is that although many staff have SEED in their classrooms, they have not actually used it. SEED has had no discernible impact on them, nor — it follows — on their pupils.

(C) Cooloffham

In Cooloffham the initial reaction of staff was not as good as at Brashbury. But at least it was gratifying to see teachers who took up SEED did immediately start using the package, and were extremely enthusiastic. We have received an impressive number of glowing letters. Yet sadly I have to admit to you that once the initial euphoria had died down SEED was basically tidied away. The position now, a few months after the project, is that SEED is no more used at Cooloffham than it is at Brashbury.

(D) Deapchangeley

Deapchangeley, I am happy to report to you, has been a real success story. SEED is being widely used throughout the school, and it is transforming people's lives. There has been an explosion of classroom newspapers, and of school newsletters and bulletins. There are — so to speak — several small publishing houses, producing stories, auto-biography and poetry written by the pupils and by local people. There are vigorous new networks and relationships throughout the school, and very large numbers of pupils, teachers, parents and local com-munity people are gaining fulfilment through writing, printing, pub-lishing and sharing their ideas and their stories. SEED stands, you recall, for SENSITIVITY, ENLIGHTENMENT, EMPOWERMENT and DELIGHT. It has certainly lived up to its name at Deapchangeley.

We are — I will be frank with you — puzzled by these four differing responses to the same package. For I repeat and emphasise, the four schools are apparently very similar to each other. We are very keen to have light thrown on this matter, if at all possible.

We wonder, therefore, whether any of you here today have any comments or suggestions? Have you ever heard a story which was at all similar?

14

Yes Of Course, Of Course

dreaming a future

Punita was initially surprised and dismayed, but in the event pleased, when she had to write an extended essay entitled 'The Multi-Ethnic Good Society: why, what, where, how and when'. To prepare this she had to use concepts of racialisation and racist exclusion, ethnogenesis and hybrid identity, cultural politics and postmodernism, and urban policy and regeneration.

Paper provided for a conference organised by the Schools Curriculum and Assessment Authority (SCAA), summer 1995, on the teaching of English as an additional language.

14. Yes Of Course, Of Course
dreaming a future

Part One: a case study

Glowing terms

Midleigh School is a 5-11 primary school with 12 staff. About half the pupils have learnt or are learning English as an additional language. An Ofsted inspection report earlier this year praised the school in glowing terms, referring in particular to English and language development. It attributed the school's high standards in English largely to its involvement in a five-year Learning and Language Programme, which began in autumn 1992.

Time and energy

For the whole of the school year 1992-93 Midleigh School's language coordinator, Punita Gill, was taken off regular class teaching and she devoted all her time and energy to leading, developing and assisting her colleagues. In order that she could do this, she received considerable support from outside the school as well as, of course, from Midleigh's headteacher.

Enjoyment and rejoicing

Every Monday throughout the year Punita was away from school on a course. The other course members were people very similar to herself — language coordinators in their respective schools. They were from several different LEAs, by the way. The course content had three separate aspects. First, there was great emphasis on language. Punita and the other course members were intrigued and pleased by the new terms and ideas they encountered 'semantic agility', 'rich scriptin'g, 'meaning negotiation', 'shared imaging' and so forth — and they extended their own enjoyment of, and rejoicing in, the sounds, senses and powers of words. Second, there was much reference to school effectiveness and school improvement, and to the skills and strategies required of change agents, for example — and particularly — change agents such as Punita herself. Third, there was quite a lot of sociology and political philosophy. Punita was initially surprised and dismayed, but in the event pleased, when she had to write an extended essay entitled The Multi-Ethnic Good Society: why, what, where, how and when. To prepare this she had to use concepts of racialisation and racist exclusion, ethnogenesis and hybrid identity, cultural politics and postmodernism, and urban policy and regeneration.

Her own research

Not that theoretical essays were the principal kinds of written assignment on the course. Mainly the course members had to engage in classroom-action-research projects in their own schools. Punita's own research was into children's imaging of word meanings in mathematics and into the use of texts with Year Four children about inter-ethnic conflict and the negotiation of ethnic identity. The course tutor visited Punita at Midleigh at least once each term during the year, and met and talked at length with the headteacher as well as with Punita herself. At the end of the year Punita received the Advanced Diploma in Primary Language Education and credits towards the master's degree which, incidentally, she is just completing now in summer 1995.

Friends and critics

That, then, was how Punita spent her Mondays. On Tuesday mornings she visited other course members in their respective schools or in her turn received visits from others. The concept of critical friend was central to the course and it was on Tuesday mornings that course members developed and practised their skills as critics and friends, and the skills of receiving and acting on what their friends told them.

Colleagues

For five of the other seven sessions each week Punita was involved in collaborative or partnership teaching with her colleagues. For two of them she acted as a supply teacher so that colleagues could attend off-site ten-session courses. By the end of the year six different colleagues had attended such courses. Two of the courses were on linguistics and language development. The other four were on national curriculum subjects music, science, art and maths.

Turns

That was 1992-93. The following year Rahila Malik, the head of infants, was released from regular class teaching and she operated in much the same way. This year it's the turn of Chris Webber, who is Midleigh School's maths coordinator. Next year it will be Pat Avery, who is taking over from Punita as the school's language coordinator. Punita herself, it so happens, will from September onwards be the school's new deputy head.

Standards

As already mentioned, the school received a glowing Ofsted report earlier this year, commenting in particular on children's high standards of literacy. An interim report from the School Effectiveness Research Unit at a nearby university has recorded objective quantifiable evidence that standards of English are higher at Midleigh than at otherwise similar schools. The research also shows, by the way, that there has been less staff illness and turnover at Midleigh than at other similar schools these last three years, less disruptive behaviour by pupils, and more and livelier parental involvement.

Part Two: questions arising

1   Q   Is there a sound theoretical base for this programme?
      A   Yes.
2   Q   Is the programme expensive?
      A   No.
3   Q   What is the role of the LEA?
      A   Considerable.
4   Q   How many schools in Britain are involved in this programme?
      A   Hundreds.
5   Q   Is the programme fact or fiction?
      A   Fiction.
6   Q   But could the programme be real?
      A   Yes, of course.

15

What We May Be

curriculum for national identity

As we see and approach the horizon which leans forward
in Britain, and as we place new steps of change, we need
— amongst many other roles and identities — the
Teacher, he or she whose life-work is to shape, to impart
and to re-create a curriculum in the nation's schools,
colleges and universities. The curriculum in its turn helps
to build a sense of shared future and agenda, and shared
courage and determination, in the nation as a whole.

*Reflections on the nature of national, cultural, ethnic and
personal identity, and an account of a specific project
concerned with citizenship education in schools.*

15. What We May Be
curriculum for national identity

TEACH THEM TO BE BRITISH ran the huge headline in the *Daily Mail* in summer 1995.[1] 'Children,' said the article beneath the headline, 'should be taught to be British — whatever their cultural or ethnic background.' The paper was reporting on a speech to headteachers given by the chief executive of the School Curriculum and Assessment Authority (SCAA).[2] Headlines about the same speech in other papers included 'Teach All Pupils to be British' *(Daily Telegraph)*, 'Putting Britain Back in the Classrooms' *(Northern Echo)* and 'It's Time to Teach Our Young How to be British' *(Birmingham Post)*. There was little discussion in the reportage of the difference between 'Britishness' and 'Englishness', no reference to multiple identities and multiple ways of being British, and little or no focusing on shared futures. Many journalists and commentators seemed to assume that a sense of national identity is the same as mindless and narrow patriotism, and that it is threatened by what they chose to call multiculturalism. The speech, said the *Daily Mail,* set SCAA 'on a collision course with the race relations industry and left-wingers, by insisting the multicultural approach to education should be swept away and replaced by a national sense of identity and purpose.'

The simplistic reporting was to a certain extent, alas, licensed by a careless and simplistic use of polemic and rhetoric in the SCAA speech itself. For example, the speech seemed seriously to suggest that the only alternative to its own sketchy proposals is 'some kind of watered down multiculturalism' and that there are many teachers who believe that 'there is no more need to teach Latin than Sanskrit, classical civilisation than the history of the American West, Milton than Mills and Boon, Christianity than New Age cults'. For there are too many teachers and teacher educators, the speech alleged, who have been influenced by relativism and post-modernism. Traditional moral values, it claimed, 'have been pushed aside by an individualistic, relativistic and hedonistic view of morality previously associated with the underclass but which in the twentieth century has been taken up and promoted by the intelligentsia in its attack on bourgeois values'.

This simplified portrayal of teachers and of contemporary thought (and also, indeed, of the so-called underclass) occurred in a speech in which there was no reference to concepts of political literacy and competence, and no discussion of concepts of social justice, participation and democracy. To discuss notions of national identity independently of political competence, and independently of the structures of inclusion and exclusion in which such competence may or may not be exercised, is to risk collusion with the crassest kinds of authoritarian rule and thinking. In due course, it must be hoped, SCAA will provide on this subject the kind of moral and intellectual leadership which teachers and headteachers need and deserve. In the meanwhile, this chapter mentions some of the principal issues which such leadership will have to address, and describes one particular project in which they were explored. To get a preliminary purchase on the main issues, we may appropriately look in the first instance across the Atlantic.

For 20 January 1993, the day that the United States formally acquired a new president, Maya Angelou was commissioned to present a poem about her dreams for a new social order.[3] She wrote and performed a celebration of American national identity, and of both collective and individual endeavour and hope. Her hymn vividly evoked the context in which concepts of ethnicity and national identity, and of education for national identity in a multi-ethnic society, have nowadays to be considered. There are many ways, she said, of being American: '... the Asian, the Hispanic, the Jew, the African, the Native American, the Sioux, the Catholic, the Muslim, the French, the Greek ...' She pictured the overall American polity as a community of communities. Each community has its own cultural markers and its own stories about the past. But each interacts with many others on a daily basis and therefore the first key element of being American lies in the fabric of customs and procedures, the *modus vivendi*, which the various communities have negotiated with each other and which they continue to re-negotiate day by day. A second element of Americanness lies in commonalities in different narratives about the past — some communities came to the United States 'arriving on a nightmare' but all came 'praying for a dream'. All tell stories about the past in order to face a shared present and a shared future. A third element lies in the shared situation of the present and therefore in the shared future. It is essentially the shared future which matters, the poem emphasised, not heritage and history, profoundly important though these undoubtedly are. To focus on the future rather than on history requires qualities of honesty, rigour and courage: 'History ... cannot be unlived, but if faced with courage, need not be lived again.'

The boundaries between communities within the overall community of communities are frequently fuzzy as distinct from hard and fast: there may be a no-person's-land, in-between space or grey area between them, for it is possible for one person to belong to two or more ethnic communities at one and the same time, and it is possible for a person to pass from one ethnic identity to another.[4] In any case the boundaries between ethnic identities are not the only significant boundaries within the overall community of communities. Also there are boundaries which criss-cross the ethnic categories, for example those which are to do with religion, occupation, gender, age, sexuality, ideology, single-issue campaigning, region and class.

In a listing of many kinds of personal identity within the overall category of American identity, Maya Angelou referred to a single secular occupation, that of the teacher. She needed a rhyme for preacher, admittedly, and for this reason if for no other could not have as readily chosen civil servants, computer programmers or film directors as significant architects of the new world of which she dreamed. ('The horizon leans forward,' she said, 'offering you space to place new steps of change.') It nevertheless seems significant as well as heartening that she chose to salute teachers, and the dignity of the work of teachers in nourishing courage for the future:

> The Irish, the Rabbi, the Priest, the Sheik,
> The Gay, the Straight, the Preacher,
> The privileged, the homeless, the Teacher ...

As we see and approach the horizon which leans forward on this side of the Atlantic, and as we place new steps of change, we too need — amongst many other roles and identities — the Teacher, he or she whose life-work is to shape, to impart and to re-create a curriculum in the nation's schools, colleges and universities. The curriculum in its turn helps to build a sense of shared future and agenda, and shared courage and determination, in the nation as a whole. In this way it promotes — to cite the aims of education in modern Britain set out in the Education Reform Act 1988 — the spiritual, moral, cultural, mental and physical development of each child and young person and of society as a whole. The Act's statement of the two interacting and complementary aims of education, the development of individuals and the development of society, is clear, ambitious and unexceptionable without being also merely bland. The teacher's role, in partnership and dialogue with all others, is to work out the two aims in the turbulence of daily practice. SCAA's role, it is reasonable to expect, is to support and lead teachers as they undertake it.

SCAA was created through a merger of the National Curriculum Council (NCC) and the Schools Examinations and Assessment Council (SEAC). When these bodies were set up by the Education Reform Act in 1988, the then Secretary of State, Kenneth Baker, wrote to both organisations instructing them to 'take account of the ethnic and cultural diversity of British society, and the importance of the curriculum in promoting equal opportunity for all pupils, regardless of ethnic origin or gender'. Three years later, when Her Majesty's Government was required by the United Nations Committee on the Elimination of all Forms of Racial Discrimination (CERD) to itemise what it had done recently to combat and reduce racism within its boundaries and jurisdiction, it included a proud reference to the writing of this letter.[5] The pride was not unreasonable. The report expressing it, however, was economical with the truth, for neither the NCC nor SEAC ever issued any detailed clarification on this topic.

The NCC did do what most people in education do when they don't know what to do: it set up a working party.[6] The intention was to issue guidance and clarification across the full range of national curriculum subjects. Budget provision of £49,000 was made for the guidance to be published and circulated widely. The terms of reference of the working party are worth quoting in full, for they show clearly and significantly that the NCC defined the essential task as being to do with national identity and common citizenship:

> To consider (a) ways in which the National Curriculum can broaden
> the horizons of all pupils so that they can understand and respect, learn
> from and contribute to the multicultural society around them and
> realise that they do share a national identity and common citizenship
> and (b) the particular curriculum needs of pupils from ethnic minority
> backgrounds. Here issues relating to bilingual pupils will be an urgent
> priority.[7]

The working party met on several occasions in 1989 and 1990 and in due course produced written guidelines. These were introduced with an unambiguous indication that the members of the working party, supported by officers of the National Curriculum Council itself and by a member of Her Majesty's Inspectorate, understood that their remit had been to prepare a document which would be issued widely to schools throughout the country: 'NCC offers this document,' they said, 'as preliminary guidance on using the framework of the National Curriculum to promote multicultural education. This is a discussion document intended for use in schools ... Schools need to be clear about the reasons for multicultural education ...'

The document was shredded in the offices of the NCC, however, before it could see the light of day — apparently because it was felt to be too controversial: it stirred up too many cans of worms and nests of hornets, in relation not only to the national curriculum itself but also to the nature of this 'nation' whose curriculum is said to be national. The official reason for suppressing the document was of course rather different. 'It is not our intention,' ran the official line, ' to publish guidelines on multicultural education because that runs the risk of this vital work being seen as a separate and perhaps side issue.'[8]

There is sound reasoning in this official statement if the proposition is that multicultural education is not a separate subject similar to, but additional to, the ten subjects of the National Curriculum. But there was nothing in the draft document, its authors maintain, which could conceivably have fostered this misunderstanding. News that the document had been shredded slowly spread in autumn 1990 and spring 1991. In April 1991 there happened to be a conference at the University of Warwick entitled 'Race, Gender and the Education Reform Act'. One of the speakers was an officer from the National Curriculum Council who was forced to admit in public what had happened. More than a hundred people were present and there was a critical mass of indignation, indeed of anger. 'Let's break into the NCC offices,' urged some of the more revolutionary spirits present, 'and find and steal the one remaining file copy, and let's publish it.' There were others at the conference, however, who had heard that the authors of the document had censored themselves in the writing of it and had been less explicit and forthright than they had in fact wished. Rather than print the old document, it was suggested, the task was to develop a completely new document. An independent organisation was accordingly approached, and was requested formally to set up a new working party and to start entirely afresh.[9]

At its first meeting, the new working party made two unanimous decisions. One was that the eventual book would be entitled 'Equality Assurance', and so it was. The phrase was a pun on the phrase 'Quality Assurance', and expressed in a neat subliminal nutshell the working party's concern with high standards (quality) and with rigour and seriousness (assurance). Further, it emphasised that the essential concept, to focus and articulate the group's understandings, was equality, not culture or multi-culturalism. Of course, conceptual problems begin, not finish, when a choice is made for equality as a fundamental value as distinct from culture. But these were the problems, the group was asserting, which it wished to work on and consideration of which it wished to promote and support in schools.

The second unanimous decision was that the eventual publication should not start with quotations from the Education Reform Act, nor from official documentation issued in the Act's wake. Instead, the eventual document would start with, as the minutes of the first meeting put it in a headline, 'the voices of the young', real quotations from real children and young people about how they saw themselves and their futures. Later, this second decision was reversed. The group came to believe that it was crucial, if the book were to have substantial authority and wide influence, that it should be situated fair and square within the law of the land, and within the new legislative framework for education. The first section of the book accordingly consisted of a series of brief quotations from the Government's own publications. The last of these was from the new *Framework for the Inspection of Schools*. In its version published in summer 1992 this explicitly required that schools should be evaluated with regard to the Race Relations Act 1976 and the Sex Discrimination Act 1975.[10]

The book then presented a framework involving three main themes, summarised with the three words Quality, Identity and Society: it was concerned with high academic standards in each subject of the curriculum (quality); with helping children and young people develop their own personal, cultural and ethnic identity, and sense of nationhood (identity); and with developing the skills and knowledge required of responsible citizens, locally, regionally, nationally, internationally (society). The book applied its three key themes to school management and organisation as well as to each, in turn, of the ten subjects in the national curriculum, and to religious education. It gave examples of classroom activities for all age-levels amongst pupils and students, in both primary schools and secondary. A selection of these, focusing in particular on primary education, is shown in Table A. The three themes were presented visually in a Venn diagram of three overlapping circles, to emphasise that they are intricately connected to each other, and that it is frequently counter-productive and self-defeating to attempt to address any one of them independently of the other two. The diagram is reprinted here as Figure 1.

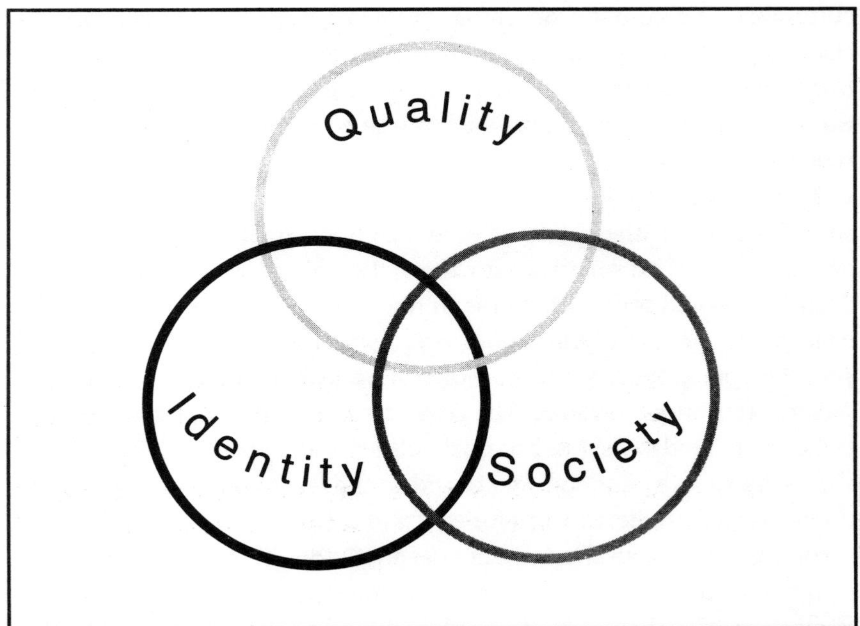

Figure 1: the three overlapping themes of *Equality Assurance in Schools*

Table A: examples of classroom activities

Make a sequence of images to illustrate an incident described in a local newspaper which raises issues to do with fairness, co-operation and cultural identity.

Involve visitors with a wide range of experiences and memories to talk about their childhoods and lives. Include reference to houses, shops and buildings close to the school and to where the children live.

Make a collaborative portrait of members of the class, showing cultural and ethnic identities, and the variety of skin tones, hair-styles, clothing and eye colours.

Enact stories at school assembly which involve repeated patterns of speech and behaviour, and which express symbolically the children's own feelings about identity, growing up, tensions and quarrels, friendships and cooperation.

Use communication games and exercises which require children to listen and speak carefully to each other in pairs and small groups, and which involve handling visual and pictorial material reflecting cultural and ethnic diversity.

Study pictures and artefacts from a particular village or town in another part of the world, and construct time-lines, maps, stories and graphs to show how people there live. Imagine what daily life is like for children in the chosen place. Write real or imaginary letters to the children who live there.

Provide pictorial displays which show scientific activity (hypothe-sising, designing fair tests, predicting, theorising about causal links, etc) at all times in human history, and in a wide range of countries and cultures.

In studies of Athens and Sparta role-play relationships between citizens and slaves, and draw up a charter or constitution for a democratic classroom in Britain in the 1990s.

Use drama to enact and study ways in which language is used in everyday conversations and interactions to reflect status, sen-iority, respect and deference, and what it means to use language assertively as distinct from aggressively or submissively.

At the Conservative Party Conference in autumn 1992 the Prime Minister said that student teachers should not waste their time on 'the politics of gender, race and class' but instead should be learning how to teach reading and writing. His speechwriter secured a ready round of applause, but was guilty of two different kinds of false dichotomy. First, it was like saying 'you needn't comb your hair, just brush your teeth instead': there is absolutely no reason why teachers cannot be *both* antiracist *and* concerned with literacy. Second, it was like claiming that 'you needn't bother to breathe in, just breathe out': actually you cannot teach children to read and write *unless* you are antiracist, and you cannot be truly antiracist *unless* you care passionately about literacy. This is all by way of saying and repeating that the first concern in *Equality Assurance* was with high standards — 'quality' — as defined and determined by the national curriculum itself.

Then second, the concern was with the concept of identity, or identities. The book noted that all people have a range of loyalties and obligations, and therefore draw their sense of personal identity from a range of different sources. It cited at one stage the Russian-dolls or concentric-circles notion of belonging, which involves picturing smaller and more local loyalties nesting inside those which are larger and wider — family, street, neighbourhood, community, region, country, continent, the world. It recalls in this connection, however, that conflicting loyalties and obligations exist *within* each circle, doll or layer, even — or especially — in the bosom of one's own household.

'My name is Karim Amir,' writes the young narrator of Hanif Kureishi's *A Buddha of Suburbia,* introducing himself in the novel's first sentence, 'and I am an Englishman born and bred, almost.' He introduces also the notion that multiple identities and loyalties have addresses very close to home. His mother is English and his father is from South Asia. It so happens that there are many people in modern Britain who, like Karim Amir, are 'English born and bred, almost' — people who are 'a funny kind of English person, a new breed as it were, having emerged from two old histories', with an 'odd mixture of continents and blood, of here and there, of belonging and not'.[11] Such people affect their friends, contacts, neighbours and relations. Also, however, they are mirrors to their friends, contacts, neighbours and relations, for all of us experience analogous tensions and hybridities in our upbringing and in our sense of self. All of us, as we go about our daily lives and as we face the future, are a mixture of here and there, of belonging and not: we are all hybrids. We have to make choices amongst and within the heritages to which we have been born, and in which we take part. Such choices are made within certain parameters and constraints, of course. They are nevertheless real, and therefore have to be periodically renewed and confirmed, or periodically critiqued, changed or discarded. The issue is not only what to choose but how to choose it, and having chosen how to live with it, and keep it in good repair. How to picture and value 'the Self'? How to represent and anticipate 'the Other'? These are the key questions.

Equality Assurance in Schools put forward the proposition that children and young people need assistance, guidance and support, in relation to the images of Self and Other which they make, of three main kinds. A person's identity needs to be:

(a) confident, strong and self-affirming, as distinct from uncertain, ashamed or insecure;

(b) open to change, choice and development, as distinct from being unreflective, doctrinaire and rigid;

(c) receptive and generous towards other identities, and prepared to learn from them, as distinct from feeling threatened and hostile, and wishing to exclude or to be separate.

The implications of this summary for practical curriculum planning are unpacked in the list of knowledge, skills and attitudes shown in Table B. The list includes reference, of course, to narratives about the past — 'history'. For the concept of identity is barely separable from the concept of narrative. What stories about the past, then, should be selected? What principles should guide their selection? These fundamental questions were raised and discussed at length by Marina Warner in her 1994 Reith Lectures.

Modern Britain was made, said Marina Warner, by 'invader and invaded, coloniser and colonised, migrants and residents'.[12] National identity was forged, and continues to be forged, by and through these three sets of essential tensions — as also, of course, by other tensions such as those of class, gender, age and region. Shared courage to face and build a shared future involves working with and from such tensions, not from denying them. Warner's sixth and final lecture, entitled 'Home: Our Famous Island Race', drew towards its end with some lines by Derek Walcott, who was born in St Lucia and whose forebears included both black slaves and white colonists, both invaded and invader, both resident and migrant.[13] In his poetry and plays, Marina Warner said, Walcott has 'worked back and forth over the relations of home and history ... His work puts the dominant and anguished questions of this end of the millennium: what does it mean to belong and not to belong? What way can history be told and experience be lived to bring about a sense of belonging? How does one come home?'[14]

In the asking and probing of such questions, imaginative literature has a vital role to play: for 'stories held in common make and remake the world we inhabit'. And the lecture continued: 'Walcott reproduces the dense mesh of modern identity, with its multiple compass points, its layered experiences; he stands witness to a rich — and painful — story made in common by both invader and invaded, coloniser and colonised, migrants and residents ...' How, in this shared heritage of suffering and achievement, are we to view the past in which our forebears took their respective parts, and how are we to view, and relate to, and learn from, each other in the present and future? 'There's no safe place,' observes Warner, 'from the injuries of history; home as a place or a time of innocence can only be an illusion. But ... [Walcott] doesn't recover the bitter past to serve present grudges — his acts of remembering, his quest for identity, are grounded in generosity.' In its broadcast version, this was the last lecture's last word, 'generosity'. It was also a fundamental keyword, as mentioned above, in *Equality Assurance in Schools* .

The lesson taught by Walcott, Marina Warner concluded in the printed version of her text, as also by other great writers of modern times, is that 'no home is an island; no home-grown culture can thrive in permanent quarantine. We're all wayfarers and we make our destinations as we go.' In her final paragraph she cited a remark made by a character in Walcott's version of *The Odyssey,* 'We earn home, like everything else'. The lecture and the whole series of lectures ended thus:

> Walcott doesn't mean paying the rent or the mortgage. He means taking part in the journey, using memory, imagination, language to question, to remember and to repair, to wish things well without sentimentality, without rancour, always resisting the sweet seduction of despair.[15]

In Marina Warner's terms, a curriculum for national identity is a curriculum for 'taking part in the journey'. The journey moves from a past which needs repairing as well as merely remembering, and which requires exercise of the imagination as well as the memory. It stretches into a future

Table B: curriculum planning and cultural identity

Knowledge and Understanding

- Knowledge of the history and development of one's own cultural traditions, and of the ways in which these both foster and constrain one's own personal identity.

- Knowledge of the history of different cultural traditions within Britain, Europe and the wider world.

- Knowledge of the physical, social and psychological needs which human beings have in common, including nutrition and shelter, and values relating to freedom, self-respect, belonging, and a sense of meaning and purpose.

- Knowledge of the various ways in which different cultures, communities and societies respond to these fundamental needs and moral concerns.

Skills

- Ability to contribute to one's own cultural traditions, including the traditions of mainstream public, cultural and political life.

- Ability to learn from different cultural experiences, norms and perspectives, and to empathise with people with different traditions.

- Ability to analyse and criticise features of cultural traditions, and to identify instances of prejudice, intolerance and discrimination.

- Ability to engage in discussion, argument and negotiation with people with traditions other than one's own.

Attitudes

- Willingness to sustain the positive aspects of one's own traditions, and therefore willingness to be constructively critical when appropriate.

- Willingness to learn from different traditions, cultures and identities.

- Willingness to challenge instances of prejudice, intolerance and discrimination.

- Willingness to accept reasonable and equitable procedures for resolving conflicts.

in preparation for which the curriculum in schools needs to be without either sentimentality or bitterness, and to be building hope not despair, sweetly seductive though the latter may frequently be.

Towards the end of *A Buddha of Suburbia* the narrator describes his friend Jamila: '... I thought what a terrific person she'd become ... I couldn't help seeing that there was in her a great depth of will, of delight in the world, and much energy for love. Her feminism, the sense of self and fight it engendered, the schemes and plans she had, the relationships -— which she desired to take this form and not that form — the things she had made herself know, and all the understandings this gave, seemed to illuminate her tonight as she went forward, an Indian woman, to live a useful life in white England.'[16] Kureishi in effect emphasises here, as did Maya Angelou in her poem for President Clinton's inauguration, that there is much more to personal and cultural identity than ethnicity. Jamila is 'an Indian woman' wanting to live 'a useful life in white England' but she is many other things too, and for herself and for her friends these are equally, or more, important. She is 'going forward', stresses Kureishi, is shaped by her future as well as, and rather than, by her heritage and past. Similarly Karim defines himself in relation to the future rather than to the past: he is, he says, 'from the South London suburbs and going somewhere'. To focus on the future is to focus also on society, and on notions not only of identity but also of citizenship, rights, social inclusion, political skill, participation. This was the third main theme, summarised with the single word 'society', in *Equality Assurance in Schools*.

The theme of society was explained with two quotations. One of these was from the Council of Europe, and was about human rights education. The other was also about rights, but was written not by an august body such as the Council of Europe but by a group of seven-year-old children. At a primary school in Manchester all the children had been involved in creating a charter of rights for themselves. Engaging in the kinds of debate which this had required, they had wrestled with major political and philosophical questions. The project had been invaluable for their learning of, in particular, history. Also it had had a major impact on reducing incidents of bullying in the playground, and anti-social behaviour in classrooms. One class of eight-year-old children wrote:

Every child has the right:

not to have to fight
to expect people to be kind
not to be made fun of
not to be made sad
not to be scared of the teachers
to have friends
not to be scared to come to school
to be safe.[17]

It was no doubt the collaborative process of hammering out this statement, rather than — or as much as — the statement itself, which was valuable. Similarly the process of hammering out the words and concepts of *Equality Assurance in Schools* was in itself valuable, involving as it did, through a lengthy consultative process, thousands of teachers throughout the country. In an analogous way, identity itself is a process or, as Marina Warner said, a journey, both for individuals and for societies and communities.

The dreams, visions and ideals sketched by writers such as Maya Angelou and Marina Warner are important as sources of inspiration, perseverance and commitment. They help us avoid sentimentality, rancour and despair. But more prosaic, pragmatic and measurable accounts of the good society, specifically of the multi-ethnic good society, need to be sketched out as well. The features need if possible to be described with sufficient precision for them to be studied and measured, such that in consequence any one country or part of a country can be compared with another, or compared with itself at different times over the years. In broad terms, a multi-ethnic good society is one in which members of different cultural, religious, linguistic and ethnic communities take an active part.[18] Not only members of the majority ethnic community (in modern Europe these are of course people whose ethnic identity is 'white') but also members of many other ethnic communities are involved in shaping, planning and organising public life. The measurable features of such a society may be grouped under five main headings, as shown in Table C.

Each of the five areas of social life listed in Table C, to repeat, could be defined in sufficient detail for measurements and objective comparisons to be made, both between and within different places. A conceptualisation emphasising measurable goals to aim for ('the good society') is surely preferable to one which refers only to evils to combat ('racism and xenophobia', for example, as in much European Union official discourse). Be that as it may, this brief sketch of the good society is a useful preliminary to consideration of the concept of education for national identity. The first recurring emphasis is on participation in national society — it would be merely frivolous and totalitarian to bother about national identity without bothering first, or any way absolutely simultaneously, about participation in social, political and economic affairs. Second, the sketch recalls that children and young people need to understand and affirm the cultural identities to which they have been born, including of course those which are widely shared and those which sustain the overall community of communities in good repair. Such understanding and affirmation must be critical as well as appreciative, in order that the young may choose, may commit themselves personally to, their heritage — or rather, their heritages, the hybrid mix of traditions and loyalties to which each has been born. Third, the sketch stresses citizenship skills and political literacy — citizenship not only as sentiment and status but also as competence.

With *Equality Assurance in Schools* as the basic background text, a study was made in 1994 of 50 of the first 56 reports to be published by the Office for Standards in Education (Ofsted).[19] The study looked in particular at how the reports handled the theory and practice of Equality of Opportunity and in this connection focused on five main sets of questions, as follows. First, to what extent are equal opportunities issues mentioned in the main findings of the reports and in the key issues which they outline as priorities for action by school governors and senior management? Second, what do the reports say about equal opportunities in their treatment of pupils' spiritual, moral, social and cultural development? Third, how do the reports refer to ethnic, cultural and religious diversity — for example, in how they describe pupils' backgrounds and the local communities which schools serve, and in their descriptions of the teaching of language and literature, and of religious education? Fourth, do the reports see behaviour and discipline as equal opportunities issues, and to what extent do they refer to the concerns of African-Caribbean parents about the disproportionate numbers of African-Caribbean boys excluded from schools? Fifth, when they refer to equality of opportunity, what kinds of specific issue do the reports mention? For example, what do they say about the content and quality of documents and policy papers? How if at

Table C: five features of a multi-ethnic good society

Politics and government

People with a range of ethnic identities ('minority' as well as 'majority') can and do take a full part in party politics at local, national and European Parliament levels, as party activists, candidates and elected members, and in the planning and running of public services and bodies, at all levels of seniority and responsibility.

Employment and occupations

People with a range of ethnic identities can and do participate fully in the economy, across a wide range of manufacturing and service industries, and at all levels of the occupational class system, including the professions and management. Members of ethnic minorities are not concentrated in particular sectors of the economy or at the lowest levels of responsibility and remuneration and are not affected disproportionately by unemployment.

Crime, law and justice

Levels of inter-ethnic tension and violence are low. People with a range of ethnic identities can and do play a full part in running the justice system, in all its branches. No ethnic minority is disproportionately the victim of threats and violence or disproportionately involved in crime and deviance.

Material conditions of life

People with a range of ethnic identities live in close proximity to each other and share the same public spaces such as shops, markets, schools and recreational areas. No community is disproportionately affected by poor material conditions of life, for example overcrowded and undesirable housing, inadequate access to transport and services, or a deprived physical environment.

Education, arts and culture

People with a range of ethnic identities can and do participate in the creation of public mainstream culture, including the curriculum of schools and universities; the production of literature and of the performing and visual arts; journalism and the media; and recreation, sports and entertainment.

all do they discuss social circumstance — for example, poverty and deprivation — as an equal opportunities issue?

If Ofsted inspections do pay serious attention to equal opportunities issues such as these, they could have a considerable effect on schools. They will raise awareness amongst governors, senior management teams and teachers, by literally putting equality issues on the agenda. More importantly still, they will help to stimulate and support valuable change. If, however, Ofsted inspections do not give much attention to these issues, they will give tacit approval to the view that equality is of little or no importance, and that the issues can be safely ignored. The study concluded regretfully, in relation to most of the reports, that headteachers and governing bodies could assume that equal opportunities are of very slight importance, at least so far as Ofsted is concerned. The 50 different Ofsted teams were either ignorant or over-cautious, or else in their haste and inexperience were merely negligent. But all the reports, as someone glancing at them observed, could be described as 'tales of the uninspected'.

Half the reports made no reference to issues of cultural diversity in their reviews of what schools do to promote pupils' cultural development. Less than ten per cent of the reports indicated that moral and social development might or should include learning about justice, fairness and equality. No report indicated or implied that moral and social issues should be seen in international and global contexts. In descriptions of pupil intakes and local communities, only one report (two per cent) referred to African-Caribbean pupils and parents. Only two reports (four per cent) made distinctions within the term 'ethnic minority'. Apart from a reference to a language said by the inspectors to be 'Pakistani', no report mentioned a single South Asian home or community language. No report mentioned pupils' religious affiliations and involvements. Ten of the reports were about schools with sizeable proportions of black and ethnic minority pupils. In their sections on the teaching of English, the teaching of religious education and links and contacts with parents, there were very few references to cultural, linguistic and religious diversity amongst the pupils and their families. No report treated behaviour and discipline as equal opportunities issues. In a few schools it was clear that ethnic minority pupils had been disproportionately excluded, but no report commented on or discussed this matter. The study showed that clearly there was — and no doubt is — still much progress to be made.

To seek to make progress is to be involved in many kinds of turbulence, in personal and local as well as national life, and in the lives of all organisations and institutions, including schools. To guide the progress Britain will need, it has been said, 'politicians who are willing to enter this turbulence and find ways of telling national stories that are inclusive and open-ended'.[20] Also, it will need the Teacher, similarly questing to tell and share inclusive and open-ended stories. Teachers for their part will need and use — amongst many other things — the computer screen and the computer mouse, as will the nation's children and young people:

> The importance of the new screens is not merely that they have the potential to disseminate and democratise knowledge about the nation. They remind us all of the provisionality of what appears on them, and of our power to act on them in ways that may aid us. This electronic world may provide us with an opportunity to imagine British national identity not as something immovable as a monument nor something that needs to be tended as a lawn but as something provisional and capable of transformation as a wave; a wave which we all might ride.[21]

As teachers contemplate and engage in the ride they will require not only computers and not only handbooks such as *Equality Assurance in Schools*. They will require also, and indeed much more importantly, qualities of determination, persistence and hope. It is fitting and inspiring to recall in this connection how Maya Angelou ended her poem for the inauguration of the new American president in early 1993. 'Here on the pulse of this new day,' she wrote, 'you may have the grace to look up and out and into your sister's eyes, and into your brother's face, your country, and say simply very simply with hope — good morning.'

The words may be read and heard as addressed to collaborative processes of all kinds. For example, they are relevant for a group of young children negotiating a charter of rights about behaviour in their own playground; for a working party of teachers and educators fashioning curriculum guidelines on equality, identity and social inclusion; and for a whole population working to build and sustain shared courage and determination, for a shared future.

16

Permits and Power

checklist for the journey

They told the other rabbits, and legal experts searched through all of Badgerland's constitutional law, and drew up all the right legal paperwork. Three of them decided to leave. 'And where do you think you're going?' asked the badger official on duty at the border control. 'Liberation,' replied the three rabbits, and they showed all the correct legal paperwork. 'And where is this place called Liberation, and what's it like?' asked the official. The rabbits couldn't answer and were sent back home.

Fable about ingredients and factors making for success. Relevant to, amongst others, chapter 12 ('They Struggled Here') and chapter 15 ('What We May Be').

16. Permits and Power
checklist for the journey

The rabbits in Badgerland were very unhappy, and one of them decided to leave. 'And where do you think you're going?' asked the badger official on duty at the border control. 'Liberation,' replied the rabbit. 'And what's wrong with Badgerland?' asked the official. The rabbit couldn't answer, and was sent back home.

She told the other rabbits, and they held a research seminar, and analysed with precision everything wrong with Badgerland. Two of them decided to leave. 'And where do you think you're going?' asked the badger official on duty at the border control. 'Liberation,' replied the two rabbits, and they explained what was wrong with Badgerland. 'And where is your licence and written permission?' asked the official. The rabbits couldn't answer, and were sent back home.

They told the other rabbits, and legal experts searched through all of Badgerland's constitutional law, and drew up all the right legal paperwork. Three of them decided to leave. 'And where do you think you're going?' asked the badger official on duty at the border control. 'Liberation,' replied the three rabbits, and they showed all the correct legal paperwork. 'And where is this place called Liberation, and what's it like?' asked the official. The rabbits couldn't answer, and were sent back home.

They told the other rabbits, and a vast arts festival was organised, full of pictures and stories about a better world. Four rabbits decided to leave. 'And where do you think you're going?' asked the badger official on duty at the border control. 'Liberation,' replied the four rabbits, and they showed all the pictures and stories about a better world. 'And how are you going to get there?' asked the official. The rabbits couldn't answer, and were sent back home.

They told the other rabbits, and a committee structure was set up with interdisciplinary working parties, and each committee formulated a development plan. Five rabbits decided to leave. 'And where do you think you're going?' asked the badger official on duty at the border control. 'Liberation,' replied the five rabbits, and they showed all their maps and development plans. 'And where is your strength?' asked the official. The rabbits couldn't answer, and were sent back home.

They told the other rabbits, and a mass rally was held. The rabbits decided that their strength lay in their numbers and in their determination, and they all of them decided to leave. 'And where do you think you're going?' asked the badger official on duty at the border control. They none of them answered. They just kept on walking, to Liberation.

Beginnings

17

A Week in a Life

*influencing friends and
making people*

Thursday
Reorganised higher and further education in morning, and
Labour Party and all other left of centre parties in
afternoon. In evening wrote a haiku.

From an idea by Roger McGough, the diary of a friend.

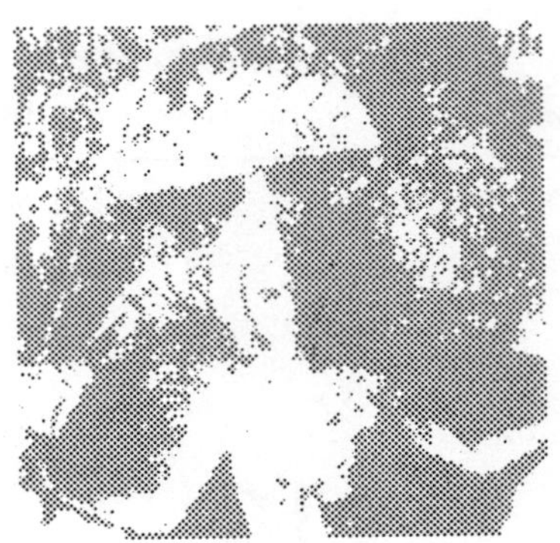

17. A Week in a Life
influencing friends and making people

Sunday

Breakfast with the editor of *The Times,* wrote two plays and an opera, lunch with editor of the *Independent,* wrote trilogy of novels, in evening organised race riot in Bournemouth.

Monday

Wrote documentary TV series on nature of justice, lunch with editor of the *Mail on Sunday,* reorganised Conservative Party in afternoon, in evening arranged mass rally in Trafalgar Square on putting an end to unemployment, half a million people present.

Tuesday

Wrote four articles for *London Review of Books,* had breakfast with Prince Charles, organised national strike, had lunch at Garrick Club with the chief rabbi and the prime minister, in afternoon played scrabble with the editor of the *Sun* (and lost), in evening organised pop concert at Wembley Stadium.

Wednesday

Addressed United Nations Race Relations Conference in morning, won case of gender discrimination at European Court of Human Rights in afternoon, led meditation at World Islamic Congress in evening.

Thursday

Reorganised higher and further education in morning, and Labour Party and all other left of centre parties in afternoon. In evening wrote a haiku.

Friday

Gave birth to my mixed-heritage twins, a daughter and a son. Was offered Nobel prizes for peace, literature and economics. Accepted all three, gracefully.

Saturday

Rested, briefly.

18

The Two Towns

self, other and looking forward

'I'm happy to be able to tell you,' said the wise woman,
'that you'll find the place you're going to is very similar
indeed to the one you are coming from.' The teacher
travelled on, even more happy and hopeful than before.
The future would be one fruitful encounter and
exchange after another.

After Aesop, on looking backwards and forwards.

18. The Two Towns
self, other and looking forward

This is an ancient tale of two towns, Selfbury and Otherham. A lonely road connected the two. By the roadside sat a wise woman. Travellers on the road from Selfbury to Otherham would sometimes ask her for guidance and advice.

One day a teacher travelling on the road stopped to speak to her. 'I am travelling to Otherham to take up a new post in one of the LEA's schools,' said the teacher. 'What's it like there?'

'Well,' said the wise woman, 'what was it like in the school you're coming from?'

'Terrible,' said the teacher. 'My colleagues were for ever gossiping behind my back, I never got the slightest support from my headteacher, who basically was a cross between Saddam Hussain and Napoleon Bonaparte, and the children were a pack of dirty-minded and vicious barbarians, always trying to wear you down, and totally incapable of learning anything at all. The LEA inspectors, advisers and administrators were dalek-like robots in grey suits, totally impersonal and mechanistic. I shall be only too pleased to get away from everyone, I can tell you. But any way, what's it like in Otherham?'

'I regret to have to tell you,' said the wise woman, 'that you'll find the place you're going to is very similar indeed to the one you are coming from.'

The teacher travelled on, even more depressed and despairing than before. The future would be one power conflict and battle for control after another.

A few hours later another teacher travelling from Selfbury to Otherham stopped to speak to the wise woman. 'I am travelling to Otherham to take up a post in one of the LEA's schools,' said the teacher. 'What's it like there?'

'Well,' said the wise woman, 'what was it like in the school you're coming from?'

'Wonderful,' said the teacher. 'My colleagues couldn't have been more helpful, the headteacher gave me lots of space to learn and grow, the children were fabulous, full of hope and eagerness, thrilled by stories and history, always reaching out into the future. The LEA staff were constantly available, good listeners, keen to give you a helping hand. I'm really sorry to be going away from everyone, I can tell you. But any way, what's it like in Otherham?'

'I'm happy to be able to tell you,' said the wise woman, 'that you'll find the place you're going to is very similar indeed to the one you are coming from.'

The teacher travelled on, even more happy and hopeful than before. The future would be one fruitful encounter and exchange after another.

19

A Day to Remember

headlines for a young friend

All praise soars, now and for ever,
Over words like *any way, but, however:*
Hopefulness, peace, serenity, light
Grow amongst *all the same, yet, despite.*
Murk, murder, madness, mess:
We choose life, *nevertheless.*

*Speech at the occasion when Ester Gluck celebrated
becoming Bat Mitzvah at the West London Synagogue on
the Saturday following her thirteenth birthday in the
Hebrew calendar. The speech introduced and referred
throughout to a copy of the* Guardian *newspaper
published on the day when Ester was born, 26 April 1982.*

19. A Day to Remember
headlines for a young friend

Well, Ester, there's a newspaper here for you
Dated the 26th of April, 1982.

A day to remember, with heart and voice,
The day the Prime Minister said 'Rejoice!'
Though alas the celebratory cause she had in mind
Wasn't really all that good or kind:
SOUTH GEORGIA SEIZED we read. The paper then says
Quoting a foreign diplomat, Nicanor Costa Mendez,
Sounding subdued and sane, not fierce or frantic,
That Britain is at war in the South Atlantic.

A day for rejoicing, we do here all agree,
But not for the reason Mrs, now Baroness, T
Proclaimed (for since when was the short fuse
Of Her Majesty's Government Good News?)
But because the event which really blessed her,
And the whole world too, was you, Ester.
You were the event for which rejoicing was due
On the twenty sixth of the fourth, nineteen eighty two.

(We ought to register, by the way,
That also peace was front page news that day,
But unenthusiastically, almost mournful, moping:
ISRAEL RESIGNS ITSELF TO HOPING.)

Inside the paper I seek signs to see
If humankind saw cause for fes-tee-vee-tee
That day, yes, if the human species knew
What really mattered, on two six April, '82.
And well, er, no, everything's pretty dire
There's awfully little to enthuse or inspire.
E.g. BRITAIN SOON TO BE A THIRD WORLD NATION
Unless it puts an end to progressive education:
That is the view and the voice on
Page 3 of Mr, now Sir, Rhodes Boyson.
(On a later page, by the way, this day
There's a job advert from the ILEA —
Three posts vacant for a TV director
Presumably to make politically incorrecter
Programmes, progressive yes and proud,
Than nowadays, Ester, would be allowed.)

There's a chance to cheer our kin and kith
Through a TV review by Nancy Banks Smith,
Though it's not the Falklands showing right from wrong
But the Eurovision contest for a Euro-song.
The Royaume Uni did well, more or less — *plus ou moins*
But Finland, poor old Finland: *nul points*.
They used to be musically gifted, but now, we see,
Finns ain't what they used to be.

(You may think I'm now ending, so it says here,
And may throw me kisses, and clap and cheer,
Or you may fearfully suspect, apropos of this verse,
That it won't get better before it gets worse.
In which case, I daresay, you'll throw me a bomb,
Since there could be more, where that came from.)

I turn to moral issues, here's Jill Tweedie, er,
She writes about discussion programmes in the media:
Complains, um, about 'balanced' presentations of views,
Says, er, you can't have balance about all of the news.
She seems, um, er, to be making, in those distant days,
A prophetic critique of *The Moral Maze*.
As for the rest of the paper, mainly let's skip it,
I'll just give you the occasional snippet —
I'll have to be partial, I can't be thorough.
I note MARXIST MENACE IN A LONDON BOROUGH,
And there's PEACETIME TUMBLES, it's about a horse
And MESSIAH DEADLINE REVEALED, about an ass, of course.
We are told that SLOUGH FINDS CONSOLATION —
It's all about hockey, not the dark night of the nation.
And since basket ball is what it's about
ENGLAND BOUNCE BACK inspires no shout.

As for TV that evening, on the whole
There is nothing there to gladden the soul.
We need bounce and shout and serenity too
But BARRY MANILOW IN BRITAIN will scarcely do.
Nor will it help us to feel at all calmer
To watch the prime minister on *Panorama*.

But any way, any way, any way, any way,
We do rejoice as we remember that day.

(All praise soars, now and for ever,
Over words like *any way, but, however*:
Hopefulness, peace, serenity, light
Grow amongst *all the same, yet, despite*.
Murk, murder, madness, mess:
We choose life, *nevertheless*.)

We sing and we bless, we do, we do.
So let's hear it for the twenty sixth of April,
Nineteen eighty two.

For Ester with love, on another day you're specially alive,
6 May 1995.

20

Unfinished

toward a theory of justice

She strokes the child's face gently, and gazes into the depths of the child's eyes. 'Let us go,' she says, 'to the country where the power and the energy in this child will have the best chance of unfolding into a human being fully alive.' And she adds: 'The way to cherish and nourish that power and energy is through telling stories'.

A debating situation reminiscent of an image in John Rawls's 'A Theory of Justice'. But about personal and inner qualities of individuals as well as about the features of the just society.

20. Unfinished
toward a theory of justice

There is this family in the world somewhere today, thinking, talking, dreaming, hoping.

Through cruel ill fortune, the members of this family have suddenly found themselves to be refugees from their homeland. They have nowhere to dwell, nowhere stable to go out from, nowhere trusted to return to. They can only move onwards, outwards, can only be footloose, wandering migrants now for the rest of their lives. There is an old grandmother, close to the end of her days; various grown-up children and their partners; and about a dozen grandchildren, including a tiny infant, a few weeks old.

What is to become of them? Where will they find asylum? They debate and deliberate. In the very heart of their trauma they share their dreams and their hopes. In what kind of new country would they most like to settle?

'Basically,' says one of them, fingering a smooth stone, 'this conversation is pointless. Obviously we must look after ourselves as well as we can, and we must keep ourselves strong. But at the end of the day there's nothing we can do and all societies are as good or as bad as each other. This lifeless stone reminds us that our feelings and thoughts are irrelevant. All this talk is a waste of our precious time.'

'Well yes, I do agree in many ways,' says a second, holding up an old lottery ticket. 'But we need wealth and riches if at all possible and that means that we need good luck. Let's go to a country where we are likely to have good luck, and where we shall become rich and wealthy.'

'That's all very well', says a third, opening a small prayerbook, 'but happiness doesn't just depend on money and wealth. It depends on whether we are are left alone to be ourselves, and to stay exactly as we are. Let's go to a country where we're allowed to continue to speak our own dear language, tell our children our own special tales and truths, and be protected in all our ways by our own dear God. This little book written in our own language and praising our own God will always remind us: nothing is more important than continuity and stability, and the cherishing and preserving of our past.'

'Yes of course,' says a fourth, taking out a compass, 'that is quite right. But we've got be streetwise, too. This compass I'm holding is a reminder to us that we've got to be sharp and cunning, and trust our own sense of direction. Often we shall have nothing to depend on apart from our own courage and our own quick thinking. Let's go to a country where we can make really good use of our own wits and cunning.'

'That's right in lots of ways,' says a fifth, showing the others a wedding ring. 'It's important that we should be clever and cunning, yes of course, and not be afraid to take risks. But it's even more important to love each other. This ring is a symbol of never-ending love. We should let nothing ever get in the way of love. If necessary, it is more important to sacrifice one's own life than to stop loving. That's real bravery, and that's what is perhaps going to be required of us. Let's go to a country where people are allowed and encouraged to love.'

'Of course it is important,' says a sixth, touching a flower in bud, 'that we should love each other. But finally what we are going to need is hope — we need to believe that finally, and deep down, all will be for the best. Look at this bud. It will one day become a beautiful flower. Then one day the flower will change into seeds, and the seeds will fall into the earth, and a new plant will grow. So life will go on, and on and on. There is death, yes, all the time, and terrible misfortune. But also there is always new life. Let's go to a country where the people are not despairing, but are full of hope.'

The six of them turn to the old grandmother, each of them wanting and expecting her to support their own views. She happens at this moment to be holding the infant, the youngest and the newest of the whole extended family. She strokes the child's face gently, and gazes into the depths of the child's eyes. 'Let us go,' she says, 'to the country where the power and the energy in this child will have the best chance of unfolding into a human being fully alive.' And she adds: 'The way to cherish and nourish that power and energy is through telling stories'.

She pauses. 'And the stories need to be, you know, about the six small objects which you have all just been showing. 'Once upon a time there was a stone, a lottery ticket, a prayerbook, a compass, a wedding ring and a flower in bud.' That's how all stories ought to begin. Drenched in stories such as that, this child will become a human being fully alive.'

The child in her arms smiles. But is the smile grateful and approving, or is it ironic and resigned? No member of the family can at this stage tell. The future stretches out before them, unknown and featureless, like an untold story.

21

The Keys of the Country

we hold them in our hands

Dream in the war, war in the world, world in the child,
child in the teacher, teacher in the school, school in the
borough, borough in the city, city in the country.
These are the keys of the country.
We hold them in our hands.

*Presentation at a conference entitled 'Education for
Democracy, Equality, Justice and Peace', organised by
Haringey Council Education Services, Alexandra Palace,
May 1995.*

21. The Keys of the Country
we hold them in our hands

These are the keys of the country. We hold them in our hands.

In that country is a city. In the city known as Greater London there have been, since May 1994, 1,917 borough counsellors. If I said, in this place and on this occasion and at this moment, let's hear it for the 1,917 elected members of Greater London councils, for they are the pillars of democracy, equality, justice and peace in this city, there could be a silence. A silence which would be a tad embarrassing and, in the circumstances of the present moment, a bit mega-depressing. So I won't say it. But I do give due warning that if we are truly to celebrate success in the education system of this country there must be a place in our song and in our story for public forums, committee rooms and town halls, and for locally elected delegates, revocable and accountable.

In that country is a city. In that city is a borough. I do not have at my fingertips much information about the 1,917 borough counsellors of Greater London, their personal stories and trajectories, what sort of dreams they have, within and between them, real dreams, the kinds of dream that politics exists minimally to manage but maximally to incarnate. I don't even have to hand data on their political affiliation let alone on their gender, or generation, or social location vis-a-vis, as the phrase until recently was, the ownership and control of the means of production, distribution and exchange. But I do happen to know that in a recent survey relating to notions of ethnic identity it was found that 63 of them (3.3 per cent) described themselves as African or Caribbean and 139 as South Asian (7.2 per cent). One counsellor, by the way, rejected the term 'white' as a classification and declared himself to be 'Aryan'. That is 0.052 per cent. Anyone who came to this conference with the sole intention of collecting one piece of useless factual information may at this point, they may think, leave. But watch this space. In the meanwhile, in the borough is a school.

In that country is a city. In that city is a borough. In that borough is a school. Let us celebrate headteachers, no seriously. I had, if I may please make a brief confession at this point, a mis-spent youth. One consequence was that many of the people with whom I consorted in those days subsequently became headteachers, for they too had mis-spent youths. I recall an evening about 25 years ago when a group of us who had been young teachers together had a reunion. One member of the group was already a headteacher. At one point in the evening he said, reflectively, slowly, 'Strange, but since I became a headteacher I have started believing in God.' Everyone else collapsed in helpless hilarity. One person (who subsequently became a head himself, it so happens) literally rolled about. When the laughter and rolling eventually died down our friend said, in exactly the same tone as before, 'I don't see what's so funny.' This time, not everyone laughed quite so much or for so long. Compared with running a school, running the odd universe is a doddle. So let's celebrate head-teachers, seriously. In the borough is a school.

In that country is a city. In that city is a borough. In that borough is a school. In that school is a teacher. In the exhibitions here today there is a display created by a teacher about the work she has been doing with her pupils about Black History. There are quotations from course materials, theoretical observations about history in the national curriculum, and extracts from the young people's work. Also the display contains reflections about the nature and purpose of history written by the teacher, including the following: 'Methodology is as important as content. If a course on Black History does not promote access, does not enhance oracy, does not offer a variety of ways of learning, does not allow students to learn with and from each other, and does not lead to success, is it worth it?' We celebrate the country's teachers here today. In the school is a teacher.

In that country is a city. In that city is a borough. In that borough is a school. In that school is a teacher. In that teacher is a child. Of course, outside the teacher there are children too — pupils, students, learners — and, yes of course, they are to be taught. I am not, in celebrating the child in the teacher, celebrating the teacher as ego-tripping solipsist. Though that is a risk I run, with the form as well as the content of this presentation here this morning. ('These are the keys of the country. We hold them in our hands ...') I am recalling that the politics of building democracy, equality, justice and peace, and keeping them in good repair, requires teachers to be learners. This includes teachers keeping in touch with the experiences of oppression which they themselves had as children and young people — the times when they lived the absence or withdrawal of democracy, equality, justice and peace — and keeping in touch with play, with story, with dreams, inside themselves. In the teacher is a child.

In that country is a city. In that city is a borough. In that borough is a school. In that school is a teacher. In that teacher is a child. In that child is a world. In the great days of the Inner London Education Authority some teachers put together a book of poems for children entitled *Yesterday, Today, Tomorrow*. The title poem was by Rojada Ledge and it went as follows: 'Yesterday/ we thought/ the vote/ would change/ our lives/ Today/ we know/ there's more/ to power/ than/ voting/ Tomorrow ...' In the child is a world.

In that country is a city. In that city is a borough. In that borough is a school. In that school is a teacher. In that teacher is a child. In that child is a world. In that world is a war. Statistics of war — of the struggle to build and keep in good repair democracy, equality, justice and peace — include statistics about how human beings classify themselves and each other. Who are 'we'? Who are 'not-we'? The statistic that 0.052 per cent of Greater London elected members classify themselves as Aryan is, indeed, not terribly important. But it would be interesting to know the self-classifications of the editors, sub-editors, reporters and photographers of the British mass media, particularly those who wrote the reports in summer 1995 about the Victory in Europe celebrations. PROUD OF OUR HEROES PROUD OF OUR NATION ran the headline over a sea of union jacks all over the front page of the *Sun*. The report spoke of 'a shared pride in our country and in our honoured past ... For a few moments, when the Queen Mother, the Queen and Princess Margaret stepped out on the balcony at Buckingham Palace, we became a nation suspended in time. We forgot about vandalism, crime, inner-city problems and the state of society. We were united and proud to be British.' In other words, 'we' forgot reality and took pride in doing so. Who are 'we' in this country? Who are 'not-we'? In the world is a war.

In that country is a city. In that city is a borough. In that borough is a school. In that school is a teacher. In that teacher is a child. In that child is a world. In that world is a war. In that war is a dream. During the conflict whose cessation 50 years ago has been commemorated in this summer of 1995, an oratorio was written with a title taken from an antiracist, antifascist book written in German in the 1930s entitled *Ein Kind Unserer Zeit,* A Child of Our Time. The oratorio ended with a dream of freedom created by Black people in the United States during slavery times, about the deep river to be crossed before democracy, equality, justice and peace may be truly lived. It introduced the dream of freedom thus: 'I would know my shadow and my light, so shall I at last be whole. Then courage, sisters and brothers, dare the grave passage. Here is no final grieving but an abiding hope. The moving waters renew the earth. It is spring.' A child of our time: in that war is a dream.

Dream in the war, war in the world, world in the child, child in the teacher, teacher in the school, school in the borough, borough in the city, city in the country. These are the keys of the country. We hold them in our hands.

Endings

22

Reprise

taking stock, again

Her father loved me; oft invited me;
Still questioned me the story of my life,
From year to year — the battles, sieges, fortunes
That I have passed.
Othello, Act I, scene iii.

Mutato nomine de te
Fabula narratur.
*With a change of name it's about yourself
This tale is told.*
Horace, Satires.

*The title pages of the previous 21 chapters, and the
quotations on the frontispiece, as reminders and farewell.*

22. Reprise
taking stock, again

1.

On the night before the battle of Agincourt, according to Shakespeare, the King of England rallied his troops not by winding them up to hate the external enemy but by emphasising that the real battle was on their own shores. The battle was to forge a new national identity in a divided and diverse society. The king pictured for his people their own story over the years to come, its import and dignity.

2.

Let us praise teachers who fill their schools with unfinished stories; know a good story when they see one; tread deep into the underworld for the sake of love; bargain and negotiate; are both spiritual creatures and political animals; are unknowing; have bodies; give seed and birth to carnivals; take part in politics and attendant word-smithery; develop their governors; are multicultural persons; are midwives of new ethnicities; make images of exuberant and generous beauty; experience dismemberment yet rejoice; and sing.

3.

Processes of otherising, demonising and racialising are kept alive and well, in any one community or society, by a range of stories and narratives — including grand narratives about the history and destiny of the nation as well all sorts of fables, legends and imagery, and anecdotes, gossip and travellers' tales. They therefore have to be resisted by, amongst other things, alternative narratives, alternative imagery.

4.

To be very grand, indeed over the top, but seasonal: the stand-up comic deals in epiphanies. 'The most delicate and evanescent of moments,' said Joyce, 'when the soul or whatness of a thing leaps to us from the vestment of its appearance. The soul of the commonest object ... seems to us radiant. The object achieves its epiphany.'

5.

'In this speech now in December 1999, I propose to look back over our principal achievements of the decade which is drawing to a close and to highlight the main components of our success. I hope and intend in this way to clarify and to consolidate the policy priorities for our race and for our nation in the century, or rather — to speak more frankly and less modestly — in the millennium, which stretches before us.'

6.

'The Government is firmly wedded to quality excellence for absolutely every single child. The greater the excellence of the quality, the greater the quality of the excellence, and the more absolute the singleness. The more absolute the singleness, the more wedded the firmness. But let there be no confusion.'

7.

How are we to use our rage and anger — the rage and anger which we feel when we suffer defeat, failure or rejection, or when those whom we love and care for are crushed and broken? The task is to avoid demonising our opponents, and on the contrary — so to speak — to humanise ourselves. So the energy of rage has to be directed against defeat and defeatism, not against opponents. Also, the energy of rage has to be directing into making things, and into the building and maintaining of hope.

8.

What do we do, as teachers, for and with learners? What stories, pictures, music, games, tasks, activities, do we use? What groupings? What balances of exploration and information, finding and telling? And how do we make these choices in ways which really do lead to children learning, as distinct from merely adding to our own power and pride?

9.

'I absolutely hate my work,' explained the headteacher. 'I feel I'd like to dig up old Father Adam's grave and dance on the blighter's bones.' — 'Mm,' said the angel, 'that wouldn't really help, you know. But I can arrange, if you like, for you to go and live in a wonderful place which I know, and you'll have there a life of complete leisure. You'll never have to do a stroke of work if you decide to live there.' — 'It sounds wonderful,' replied the headteacher. 'When can I start?' — 'Straightaway,' said the angel.

10.

Stories make the inner world real, show us what transformations look and feel like. They are distinctively capable of exploring the difference between fact and fiction, faith and superstition, miracle and magic. To explore and discern this difference is a formidable but inescapable task in all phases and seasons of our lives. A recurring character in stories is the holy fool, the prince of jesters, the clown ...

11.

Care

From Old English *caru,* grief, lament, burdened state of mind. Later: serious attention, charge, oversight, concern. An inclination to look after, take care of, see to, mind, be prudent, be a steward. Something has been entrusted to you, and you look after it, and in due course you pass it on. Traditions, customs and structures. Ideals, dreams. People. Developing care: a key task throughout the middle years of life.

12.

It's a story, is this, of defeat and destruction. Such stories can be, of course, merely depressing, demoralising. But also they can recall the dignity and importance of struggling for certain values, certain ideals, and they can portray, commend and celebrate the values and ideals themselves. They recall thus the dignity of recollection, of storytelling: the dignity of bearing witness, of telling the tale.

13.

'We are very keen to have light thrown on this matter, if at all possible. We wonder, therefore, whether any of you here today have any comments or suggestions? Have you ever heard a story which was at all similar?'

14.

Punita was initially surprised and dismayed, but in the event pleased, when she had to write an extended essay entitled 'The Multi-Ethnic Good Society: why, what, where, how and when.' To prepare this she had to use concepts of racialisation and racist exclusion, ethnogenesis and hybrid identity, cultural politics and postmodernism, and urban policy and regeneration.

15.

As we see and approach the horizon which leans forward in Britain, and as we place new steps of change, we need — amongst many other roles and identities — the Teacher, he or she whose life-work is to shape, to impart and to re-create a curriculum in the nation's schools, colleges and universities. The curriculum in its turn helps to build a sense of shared future and agenda, and shared courage and determination, in the nation as a whole.

16.

They told the other rabbits, and legal experts searched through all of Badgerland's constitutional law, and drew up all the right legal paperwork. Three of them decided to leave. 'And where do you think you're going?' asked the badger official on duty at the border control. 'Liberation,' replied the three rabbits, and they showed all the correct legal paperwork. 'And where is this place called Liberation, and what's it like?' asked the official. The rabbits couldn't answer, and were sent back home.

17.

Thursday. Reorganised higher and further education in morning, and Labour Party and all other left of centre parties in afternoon. In evening wrote a haiku.

18.

'I'm happy to be able to tell you,' said the wise woman, 'that you'll find the place you're going to is very similar indeed to the one you are coming from.' The teacher travelled on, even more happy and hopeful than before. The future would be one fruitful encounter and exchange after another.

19.

> All praise soars, now and for ever,
> Over words like *any way, but, however:*
> Hopefulness, peace, serenity, light
> Grow amongst *all the same, yet, despite.*
> Murk, murder, madness, mess:
> We choose life, *nevertheless.*

20.

She strokes the child's face gently, and gazes into the depths of the child's eyes. 'Let us go,' she says, 'to the country where the power and the energy in this child will have the best chance of unfolding into a human being fully alive.' And she adds: 'The way to cherish and nourish that power and energy is through telling stories.'

21.

Dream in the war, war in the world, world in the child, child in the teacher, teacher in the school, school in the borough, borough in the city, city in the country. These are the keys of the country. We hold them in our hands.

22.

Her father loved me; oft invited me; /Still questioned me the story of my life, /From year to year — the battles, sieges, fortunes /That I have passed. (*Othello, Act I, scene iii.*)

Mutato nomine de te /Fabula narratur.

With a change of name it's about yourself / This tale is told.
(Horace, Satires.)

Notes and references

Chapter 1: Fabulous

1. Vaclav Havel, in *Disturbing the Peace* (1990), page 181. Quoted by Seamus Heaney in *The Redress of Poetry* (1995), page 4: Heaney says 'what Havel has to say about hope can also be said about poetry'.

2. There are reports from time to time in the press that senior civil servants have strong reservations about the directions and consequences of government policy. See for example Wastell (1995): 'Whitehall's most senior servants have blamed Government policy for the growth of an underclass within Britain ...' Wastell quotes the civil servants' report verbatim as it reviews the 1980s: 'There was frequently a trade-off between policies designed to widen choice, as in housing, education and health, and policies targeted on the most deprived. It was often the better-off who were able to take advantage of wider choice.' A review of the 1980s by a former member of Mrs Thatcher's government concluded that policies at that time 'were unrelentingly divisive and discriminatory against the poor, whose human dignity was relentlessly ignored'. (Gilmour 1992, page 172). When Alan Howarth MP crossed the floor of the House of Commons in October 1995 his published statements and articles showed critiques of Government policy from within the heart of one-nation Conservatism, a tradition whose principal figures, he said, included Burke, Disraeli, Salisbury, Butler, Macmillan and Macleod. In an article in the *Guardian,* 9 October 1995, he wrote that 'we should be ashamed that the poorest 20 per cent ... have not shared in the overall growth of wealth in Britain'.

3. Will Hutton (1995) describes a three-speed society in vivid detail. Smith and Noble (1995) document with up-to-date statistics the links between inequalities in society and inequalities in the education system. Lasch (1994) describes the tendency for

wealthier and more fortunate members of society to opt out from involvement in the community as a whole. Handy (1994) outlines the growing insecurities of the middle classes caused by 'down-sizing' and 'delayering'.

4.   Klein (1993) provides a clear outline of debates and developments in multicultural education over the last twenty years. Gillborn (1995) focuses the key issues with regard to specific schools. The Runnymede Trust's *Equality Assurance in Schools* (1993), described at length in chapter 15 ('What We May Be'), provides many practical ideas for teaching about citizenship and identity in a multi-ethnic society.

5.   Dennis Brutus's poem 'Somehow We Survive' was first published in his compilation *A Simple Lust,* Heinemann Educational. It subsequently gave its name to an anthology edited by Sterling Plumpp, 1982, and appears there on page 92. I came to know it through a teacher in Brent, Judith Seecoomar, and quote it here as a tribute to her.

6.   This story, derived from a tale told by Aesop about the orator Demades, is used to introduce the compilation of stories by Wood and Richardson (1992). It is cited in Bausch (1984), page 30.

7.   Benjamin's essay on storytelling (1936) appears in Connerton's compilation *Critical Sociology* (1976). The quotation is on page 277.

8.   Cupitt (1991), page 19. The two quotations about Scheherazade are respectively from pages 67 and 80. Cupitt's whole book is a fascinating meditation on the nature of narrative. There is also reference to the Scheherazade story in chapter 8 ('All the World's a Keystage'). In chapter 2 ('Let Us Now Praise Teachers') there is a checklist of the features of a good story, based on a recollection of the Orpheus and Eurydice narrative, and in chapter 10 ('The Monarch and the Inner Life') there are reflections on the role of story in religious education. Chapter 20 ('Unfinished') also has a kind of checklist, in its enumeration of six symbolic objects, of the recurring themes and tensions in traditional folktales.

9.   The quotation is from page 99 of the Picador edition of Morrison's novel.

10. Clark (1993), page 27. Her article is a fictionalised account of real events and people.

Chapter 2 Let Us Now Praise Teachers

1.   Tippett (1974) page 156, quoted by Meirion Bowen (1985) page 134.

2.   The image of a parade in which height is proportional to income was first developed by Pen (1971). It was graphically illustrated in the Rowntree report on income distribution (1995). See also Hills (1995).

3.   The facts about poverty presented here are from the Rowntree report and Hills, op cit.

4.   Teresa Smith and Michael Noble (1995) have documented the growing inequalities in the education system.

5. Stan and Mari Thekaekara (1995) describe poverty in UK through Indian eyes. 'At first, the people didn't seem poor, used as we are to Indian poverty. No one's in danger of starving to death. But there's a heaviness in the air which you don't experience in an Indian slum. The abandoned apartment blocks have an air of decay. Of menace.' (Page 7 of their report).

6. Quoted in Bayley (1995).

7. Adapted from Adrian Mitchell's poem 'Dear Sir' in *Ride the Nightmare,* page 46.

8. Department of the Environment (1994), *Index of Local Conditions.*

9. Gordon and Forrest (1994).

10. Maya Angelou, *On the Pulse of Morning.* See also the end of chapter 15 ('What We May Be').

11. Hanif Kureishi (1995) *The Black Album,* London: Faber and Faber.

Chapter 3 Never Mind the Crisis, Feel the Quality

1. The story was used and developed by a small working party in Tower Hamlets in early 1994, in the wake of the electoral success in a local by-election of a candidate representing the British Nationalist Party. The concept of otherising is explored also here in chapter 18, through the re-telling of one of Aesop's fables. One of the principal theorists of otherising and racialising is Robert Miles: see in particular his 1989 and 1993 texts.

2. Shearer (1991) quoted in Pfeffer and Coote (1991), page 14. Generally Pfeffer and Coote, also John Stewart (1993), make excellent critiques of much current discourse about so-called quality in public services. Eisenstadt (1994) critiques market analogies applied to voluntary organisations.

3. Interesting accounts of customer satisfaction surveys in relation to libraries have been published by Davies and Kirkpatrick (1994), pages 88-89, and the Library Association (1994), pages 34-35. See also the article about the latter survey by Guy Daines (1994), page 37. Germaine Greer (1994) has complained: 'Last November the Government published a model charter for public libraries, so cunningly that no librarian I have asked has ever been able to find a copy of it.'

4. For recent studies of increases in poverty, deprivation and inequality in British society see Goodman and Webb (1994), Jenkins (1994), Hills (1995), Hutton (1995) and Russell (1995).

5. Gill Barrington, the Library Association president, writes: 'In providing materials which reflect and validate the beliefs of diverse cultures libraries contribute to a more tolerant and understanding world. By making information accessible to people who cannot use traditional texts, they promote equality of opportunity...' (Barrington, 1994, page 79). Rowena Arshad (1994) has outlined some important priorities for libraries serving multicultural communities.

6.   'New Eyes Each Year', by Philip Larkin, written in February 1979, page 212 of his collected poems.

7.   The quotations from Pat Barker's *Regeneration* appear on pages 241-242 of the Penguin Books edition.

8.   Important theoretical studies of 'hybridity' have been made by Hall (1992), Gilroy (1993), Modood (1992), Said (1993) and Bhabha (1994). The essays in Back and Nayak (1993) contain several interesting references to a wider European context. See also Rattansi's major 1995 essay. Edward Said remarks that 'imperialism consolidated the mixture of cultures and identities on a global scale. But its worst and most paradoxical gift was to allow people to believe that they were, only, mainly, exclusively, white, or black, or Western, or Oriental.' (Said, 1993, pages 407-408.)

9.   This formulation in English of Aimé Césaire's famous statement, originally published in *Cahier d'un Retour au Pays Natal* (1947) was made by C L R James in *The Black Jacobins*. It is cited and emphasised by Edward Said (1993). A plea for more generous forms of liberalism has been made by Bhikhu Parekh (1994).

Chapter 4 Who's the Partridge in the Peartree?

1.   A S Byatt's story was first published in her 1994 collection entitled *The Djinn in the Nightingale's Eye*.

2.   Rich (1987), page 169.

3.   These quotations are from Fuller (1993) and Potter (1994).

4.   Tyler (1991), page 5.

5.   Tweedie (1993), page 89.

6.   The poem 'Holding My Beads' is in Grace Nichols's *The Fat Black Woman's Poems*, page 63.

7.   R S Thomas's poem 'The Word' was first published in his collection *Laboratories of the Spirit*, page 3.

8.   The quotation is from Nelson Mandela's *Long Walk to Freedom*, page 615.

9.. The report of the Opsahl Commission was compiled and edited by Andy Pollak. The quotation is from page 38. Tony Parker's oral histories (1993) provide a vivid picture of the background.

10. McEwan's article was entitled 'The Plot Thickens '.

11. Rosen's story 'Not Yet' about an episode at the East End grammar school which he attended in the 1930s, was included in *Stories and Meanings*, published in the early 1980s by the National Association for the Teaching of English. The quotation about sentences and full stops is from an essay in the same booklet.

12. Page 139 in the hardback edition of Anne Fine's *Goggle-Eyes*.

13. Page 211 of Salman Rushdie's *East, West*.

14. The report of the Commission on Social Justice, chaired by Sir Gordon Borrie, was entitled *Strategies for National Renewal.*

15. A play based on James Joyce's story 'The Dead' was broadcast on BBC radio during the twelve days of Christmas 1994/95. The quotation from the story given here is from pages 224-25 of the Penguin Books edition of *Dubliners.*

16. Italo Calvino's story about Christmas appears in his collection *Marcovaldo.* The quotation is from pages 120-21.

Chapter 5 Review of the Decade

As mentioned in its introductory note, this piece formed part of a lecture for a conference at the University of Warwick entitled 'Race, Gender and the Education Reform Act', held in April 1991. At the same conference there was considerable discussion of the National Curriculum Council's decision not to publish guidelines on multiculturalism. This decision is referred to in greater detail in chapter 15. The piece entitled 'A Week in a Life' (chapter 17) was also written for this conference. The idea of starting the review of the decade with a reference to 'treachery' in the Conservative Party in autumn 1990 was derived from a letter about Mrs Thatcher's departure written in early 1991 by Roger Scruton, addressed to readers of the *Salisbury Review.*

Chapter 6 A Great White Paper

This rather heavy-handed commentary on the White Paper of summer 1992, entitled *Choice and Diversity: a new framework for schools* (Cm 2021), tries to highlight the Paper's non-sequiturs and disingenuous simplifications. The last paragraph ('The Government's Vision') tries to highlight the Paper's curious use of metaphors.

Chapter 7 Returning Home

1. This version of the traditional story was reprinted in Wood and Richardson (1992). See also the title story in *The People Could Fly: Black American Folktales,* Walker Press, 1986.

2. Maya Angelou, 'Best of a Bad US Judge', reprinted in the *Guardian,* 5 September 1991, from the *New York Times.*

3. Mal Leicester's tribute was first published in the journal *Multicultural Teaching,* autumn 1990.

4. Section 11: the reference is to a provision in the Local Government Act 1966, which empowered central government to provide additional funds to local authorities in relation to the general fields marked by terms such as 'ethnic minorities', 'teaching English as an additional language' and 'multiculturalism'. There is further recurring reference to Section 11 in chapter 12. The quotation from an article by Teresa Clark, near the end of chapter 1, refers to the work of a Section 11 teacher. The story printed as chapter 14 ('Yes, Of Course') is about an alternative way of using Section 11 resources.

5. Gabriel Garcia Marquez, *Love in the Time of Cholera,* 1985, page 165 of the Penguin Books edition.

6. Italo Calvino, *If On a Winter's Night a Traveller,* Picador Books 1982, page 204.

7. Chapters 8 and 10 discuss at length this approach to religious education, emphasising the spiritual development of individuals.

8. There was fuller discussion of this news coverage, and points arising, in an article entitled 'Religious Education, Letter and Spirit 1991' in *Race and Immigration,* The Runnymede Trust, October 1991.

9. Adrienne Rich, *The Fact of a Doorframe,* Norton and Company, 1984, page 273.

10. Ben Okri, 'Redreaming the World', the *Guardian,* 9 August 1990.

Chapter 8 All the World's a Keystage

1. From the novel *Stars and Bars* by William Boyd, the first page.

2. The pieces by Rachel and Yusuf are reprinted with acknowledgement to the Raising Achievement Project, London Borough of Lambeth. They were written in summer 1993.

3. The version of the Scheherazade story used here is from Wood and Richardson (1992). For further references to the Scheherazade story, see the quotations from Don Cupitt in chapter 1, note 8.

4. Quoted in Yaffa Eliach (1982) and in Wood and Richardson (1992), page 120.

5. These three quotations are respectively from Murdoch (1992) pages 73, 83 and 82. Also Seamus Heaney (1995) uses the term 'spiritual' repeatedly in his discussions of poetry, but without implying commitment to a specific religious tradition.

6. For example, National Curriculum Council (1993) and Ofsted (1994). There are useful quotations from these in chapters one and seven of Inman and Buck (1995). The City of Westminster guidelines on school worship (1994) are not only skilful politically but also sound and stimulating philosophically and inspiring and practical pedagogically. Also on the subject of school worship see Angela Wood's *Assembly Kit,* a treasure-trove of practical ideas for promoting and supporting pupils' spiritual development.

7. Erik Erikson, chapter 7 of *Childhood and Society.* His notion that development of identity has eight main components or stages is illustrated in chapter 10 ('The Monarch and the Inner Life'). Eight components (similar to but not precisely the same as those identified by Erikson) are listed in chapter 11 ('Roots and Routes'). David Cohen's *The Circle of Life* contains many striking illustrations and quotations on the general theme of the human life cycle.

8. The reference is to James Fowler and his followers and commentators, including Deboy, Droege, Leavitt and the Woodheads. Their work often refers to secular writers such as Erikson (note 7), Levinson and Gail Sheehy. Conn and Conn (1990) apply concepts of developmental psychology to Christian theories of spirituality.

9. Christopher Bryant, page 566 in the book edited by Jones et al.

10. Wood and Richardson (1992), in the structure of the anthology itself.

11. The Ecumenical Association of Third World Theologians, meeting at Nairobi in 1992.

12. Steven Berkoff (1992), page 10. The second quotation is from page 37.

13. Quoted in Brian Moore's novel *Cold Heaven,* page 246.

14. Gerard Hughes, *God of Surprises,* pages 8-9.

15. Christopher Bryant, page 565 in Jones et al. Sheldrake (1991) discusses the history of the term spirituality and shows that its modern usage derives from Roman Catholic writers in France in the early years of the twentieth century.

16. Garner (1986), in Robson and Lonsdale, page 5.

17. Stephen Barton (1992), page 1.

18. Jim Thompson (1990), page 79. Thompson adds: 'Our prayer is the expression of that relationship as we look for a cure for our soul, and God responds through the knowledge, the thoughts and the feelings which we can share with Him.'

19. Kathleen Fischer (1989), page 5.

20. Iris Murdoch (1992), page 505.

21. Quoted by Thomas Merton (1977), page 114.

22. Jim Thompson (1990), page 263. A broadly similar view is outlined by Joanna Macy. She writes about spirituality and the inner life from a mainly non-theistic perspective, however, deeply influenced by modern science and by Buddhism. Sara Maitland (1995) has many stimulating insights on connections between inner and outer life, spirituality and politics. Wink (1992) writes at length about combating domination and violence both in the self and in the outer world, and stresses that both struggles are 'spiritual'.

23. Peter Selby (1983), page 6. See also Walter Wink: 'History belongs to the intercessors, who believe the future into being. This is not simply a religious statement. It is true of communists or capitalists or anarchists as it is of Christians ... This is the politics of hope.' (Wink 1992, page 299.)

24. The words of Krishna to Arjuna, as portrayed in the drama by Jean-Claude Carrière for Peter Brook.

25. Wood and Richardson, pages 28-33. John Bowker (1991) discusses links between personal stories and religious myths, as does Mario Vargas Llosa in his novel *The Storyteller.* For cross-references to the theme of story in other chapters of this book, see note 8 for chapter 1.

26. Cupitt (1991), page 133. See also note 8 for chapter 1.

Chapter 9 Paradise Postponed

A version of the original Arab story appears in Inea Bushnaq's *Arab Folk Tales,* Penguin Books 1986. This modernised version is adapted from one which appears in *Inside Stories,* compiled by Angela Wood and Robin Richardson, Trentham Books 1992.

Chapter 10 The Monarch and the Inner Life

1. The story appears with the title 'The Wooden Sword' in *Elijah's Violin and other Jewish Folktales,* selected and retold by Howard Schwartz, Penguin Books 1987. Hick (1994) argues that transformation 'from self-centredness to a new orientation' is the essential characteristic of all religious traditions and that this transformation is expressed in 'love, compassion, joy, peace, patience, kindness, goodness, faithfulness, gentleness, self- control'.

2. Updike's story about Roger Skunk and the wizard was first published in the *New Yorker* in the 1950s and was included in his collection *Pigeon Feathers and Other Stories,* André Deutsch 1962.

3. Erikson's famous paper entitled 'The Eight Ages of Man' was included in his *Childhood and Society.* See also the reference to Erikson in chapter 8 above, note 7.

4. 'Born Curious' was the title of a book some years ago by Robin Hodgkin, full details in bibliography. Hodgkin outlined an educational philosophy ('in the home-spun sense of the word') and pedagogy reflecting research which shows 'that new-born children have strongly patterned, innate yet flexible competence and that one aspect of this is a power to frame pre-verbal hypotheses and questions'. Heaney (1995) discusses 'Key Stage Eight', as it were, in the poetry of Philip Larkin and W B Yeats, and recalls vividly that views of death and dying affect us throughout our life-cycles, not at the end only.

Chapter 11 Roots and Routes

As mentioned in the text of chapter 10, the scheme presented here is based broadly on Erikson (1950). There are references to Erikson and his life- cycle theory of identity also in chapter 8. The derivations of words are taken from the Oxford Dictionary of Etymology.

Chapter 12 They Struggled Here

1. From Achebe's *Anthills of the Savannah,* Heinemann African Writers Series, page 128.

2. I was employed by the London Borough of Brent in the period 1985-1990 and was involved with others in the creation of the DPRE in 1986.

3. *Mail on Sunday,* 19 October 1986. There is a more detailed account of the press coverage of the DPRE in an article which I contributed to an Open University reader: see Gill et al (1991) pages 134-150.

4. Lane's report was published by the Home Office in spring 1988. Its appendices included lengthy extracts from the Programme's formal documentation.

5. The report by Her Majesty's Inspectorate was published by the Department of Education and Science (as the Department for Education and Employment was then known) in 1988.

6. Publication of the Warwick report was held up for several years. It eventually appeared as a monograph in 1991, authored by Malcolm Cross and his co-researchers.

7. The memorandum was originally private and confidential but was inadvertently included in public papers for an Education Committee meeting in autumn 1985.

8. When re-issued in the 1990s, the title of this document was changed to *Excellence and Equality*. The actual text, however, remained unchanged.

9. The poet was Tania Ahsan, a student at Willesden High School. Her poem appeared in a compilation by the DPRE entitled *Drum, Talk and Dub*, 1990.

10. The poem was published in a local compilation edited by Steven Delsol, entitled *Children's Self-Worth Poems*, Brent Education Department 1990. The author was a pupil at Chalkhill Junior School, Wembley.

Chapter 13 The Answer Lies in the School

This version of the Parable of the Sower (in, for example, the Gospel of St Matthew, chapter 13) is adapted from one which appears in Wood and Richardson (1992), pages 18-19.

Chapter 14 Yes, Of Course

The striking phrases at one stage in this story — 'semantic agility, 'rich scripting', 'meaning negotiation', 'shared imaging' — are from a fascinating and inspirational paper presented to the SCAA conference by Norah McWilliam, from Bradford and Ilkley Community College.

Chapter 15 What We May Be

1. *Daily Mail,* 18 July 1995.

2. The SCAA speech on cultural identity by Nicholas Tate, chief executive of the School Curriculum and Assessment Authority, was given on Thursday 13 July 1995 at the annual conference of the Shropshire Secondary Headteachers Association. The full text was released to the press the following Monday.

3. Maya Angelou's poem was entitled 'On the Pulse of Morning' and was published by Virago in 1993.

4. A new journal, *Social Identities,* carried three significant articles in summer 1995 about concepts of ethnic identity: see Cohen, Martin and Rex.

5. The twelfth periodic report of the UK Government to the United Nations Committee concerned with the Convention on the Elimination of all Forms of Racial Discrimination (CERD), paragraph 153.

6. There is a full account of this working party in a chapter by Sally Tomlinson in a valuable book on the national curriculum and multicultural education edited and compiled by Anna King and Michael Reiss, pages 21-29.

7. Quoted in Tomlinson, op cit.

8. Quoted in Tomlinson, op cit.

9.   The Runnymede Trust organised the production of *Equality Assurance in Schools: quality, identity, society*. The document was published in partnership with Trentham Books.

10. Subsequently (October 1995) the Ofsted Framework dropped equal opportunities as a discrete issue, but retained the overall concern under several separate headings. A brief report summarising the principal changes was included in *The Runnymede Bulletin,* September 1995.

11. All quotations here are from the first page of Kureishi's novel.

12. Warner, 1994, page 93. In *The Satanic Verses,* Salman Rushdie has a character who stammers drunkenly that 'the trouble with the Engenglish is that their hiss hiss history happened overseas, so they dodo don't know what it means.' This is quoted in Bhabha (1994), page 6.

13. Marina Warner quotes Walcott's poem 'The Schooner Flight', published in *The Star-Apple Kingdom,* 1980, and reprinted in *Selected Poems,* Heinemann Caribbean Writers series, 1981, republished 1993.

14. Warner, op cit, page 93.

15.   Warner, op cit, page 94.

16. The quotation about Jamila is from page 216 of the paperback edition of Kureishi's novel, published by Faber and Faber.

17. Quoted on page 14 of *Equality Assurance in Schools.*

18. The concept of 'a multi-ethnic good society' is illustrated with statistics in the Runnymede Trust's 1994 publication *Multi-Ethnic Britain: facts and trends.*

19. See *The First Fifty,* published by the Runnymede Trust, 1994.

20. Dodd (1995), page 50.

21. Dodd (1995), ibid.

Chapter 16 Permits and Power

This was originally written as a reflection on practical and political tasks connected with the compilation of *Equality Assurance in Schools,* described at length in chapter 15.

Chapter 17 A Week in a Life

This was originally written as an epilogue for a lecture which began with an imaginary history of the 1990s, printed here as chapter 5 ('Review of the Decade'). The diary format is derived from a poem by Roger McGough.

Chapter 18 The Two Towns

Originally written to introduce the concept of 'the Other'. Some of the imagery used by the first teacher recalls the Other as seen by a colonial and colonising mentality. For extended discussions of notions of Self and Other, see the work of Robert Miles (1989 and 1993). Martin (1995) cites self/other theories developed by clinical psychology, particularly through the work of Paul Ricoeur. The story in chapter 3 ('Never Mind the Crisis ...') recalls the human tendency to see the Other as the source of all the Self's problems.

Chapter 19 A Day to Remember

All headlines and news references are from the *Guardian*, 26 April 1982. Several were chosen because they would have a special resonance for Ester's family, and for her family's closest friends.

Chapter 20 Unfinished

This story is adapted slightly from one which appears in Wood and Richardson (1992). In an earlier version it was used to introduce reflections on human rights education, in a compilation of essays edited by Hugh Starkey for the Council of Europe, 1991. The imaginary situation of people deliberating about the features of an ideal society is taken from John Rawls's seminal work A *Theory of Justice*.

Chapter 21 The Keys of the Country

The research on Greater London counsellors in 1994 was conducted by the Runnymede Trust. The exhibition on teaching Black History was from Lilian Baylis School, Lambeth. The extract quoted from the *Sun* appeared on Tuesday 9 May 1995. The libretto for *A Child of Our Time* was written by Michael Tippett, as of course was the music.

List of works cited

Achebe, Chinua (1987) *Anthills of the Savannah,* London: Heinemann.

Angelou, Maya (1993) *On the Pulse of Morning,* London: Virago.

Arshad, R (1993) Reading into Equality, *Scottish Libraries*, Issue 42, November/ December.

Back, L and Nayak, A eds (1993) *Invisible Europeans?: black people in the New Europe,* Birmingham: All Faiths for One Race (AFFOR).

Barker, Pat (1991) *Regeneration,* London: Viking.

Barton, S (1992) *The Spirituality of the Gospels,* London: SPCK.

Bausch, William (1984) *Storytelling: imagination and faith,* Mystic, Connecticut: Twenty-Third Publications.

Bayley, C (1995) The Well-Made Playwright, *The Independent,* 7 April.

Benjamin, Walter (1936) The Storyteller and Artisan Cultures, in P. Connerton ed (1976).

Berkoff, Steven (1992) *The Theatre of Steven Berkoff,* London: Methuen.

Bhabha, Homi (1994) *The Location of Culture,* London and New York: Routledge.

Blunkett, David (1995) Merit and the Class of 1995, *Guardian,* 2 January .

Bowker, John (1991) *A Year to Live,* London: SPCK.

Boyd, William (1984) *Stars and Bars,* London: Hamish Hamilton.

Brink, André (1979) *A Dry White Season,* London: W H Allen.

Bryant, C (1986) The Nature of Spiritual Development, in Jones, C et al (1986).

Burrington, Gill (1994) Literacy Theme for President, *Record* Vol 96 (2), February, London: The Library Association.

Byatt, A S (1994) *The Djinn in the Nightingale's Eye,* London: Chatto and Windus.

Calvino, Italo (1982) *If On a Winter's Night a Traveller,* London: Picador Books.

Calvino, Italo (1983) *Marcovaldo,* London: Secker and Warburg.

Carrière, J-C (1988) *The Mahabharata,* London: Methuen.

Clark, Teresa (1993) All Our Ridwanas, *Multicultural Teaching,* Vol 12 No 1.

Cohen, David (1991) *The Circle of Life: rituals from the human family album,* London: The Aquarian Press (Harper Collins).

Cohen, Robin (1995) Fuzzy Frontiers of Identity: the British case, *Social Identities* vol 1, no 1, Oxford: Carfax.

Commission on Social Justice (1994) *Strategies for National Renewal,* London: Vintage.

Conn, J and Conn, W (1990) Christian Spiritual Growth and Developmental Psychology, *The Way Supplement,* number 69, autumn, London: Heythrop College.

Connerton, P ed (1976) *Critical Sociology: selected readings,* Harmondsworth: Penguin Books.

Cross, M et al (1991) *Racial Equality and the Local State: an evaluation of race policy in the London Borough of Brent,* University of Warwick: Centre for Research in Ethnic Relations.

Cupitt, Don (1991) *What is a Story?* London: SCM Press.

Daines, G (1994) Wide Impact Overall, *Record* Vol 96 (1), January, London: The Library Association.

Davies, Annette and Kirkpatrick, Ian (1994) To Measure Service: ask the library user, *Record* Vol 96 (2), February, London: The Library Association.

Deboy, J ed (1979) *Getting Started in Adult Religious Education,* Paulist Press, New York.

Department of Education and Science (1988) *The Development Programme for Race Equality in the London Borough of Brent,* reference INS56/12/227, 198/88, DS1/88, London: DES.

Department of the Environment (1994) *Index of Local Conditions: an analysis based on 1991 Census data,* London: Department of the Environment

Dodd, Philip (1995) *The Battle over Britain,* London: Demos.

Donald, James and Rattansi, Ali eds (1992) *'Race', Culture and Difference,* Sage Publications for the Open University.

Droege, T (1990) *Faith Passages and Patterns,* Fortress Press, Philadelphia.

Ecumenical Association of Third World Theologians (1992) *A Cry for Life: a spirituality for the third world,* Nairobi: Third General Assembly.

Eisenstadt, N (1994) Market Costs, *NCVO News,* number 54, May. London: National Council for Voluntary Organisations.

Eliach, Y (1982) *Hasidic Tales of the Holocaust,* New York: Avon Books.

Erikson, E (1950) *Childhood and Society,* W W Norton and Penguin Books (revised edition).

Field, F (1995) *Making Welfare Work,* London: Institute of Community Studies.

Fine, Anne (1989) *Goggle-Eyes,* London: Hamish Hamilton.

Fischer, Kathleen (1989) *Women at the Well: feminist perspectives on spiritual direction,* London: SPCK.

Fowler, J (1981) *Stages of Faith: the psychology of human development and the quest for meaning,* San Francisco: Harper and Row.

Fowler, J (1984) *Becoming Adult, Becoming Christian,* San Francisco: Harper and Row.

Fuller, G (1993) *Potter on Potter,* London: Faber and Faber.

Gabriel, J (1994) *Racism, Culture, Markets,* London: Routledge.

Gamer, C (1986) What on Earth is Spirituality? in Robson, J et al (1986).

Gill, Dawn et al eds (1991) *Racism and Education: structures and strategies,* London: Sage Publications for the Open University.

Gillborn, David (1995) *Racism and Antiracism in Real Schools,* Buckingham: Open University Press.

Gilmour, Ian (1992) *Dancing with Dogma: Britain under Thatcherism,* London: Simon and Schuster.

Gilroy, Paul (1993) *Small Acts: thoughts on the politics of black cultures,* London and New York: Serpent's Tail.

Goodman, A and Webb, S (1994) *For Richer, For Poorer: the changing distribution of income in the United Kingdom, 1961-1991,* London: Institute for Fiscal Studies.

Gordon, D and Forrest, R (1994) *People and Places 2: social and economic distinctions in England,* University of Bristol: School for Advanced Urban Studies.

Greer, Germaine (1994): Book Up for a Long Hot Summer in Libraryland, *Guardian,* 30 May.

Hackney Council (1993) *Inner City Focus: a series of lectures on urban policy issues,* London: Borough of Hackney.

Hall, Stuart (1992) New Ethnicities, in Donald, J and Rattansi, A eds (1992).

Handy, Charles (1994) *The Empty Raincoat,* London: Hutchinson.

Havel, Vàclav (1990) *Disturbing the Peace,* London: Faber and Faber.

Heaney, Seamus (1995) *The Redress of Poetry,* London: Faber and Faber.

Hick, John (1994) Christianity Among the Religions of the World, *Discernment* Vol 1 No 3, Oxford: Westminster College.

Hills, John (1995) *Inquiry into Income and Wealth: volume 2, a summary of the evidence,* York: Joseph Rowntree Foundation.

Hodgkin, R A (1974) *Born Curious: new perspectives in educational theory,* London: John Wiley.

Howarth, Alan (1995) In All Future Fairness, *Guardian,* 9 October.

Hughes, G (1988) *God of Surprises,* London: Darton, Longman and Todd.

Hutton, Will (1995) *The State We're In,* London: Jonathan Cape.

Inman, Sally and Buck, Martin (1995) *Adding Value? — schools' responsibilities for pupils' personal development*, Stoke-on-Trent: Trentham Books.

Jenkins, S (1994) *Winners and Losers,* Swansea: University Department of Economics.

Jones, C et al eds (1986) *The Study of Spirituality,* SPCK.

Joyce, James (1914) *The Dubliners,* Harmondsworth: Penguin Books.

King, A and Reiss, M (1993) *The Multicultural Dimension of the National Curriculum,* London: Falmer Press

King's Fund (1995) *Tackling Inequalities in Health: an agenda for action,* London: The King's Fund.

Klein, Gillian (1993) *Education Towards Race Equality,* London: Cassell.

Kureishi, Hanif (1990) *The Buddha of Suburbia,* London: Faber and Faber.

Kushner, Tony (1992) *Angels in America,* London: Royal National Theatre and Nick Hearn Books.

Lane, David (1988) *Brent's Development Programme for Racial Equality in Schools,* London: The Home Office.

Larkin, Philip (1988) *Collected Poems,* London: Marvell Press.

Lasch, C (1994) *The Revolt of the Elites,* London and New York: W W Norton.

Leavitt, D (1982) *A Faith for the Middle Years,* Washington: Alban Institute.

Leicester, M (1990) David Ruddell: an appreciation, *Multicultural Teaching* Vol 9 No 1, Stoke-on-Trent: Trentham Books.

Levinson, D et al (1978) *The Seasons of a Man's Life,* New York: Ballantine Books.

Library Association (1994) Positive Opinion Poll, *Record* Vol 96 (1), January, London: The Library Association.

Llosa, M (1989) *The Storyteller,* London: Faber and Faber.

Maitland, Sara (1995) *A Big-Enough God: artful theology,* London: Mowbray.

Macy, J (1983) *Despair and Personal Power in the Nuclear Age,* Philadelphia: New Society Publishers.

Mandela, Nelson (1994a) Joyous Night for the Human Spirit, reported in the *Guardian,* 3 May.

Mandela, Nelson (1994b) *Long Walk to Freedom,* London: Little, Brown and Company.

Marquez, Gabriel Garcia (1985) *Love in the Time of Cholera,* Harmondsworth: Penguin Books.

Martin, Denis-Constant (1995) The Choices of Identity, *Social Identities* vol 1, no 1, Oxford: Carfax.

McEwan, Ian (1994) The Plot Thickens, *Financial Times,* 24 December.

Merton, Thomas (1977) *Raids on the Unspeakable,* London: Bums and Oats.

Miles, Robert (1989) *Racism,* London: Routledge.

Miles, Robert (1993) *Racism after 'Race Relations',* London: Routledge.

Mitchell, Adrian (1971) *Ride the Nightmare,* London: Jonathan Cape.

Modood, Tariq (1992) *Not Easy Being British,* Stoke-on-Trent: Trentham Books with the Runnymede Trust.

Moore, Brian (1983) *Cold Heaven,* London: Jonathan Cape.

Murdoch, Iris (1985) *The Good Apprentice*, London: Chatto and Windus.

Murdoch, Iris (1992) *Metaphysics as a Guide to Morals*, London: Chatto and Windus.

National Curriculum Council (1993) *Spiritual and Moral Development — a discussion paper*, York: National Curriculum Council.

Nichols, Grace (1984) *The Fat Black Woman's Poems*, London: Virago.

Okri, Ben (1990) Redreaming the World, *Guardian*, 9 August.

Office for Standards in Education (1994) *Spiritual, Moral, Social, Cultural Development: a discussion paper*, London: HMSO.

Parekh, B (1994) Superior People: the narrowness of liberalism from Mill to Rawls, *Times Literary Supplement*, 25 February.

Parekh, B (1995) The Concept of National Identity, *New Community* Vol 21 No 2, Oxford: Carfax.

Parker, Tony (1993) *May the Lord in His Mercy be Kind to Belfast*, London: Harper Collins.

Pen, J (1971) *Income Distribution*, London: Allen Lane.

Pfeffer, N and Coote, A (1991): *Is Quality Good for You?: a critical review of quality assurance in welfare services*, London: Institute for Public Policy Research.

Pieterse, J (1995) Unpacking the West: how European is Europe? in Rattansi, A and Westwood, S eds (1995).

Plumpp, Sterling ed (1982) *Somehow We Survive*, New York: Thunder's Mouth Press.

Pollak, A (1993) *A Citizen's Inquiry*, Dublin: Lilliput Press.

Rattansi, Ali and Westwood, Sallie, eds (1995) *Racism, Modernity and Identity: on the western front*, Cambridge: Polity Press.

Rex, John (1995) Ethnic Identity and the Nation State: the political sociology of multicultural societies, *Social Identities* vol 1, no 1, Oxford: Carfax.

Rich, Adrienne (1984) *The Fact of a Doorframe*, New York: Norton and Company.

Rich, Adrienne (1987) *Blood, Bread and Poetry*, London: Virago.

Robson, J and Lonsdale, D eds (1986): *Can Spirituality be Taught? — exploratory essays*, London: Association of Centres of Adult Education and British Council of Churches.

Roosens, E (1989) *Creating Ethnicity: the process of ethnogenesis*, London: Sage Publications.

Rosen, Harold (1982) *Stories and Meanings*, London: National Association for the Teaching of English.

Rowntree Foundation (1995) *Inquiry into Income and Wealth: volume 1*, York: Joseph Rowntree Foundation.

Runnymede Trust (1993) *Equality Assurance in Schools: quality, identity, society*, Stoke- on-Trent: Trentham Books with the Runnymede Trust.

Runnymede Trust (1994) *Multi-Ethnic Britain: facts and trends*, London: Runnymede Trust.

Russell, Hilary (1995) *Poverty Close to Home: a Christian understanding,* Poole: Mowbray.

Sheehy, Gail (1976) *Passages: predictable crises of adult life,* New York: E P Dulton and Co.

Said, Edward (1993) *Culture and Imperialism,* London: Chatto and Windus.

Schwartz, Howard (1987) *Elijah's Violin and other Jewish Folktales,* Harmondsworth: Penguin Books.

Selby, Peter (1983) *Liberating God: private care and public struggle,* London: SPCK.

Shearer, A (1991) Dumping Dependency, *Health Service Journal,* 4 April.

Sheldrake, Philip (1991) *Spirituality and History: questions of interpretation and method,* London: SPCK.

Smith, T and Noble, M (1995) *Education Divides: poverty and schooling in the 1990s,* London: Child Poverty Action Group.

Starkey, Hugh ed (1991) *The Challenge of Human Rights Education,* London: Cassell Educational for the Council of Europe.

Stewart, J (1993) The Changing Face of Local Government, in Hackney Council (1993).

Thekaekara, Stan and Thekaekara, Mari (1995) *Across the Geographical Divide,* London: Centre for Innovation in Voluntary Action.

Thomas, R S (1975) *Laboratories of the Spirit,* London: Macmillan.

Tomlinson, Sally (1993) The Multicultural Task Group: the group that never was, in King, A and Reiss, M eds (1993).

Thompson, J (1990) *The Lord's Song,* London: Collins Fount.

Tippett, Michael (1974) *Moving into Aquarius,* London: Paladin.

Tweedie, Jill (1993) *Eating Children,* London: Viking.

Tyler, Anne (1991) *Saint Maybe,* London: Chatto and Windus.

Updike, John (1962) *Pigeon Feathers and Other Stories,* London: André Deutsch.

Wakefield, G ed (1983) *A Dictionary of Christian Spirituality,* London: SCM Press.

Wastell, D (1995) Whitehall Blames Tories for Poor, *Sunday Telegraph,* 12 February.

Westminster SACRE (1993) *Things of the Spirit: guidelines for collective worship,* London: City of Westminster Education.

Whitehead, E and Whitehead, J (1986) *Seasons of Strength: new visions of adult Christian maturing,* New York: Image Books.

Wilkinson, C (1995) *The Drop Out Society,* Leicester: National Youth Agency.

Wink, Walter (1992) *Engaging the Powers: discernment and resistance in a world of domination,* Minneapolis: Fortress Press.

Wood, Angela (1992) *Assembly Kit,* London: BBC/Longman.

Wood, Angela and Richardson, Robin (1992) *Inside Stories: wisdom and hope for changing worlds,* Stoke-on-Trent: Trentham Books.